REASON
THE ONLY
ORACLE OF MAN,
OR A
Compenduous System
OF
Natural RELIGION.

Alternately ADORNED with Confutations
of a variety of DOCTRINES
incompatible to it;
Deduced from the moſt exalted Ideas which
we are able to form of the

DIVINE and Human
CHARACTERS,
AND FROM THE
Univerſe in General.

By Ethan Allen, *Eſq;*

BENNINGTON:
STATE OF VERMONT;
Printed by HASWELL & RUSSELL.
M,DCC,LXXXIV.

Printing Statement:

Due to the very old age and scarcity of this book, many of the pages may be hard to read due to the blurring of the original text, possible missing pages, missing text and other issues beyond our control.

Because this is such an important and rare work, we believe it is best to reproduce this book regardless of its original condition.

Thank you for your understanding.

PREFACE.

AN apology appears to me to be impertinent in writers who venture their works to public inspection, for this obvious reason, that if they need it, they should have been stifled in the birth, and not permitted a public existence. I therefore offer my composition to the candid judgment of the impartial world without it, taking it for granted that I have as good a natural right to expose myself to public censure, by endeavouring to subserve mankind, as any of the species, who have published their productions since the creation. and I ask no favour at the hands of philosophers, divines or Critics, but hope and expect they will severely chastise me for my errors and mistakes, least they may have a share in perverting the truth, which is very far from my intention.

IN my youth I was much disposed to contemplation, and at my commencement in manhood, I committed to manuscript such sentiments or arguments, as appeared most consonant to reason, least through the debility of memory my improvement should have been less gradual: This method of scribling I practised for many years, from which I experienced great advantages

in

PREFACE.

in the progression of learning and knowledge, the more so as I was deficient in education, and had to acquire the knowledge of grammar and language, as well as the art of reasoning, principally from a studious application to it, which after all I am sensible, lays me under disadvantages, particularly in matters of composition: however, to remedy this defect, I have substituted the most unwearied pains, and frankly acknowledge, that I have been so mortified by my own corrections of the subsequent treatise, that I am in some measure diffident of my accomplishments in composing it, but confident nevertheless, that I have struck the outlines of a consistent system, which I recommend to abler writers to perfect.

THE Bible and a Dictionary have been the only books, which I have made use of, since I have been correcting my old manuscripts, and making the following composition; though in those manuscripts I had copied sundry passages from certain authors, many years prior to the completion of the subsequent discourse, which the reader will find transcribed with proper quotations.

I HAVE invariably endeavored to make reason my guide through the whole contents of the system, and expect that they who read it, will approve or disapprove it, as they may judge, whether it accords with that original principle or not.

*IF The arguments are rightly stated, and the inferences justly drawn, they will stand the test of truth, although they do not come recommended to the public with the prelude of "*Thus faith the Lord.*"*

PREFACE.

IN the circle of my acquaintance (which has not been small) I have generally been denominated a Deist, the reality of which I never disputed, being conscious I am no Christian, except mere infant baptism makes me one; and as to being a Deist, I know not strictly speaking, whether I am one or not, for I have never read their writings; mine will therefore determine the matter; for I have not in the least disguised my sentiments, but have written freely without any conscious knowledge of prejudice for, or against any man, sectary or party whatever; but wish that good sense, truth and virtue may be promoted and flourish in the world, to the detection of delusion, superstition and false religion: and therefore any errors in the succeeding treatise, which may be rationally pointed out, will readily be rescinded,

By the public's most obedient humble servant,

Ethan Allen.

VERMONT, July 2, 1782.

The Contents.

Chapter I.

SECTION I.
The Duty of reforming Mankind from Superstition and Error, and the good Consequences of it.

SECTION II.
Of the BEING *of a* GOD.

SECTION III.
The Manner of discovering the MORAL PERFECTIONS *and* NATURAL ATTRIBUTES *of* GOD.

SECTION IV.
Of the ETERNITY *and* INFINITY *of* GOD.

CONTENTS.

SECTION V.
The Cause of IDOLATRY and the Remedy thereof.

Chapter II.

SECTION I.
OF the ETERNITY of CREATION.

SECTION II.
The natural impossibility of a successive CREATION, evinces the ETERNITY of it.

SECTION III.
The ETERNITY and INFINITY of GOD demonstrative of the ETERNITY and INFINITY of his CREATION and PROVIDENCE.

SECTION IV.
OF the INFINITUDE and ETERNITY of PROVIDENCE in the Creation and Formation of FINITE BEINGS.

SECTION V.
The Distinction between Creation and Formation.

SECTION VI.
OBSERVATIONS on MOSES's Account of CREATION.

CONTENTS.

SECTION VII.
Of the ETERNITY and INFINITY of DIVINE PROVIDENCE.

SECTION VIII.
The PROVIDENCE of GOD does not interfere with the AGENCY of MAN.

Chapter III.

SECTION I.
The Doctrine of THE INFINITE EVIL OF SIN considered.

SECTION II.
The MORAL GOVERNMENT of GOD, incompatible with ETERNAL PUNISHMENT.

SECTION III.
HUMAN LIBERTY, AGENCY, and ACCOUNTABILITY cannot be attended with ETERNAL CONSEQUENCES either good or evil.

SECTION IV.
Of Physical Evils.

Chapter IV.

SECTION I.

Of the Aptitudes of Sensation, and of their subserviency to the Mind.

SECTION II.

The intrinsic difference between SENSATION and the PRINCIPLE of the SOUL, and of their distinct Functions.

SECTION III.

Of the Providence of GOD as it respects the important Subject of the IMMORTALITY of the SOUL.

Chapter V.

SECTION I.

Speculations on the Doctrine of the Depravity of Human Reason.

SECTION II.

Containing a Disquisition of the Law of Nature, as it respects the Moral System, interspersed with Observations on subsequent Religions.

Chapter VI.

SECTION I.

Argumentative Reflections on SUPERNATURAL *and* MYSTERIOUS REVELATION *in general.*

SECTION II.

Containing OBSERVATIONS *on the* PROVIDENCE *and* AGENCY *of* GOD, *as it respects the Natural and Moral World, with* STRICTURES *on* REVELATION *in general.*

Chapter VII.

SECTION I.
OF MIRACLES.

SECTION II.

A succession of Knowledge, or of the exertion of Power in God, incompatible with his OMNISCIENCE *or* OMNIPOTENCE, *and the* ETERNAL *and* INFINITE *Display of* DIVINE POWER, *fore-closes any subsequent Exertion of it* MIRACULOUSLY.

SECTION III.

That which we understand is NATURAL, *and that which we understand not we cannot understand to be* MIRACULOUS.

SECTION IV.

Rare and wonderful Phenomenæ no evidence of MIRACLES, *nor are diabolical Spirits able to effect them, or superstitious Traditions to confirm them, nor can ancient* MIRACLES *prove recent* REVELATIONS.

SECTION V.

Miracles could not be instructive to Mankind.

SECTION VI.

Prayer cannot be attended with Miraculous Consequences.

Chapter VIII.

SECTION I.

The vagueness and unintelligibleness of the Prophecies, render them incapable of proving Revelation.

CONTENTS.

SECTION II.

The Contentions which subsisted between the Prophets respecting their Veracity and their Inconsistencies with one another, and with the nature of Things, and their Omission in teaching the Doctrine of Immortality precludes the Divinity of their Prophecies.

SECTION III.

Dreams or Visions uncertain and chimerical Channel for the Conveyance of Revelation, with Remarks on the Communication of the Holy Ghost to the Disciples by the Prayers and laying on of the Apostle's Hands, with Observations on the divine Dictations of the first Promulgators of the Gospel, and an Account of the Elect Lady, and her new Sectary of Shakers.

Chapter IX.

SECTION I.

Of *the Nature of* FAITH, *and wherein it consists.*

SECTION II.

Of *the Traditions of our Forefathers.*

SECTION III.

Our Faith is governed by our Reasonings, whether they are supposed to be conclusive or inconclusive, and not merely by our own Choice.

Chapter X.

SECTION I.

A Trinity of Persons cannot exist in the Divine Essence, whether the Persons be supposed to be finite or infinite: With remarks on St. Athenasius's Creed.

SECTION II.

Essence, being the cause of Identity, is inconsistent with Personality in the Divine Nature.

SECTION III.

The imperfection of Knowledge in the Person of Jesus Christ, incompatible with his Divinity, with Observations on the Hypostatical Union of the Divine and Human Nature.

CONTENTS.

Chapter XI.

SECTION I.

OBSERVATIONS *on the State of* MAN *in* MOSES'S PARADISE, *on the* TREE OF KNOWLEDGE OF GOOD AND EVIL, *and on the* TREE OF LIFE: *with Speculations on the divine Prohibition to Man, not to eat of the Fruit of the former of those Trees, interspersed with Remarks on the Mortality of innocent Man.*

SECTION II.

Pointing out the natural impossibility of all and every of the diverse Species of Biped Animals, commonly termed Man, to have lineally descended from Adam and Eve, or from the same original Progenitors, with Remarks on the uncertainty, whether the WHITE, BLACK, *or* TAWNY *Nations are hereditary to* ORIGINAL SIN, *or who of them it is that needs the* ATONEMENT: *With Remarks on the Devil's beguileing Adam and Eve.*

SECTION
C

SECTION III.

Of the Original of the Devil, or of Moral Evil, and of the Devil's talking with Eve; with a Remark, that the Doctrine of APOSTACY is the Foundation of CHRISTIANITY.

Chapter XII.

SECTION I.

IMPUTATION *cannot change, alienate or transfer the personal Demerit of Sin, and personal Merit of Virtue to others, who were not active therein, although this Doctrine supposes an Alienation thereof.*

SECTION II.

The Punishment of Sin, or the Reward of Virtue, as it respects the Mind, can have no positive Existence, abstractly considered, from the Demerit of the one or Merit of the other; with an Explanation of the Scripture Doctrine of IMPUTATION.

SECTION III.

The IMPUTATION *of* MORAL GOOD *or* EVIL *is incompatible with our own Consciousness of the one or of the other of those Agencies, and therefore cannot affect our mental Happiness or Misery.*

SECTION IV.

The MORAL RECTITUDE *of Things forecloses the Act of* IMPUTATION.

SECTION V.

A state of Condemnation equally affected the Character of CHRIST, *as far as he may be supposed to have partaken of the Nature of* MAN, *as well as the rest of* MANKIND; *with Remarks on the* ATONEMENT *and* SATISFACTION *for* ORIGINAL SIN.

SECTION VI.

The Person of JESUS CHRIST *considered in a variety of different Characters, every of which are incompatible with a Participation of the* DIVINE NATURE. *That a* REDEMPTION, *wrought out by inflicting the* DEMERITS OF SIN *upon the* INNOCENT, *would be* UNJUST, *and that it could contain no* MERCY *or* GOODNESS

NESS *to the* UNIVERSALITY OF BEING, *considered inclusively.*

Chapter XIII.

SECTION I.

Of *the Impossibility of translating an* INFALLIBLE REVELATION *from its original Copies, and preserving it entire through all the Revolutions of the World, and Vicissitudes of Human Learning, to our Time.*

SECTION II.

Remarks concerning Mr. Ditton's Confessions and Conclusion respecting the Authority of the Evangelical, and other ancient Authors, and of the Errors, Corruptions and Spuriousness, to which they are exposed.

SECTION III.

The variety of the Annotations and Expositions of the Scriptures, together with the diversity of Sectaries, evinces their fallibility.

SECTION

CONTENTS.

SECTION IV.

Of the compiling of the Manuscripts of the Scriptures into one Volume, and of its several Translations. The Infallibility of the Popes, and of their chartered Right to remit or retain Sins. And of the impropriety of their being trusted with a Revelation from God.

Chapter XIV.

SECTION I.

An Historical Testimony of Miracles insufficient to prove irrational Doctrines.

SECTION II.

Morality, derived from Natural Fitness, and not from Tradition.

SECTION III.

Of the Importance of the Exercise of Reason, and Practice of Morality, in order to the Happiness Mankind.

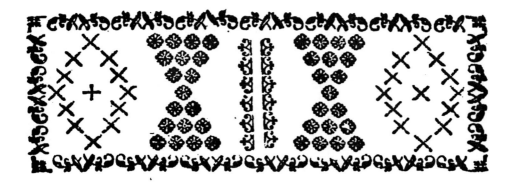

ORACLES OF REASON.

Chapter I.

SECTION I.

The Duty of reforming Mankind from Superstition and Error and the good Consequences of it.

THE desire of knowledge has engaged the attention of the wise and curious among mankind in all ages, which has been productive of

extending

extending the arts and sciences far and wide in the several quarters of the globe, and excited the contemplative to explore nature's laws in a gradual series of improvement, 'till philosophy, astronomy, geography and history, with many other branches of science, have arrived to a great degree of perfection.

It is nevertheless to be regreted, that the bulk of mankind, even in those nations which are most celebrated for learning and wisdom, are still carried down the torrent of superstition, and entertain very unworthy apprehensions of the BEING, PERFECTIONS, CREATION and PROVIDENCE of GOD, and their duty to him, which lays an indispensible obligation on the philosophic friends of human nature, unanimously to exert themselves in every lawful, wise and prudent method, to endeavour to reclaim mankind from their ignorance and delusion, by enlightening their minds in those great and sublime truths concerning God and his providence, and their obligations to moral rectitude, which in this world, and that which is to come, cannot fail greatly to affect their happiness and well being.

Though " *None by searching can find out God, or the Almighty to perfection ;*" yet I am persuaded, that if mankind would dare to exercise
their

their reason as freely on those divine topics, as they do in the common concerns of life, they would, in a great measure rid themselves of their blindness and superstition, gain more exalted ideas of God and their obligations to him and one another, and be proportionably delighted and blessed with the views of his moral government, make better members of society, and acquire many powerful incentives to the practice of morality, which is the last and greatest perfection that human nature is capable of.

SECTION II.

Of the BEING of a GOD.

THE Laws of Nature having subjected mankind to a state of absolute dependence on something out of, and manifestly beyond themselves, or the compound exertion of their natural powers, gave them the first conception of a superior principle existing; otherwise they could have had no possible conception of a superintending power. But this sense of dependency, which results from experience and reasoning on the facts, which every day cannot fail to produce, has uniformly established the knowledge of our dependence to every of the species who are rational, which necessarily

cessarily involves or contains in it the idea of a ruling power, or that there is a GOD, which ideas are synonimous.

THIS is the first glimpse of a Deity, and powerfully attracts the rational mind to make farther discoveries, which, through the weakness of human reasonings opens a door for errors and mistakes respecting the divine essence, though there is no possibility of our being deceived in our first conceptions of a superintending power. Of which more will be observed in its order.

THE globe with its productions, the planets in their motions, and the starry heavens in their magnitudes, surprize our senses, and confound our reason, in their munificent lessons of instruction concerning GOD, by means whereof we are apt to be more or less lost in our ideas of the object of divine adoration, though at the same time every one is truly sensible that their being and preservation is from GOD. We are too apt to confound our ideas of GOD with his works, and take the latter for the former. Thus barbarous and unlearned nations have imagined, that inasmuch as the sun in its influence is beneficial to them, in bringing forward the spring of the year, causing the production of vegetation, and food for their subsistence, that therefore it is their GOD: while others have located eated other parts of creation, and ascribe to them the prerogatives of God; and mere creatures and images have been substituted to be Gods by the wickedness or weakness of man, or both together. It seems that mankind in most ages and parts of the world have been fond of corporeal Deities with whom their outward senses might be gratified, or as fantastically diverted from the just apprehension of the true God, by a supposed supernatural intercourse with invisible and mere spiritual beings, to whom they ascribe divinity, so that through one means or other, the character of the true God has been much neglected, to the great detriment of truth, justice and morality in the world; nor is it possible, that mankind can be uniform in their religious opinions, or worship God according to knowledge, except they can form a consistent arrangment of ideas of the Divine character. This therefore shall be the great object of the following pages, to which all others are only subordinate; for the superstructure of our religion will be proportionate to the notions we entertain of the divinity whom we adore. A sensibility of mere dependence includes an idea of something, on which we depend (call it by what name we will) which has a real existence, in as much as a dependency on nonentity is inadmissibe, for that the absence or non-existence of all being could not have

caused

caused an existence to be. But should we attempt to trace the succession of the causes of our dependence, they would exceed our comprehension, though every of them, which we could understand, would be so many evidences (of the displays) of a God. Although a sense of dependency discloses to our minds the certainty of a Supreme Being, yet it does not point out to us the object, nature or perfections of that being; this belongs to the province of reason, and in our course of ratiocination on the succession of causes and events. Although we extend our ideas retrospectively ever so far upon the succession, yet no one cause in the extended order of succession, which depends upon another prior to itself, can be the independent cause of all things: nor is it possible to trace the order of the succession of causes back to that self-existent cause, inasmuch as it is eternal and infinite, and therefore cannot be traced out by succession, which operates according to the order of time, consequently can bear no more proportion to the eternity of God, than time itself may be supposed to do, which has no proportion at all; as the succeeding arguments respecting the eternity and infinity of God will evince. But notwithstanding the series of the succession of causes cannot be followed in a retrospective succession up to the self-existent or eternal cause, it is nevertheless

less a perpetual and conclusive evidence of a God. For a succession of causes, considered collectively, can be nothing more than effects of the independent cause, and as much dependent on it, as those dependent causes are upon one another; so that we may with certainty conclude that the system of nature, which we call by the name of natural causes, is as much dependent on a self-existent cause, as an individual of the species in the order of generation is dependent on its progenitors for existence. Such part of the series of nature's operations, which we understand, has a regular and necessary connection with, and dependence on its parts, which we denominate by the names of cause and effect. From hence we are authorised from reason to conclude, that the vast system of causes and effects are thus necessarily connected, (speaking of the natural world only) and the whole regularly and necessarily dependent on a self existent cause; so that we are obliged to admit an independent cause, and ascribe self-existence to it, otherwise it could not be independent, and consequently not a God. But the eternity or manner of the existence of a self-existent and independent being is to all finite capacities utterly incomprehensible; yet this is so far from an objection against the reality of such a being, that it is essentially necessary to support the evidence of it; for if we could comprehend

prehend that being, whom we call God, he would not be God, but muſt have been finite, and that in the ſame degree as thoſe may be ſuppoſed to be, who could comprehend him; therefore ſo certain as God is, we cannot comprehend his eſſence, eternity or manner of exiſtence. This ſhould always be premiſed, when we aſſay to reaſon on the being, perfection, eternity and infinity of God, or of his creation and providence. As far as we underſtand nature, we are become acquainted with the character of God; for the knowledge of nature is the revelation of God. If we form in our imagination a compeduous idea of the harmony of the univerſe, it is the ſame as calling God by the name of harmony, for there could be no harmony without regulation, and no regulation without a regulator, which is expreſſive of the idea of a God. Nor could it be poſſible, that there could be order or diſorder, except we admit of ſuch a thing as creation, and creation contains in it the idea of a creator, which is another appellation for the Divine Being, diſtinguiſhing God from his creation. Furthermore there could be no proportion, figure or motion without wiſdom and power; wiſdom to plan, and power to execute, and theſe are perfections, when applied to the works of nature, which ſignify the agency or ſuperintendency of God. If we conſider nature to be matter, figure and motion,

we

we include the idea of God in that of motion; for motion implies a mover, as much as creation does a creator. If from the composition, texture, and tendency of the universe in general, we form a complex idea of general good refulting therefrom to mankind, we implicitly admit a God by the name of good, including the idea of his providence to man. And from hence arifes our obligation to love and adore God, becaufe he provides for, and is benificent to us: abftract the idea of goodnefs from the character of God, and it would cancel all our obligations to him, and excite us to hate and deteft him as a tyrant; hence is is, that ignorant people are fuperftitioufly mifled into a conceit that they hate God, when at the fame time it is only the idol of their own imagination, which they truly ought to hate and be afhamed of; but were fuch perfons to connect the ideas of power, wifdom, goodnefs and all poffible perfection in the character of God, their hatred toward him would be turned into love and adoration.

For mankind to hate truth as it may bring their evil deeds to light and punifhment, is very eafy and common; but to hate truth as truth, or God as God, which is the fame as to hate goodnefs for its own fake, unconnected with any other confequences, is impoffible even to a (premifed) diabolical nature itfelf. If we advert to the feries

of

of the causes of our being and preservation in the world, we shall commence a retrospective examination from son to father, grand-father and great-grandfather, and so on to the supreme and self-existent father of all : and as to the means of our preservation or succeeding causes of it, we may begin with parental kindness in nourishing, succouring and providing for us in our helpless age, always remembering it to have originated from our eternal father, who implanted that powerful and sympathetic paternal affection in them.

By extending our ideas in a larger circle, we shall perceive our dependence on the earth and waters of the globe, which we inhabit, and from which we are bountifully fed and gorgeously arrayed, and nextly extend our ideas to the sun, whose fiery mass darts its brilliant rays of light to our terraqueous ball with amazing velocity, and whose region of inexhaustible fire supplies it with fervent heat, which causes vegetation and guilds the various seasons of the year with ten thousand charms : this is not the atchievement of man, but the workmanship and providence of God. But how the sun is supplied with materials thus to perpetuate its kind influences, we know not. But will any one deny the reality of those beneficial influences, because we do not understand the manner of the
perpetuity

perpetuality of that fiery world, or how it became such a body of fire; or will any one deny the reality of nutrition by food, because we do not understand the secret operation of the digesting powers of animal nature, or the minute particulars of its cherishing influence, none will be so stupid as to do it. Equally absurd would it be for us to deny the providence of God, by "whom we live, move, and have our being," because we cannot comprehend it.

We know that earth, water, fire and air in their various compositions subserve us, and we also know that these elements are devoid of reflection, reason or design; from whence we may easily infer, that a wise, understanding, and designing being has ordained them to be thus subservient. Could blind chance constitute order and decorum, and consequently a providence? That wisdom, order, and design should be the production of non-entity, or of chaos, confusion and old night, is too absurd to deserve a serious confutation, for it supposeth that there may be effects without a cause, viz. produced by non-entity, or that chaos and confusion could produce the effects of power, wisdom and goodness; such absurdities as these we must assent to, or subscribe to the doctrine of a self-existent and providential being. Chaos itself would necessarily include the idea of a creator, inasmuch as it supposes a positive existence, though it precludes the idea of a Providence; which cannot exist without order, tendency and design.

But Chaos could no more exist independent of a Creator than the present aptly disposed system of nature. For there could be no fortuitous jumble, or chaos of original atoms, independent of or previous to creation, as nonentity could not produce the materials. *Nothing from nothing and there remains nothing, but something from nothing is contradictory and impossible.* The evidence of the being and providence of a God, is so full and compleat, that we cannot miss of discerning it, if we but open our eyes and reflect on the visible creation. The display of God's providence is that by which the evidence of his being is evinced to us, for though mere Chaos would evince the certainty of a Creator, yet that abstracted method of argument could not have been conceived of, or known by us, was it not for the exercise of God's Providence, (by whom we have our being;) though that argument in itself would have been true whether it had been used by us or not: for the reason of propositions and just inferrences in themselves, are in truth the same, independent of our conceptions of them, abstractedly considered from our existence.

The benefit accruing to us from reasoning and argument, as it respects our knowledge and practice, is to explore the truth of things, as they are in their own nature, this is our wisdom. All other conceptions of things are false and imaginary. We cannot exercise a thought on any thing whatever, that has a positive existence, but if we trace it thoroughly it will center in an independent cause, and be evidential of a God. Thus it is from the works of nature that we explore its great author; but all inquisitive minds are lost in their searches and researches into the immensity of the divine fullness, from whence our beings and all our blessings flow.

SECTION III.

The manner of discovering the Moral Perfections and natural Attributes of GOD.

HAVING in a concise manner offered a variety of indisputable reasons to evince the certainty of the being and providence of God, and of his goodness to man through the intervention of the series of nature's operations, which are commonly described by the name of natural causes. We come now more particularly to the consideration of his moral perfections, and though all finite beings fall as much short of an adequate knowledge thereof, as they do of perfection itself; nevertheless

through

through the intelligence of our own souls we may have something of a prospective idea of the divine perfections. For though the human mind bears no proportion to the divine, yet there is undoubtedly a resemblance between them; for instance, God knows all things, and we know some things, and in the things which we do understand, our knowledge agrees with that of the divine, and cannot fail of necessarily corresponding with it. To more than know a thing, speaking of that thing only, is impossible even to omniscience itself; for knowledge is but the same in both the infinite and finite minds: To know a thing is the same as to have right ideas of it, or ideas according to truth, and truth is uniform in all rational minds, the divine mind not excepted. It will not be disputed but that mankind in plain and common matters understand justice from injustice, truth from falshood, right from wrong, virtue from vice, and praise-worthiness from blame-worthiness, for otherwise they could not be accountable creatures. This being admitted, we are capable of forming a complex idea of a moral character, which when done in the most deliberate, the wisest and most rational manner in our power, we are certain bears a resemblance to the divine perfections. For as we learn from the works of nature an idea of the power and wisdom of God, so from our own rational nature we learn an idea of his moral perfections.

BUT

But mere power and wisdom abstractedly considered from justice, goodness and truth, are not necessarily connected with a moral character, as applicable to man, as many tyrants have demonstrated, who have been wise to plan and powerful to execute unjust wars to the ruin and destruction of their species: but on the other hand when power and wisdom are in the possession of patriots they subserve mankind. But as God is unchangeably and infinitely just and good, as well as infinitely wise and powerful, he can therefore never vary from the rectitude of his moral character, and consequently his power and wisdom, though not included in his moral perfections (being his natural attributes) cannot act in opposition to his moral character. For of all possible systems infinite wisdom must have eternally discerned the best, and infinite justice, goodness and truth approved it, and infinite power effected it*.

From what has been observed on the moral perfections of God, we infer that all rational beings, who have an idea of justice, goodness and truth, have at the same time either a greater or less idea of the moral perfections of God. It is by reason that we are able to compound an idea of a moral character, whether applied to God or man;

---

* This conclusion is meant to respect the creation and providence of God only, and not to affect the liberty of man, or to infringe the morality of his actions.

it is that which gives us the supremacy over the irrational part of the creation, and it is that by which we may truly be said to be "made after the image of God."

SECTION IV.

Of the ETERNITY and INFINITY of GOD.

WE proceed next to enquire into the eternity and infinity of God. To ask how God came to be, implies a contradiction to his being as God, in as much as it supposes him to have come from, and to be dependent on some pre-existing cause, which holds up to our view the character of a finite and dependent being. But if we extend our minds retrospectively on the chain of pre-existing causes as far as human numeration can extend, still we are at as great a remove from a God as when we first attempted the order of pre-existing causes; for a mere succession of causes cannot extend themselves *ad infinitum*. If we conceive of God to have existed from eternity and that he will exist to eternity; in this conception we form an idea that God existed in time, and that in time he will cease to be, viz; from a certain Æra called eternity he existed to a second Æra called by the same name, viz; from one Epocha to another: and on this position there would have been an eternity preceding his existence, and another succeeding it, as it is often expressed from the desk "from eternity to eternity thou art God," which is diametrically inconsistent with a just idea of eternity. God did not come to be, but was, nor did he exist from eternity, but eternally existed, and will eternally exist. Though eternity includes an idea of existence or duration (as applied to God) without beginning or end, yet it is necessary, in discussing the subject of eternal existence, to divide it into the preceeding and succeeding eternity, as they may be considered seperately by the mind; but to consider it complexly, it is but one entire eternity without beginning or end. The idea of existence without beginning or end, contains in it an idea of self-existence and independence of any pre-existing cause: but an existence from eternity, necessarily implies either from a certain time, or from a certain pre-existing cause, called by the name of eternity, which runs into the absurdity of the derivation of a God from the chain of supposed pre-existing causes, which has been already sufficiently confuted.

SELF-EXISTENCE is the highest appellation we can ascribe to God, for nothing short of that can render him independent, and establish a just sense of his divinity and eternity. And though we cannot comprehend this misterious manner of existence

istence, yet we can comprehend that any manner of existence, short of, or inferior to that which is self existent, must necessarily be dependent, consequently imperfect and utterly devoid of any rightful pretensions of a God: for that which is not self-existent, must necessarily be dependent on that which is so, or it could not exist, except we suppose that a dependent existence can exist independently, which is inadmissible. It is not good sense, when we are speaking of God, to say that he is the first cause of all things; for if it was true, there would have been second, third, fourth and fifth causes in the series, and so on to the causes now in immediate exercise or influence, which would necessarily imply a beginning to the succession, and consequently to the being of God. But succession, which can operate no other way but according to the order of time or numerical calculations of the successions of causes, cannot eternally extend itself.

For instance, we will premise a mathematical eternal or endless line, which would be endless both ways, and every part of it would be equally in the middle, or more properly speaking there would be no middle or centre to it, in as much as it is supposed to be endless. So that was a cannon ball to be discharged on either direction of such a supposed line at any given time, and suppose it to continue its velocity (which is the

same

same as succession of motion) with unabated rapidity forever, it would never reach the endless extension of that line; for that which is without beginning or end is eternal, and cannot be measured or comprehended by the succession of numbers or motion, or by any thing that is capable of a calculation from the order of time: for which reason it is in nature impossible to trace the series of natural causes up to the self-existent and eternal cause. Though it is in nature possible to trace a succession of causes up to a supposed first cause; for first, second and third and so on throughout numeration belong to numbers and are in their nature capable of being explored by a succession, multiplication or division of numbers, which would be a contradiction to the eternity of God, therefore God cannot in truth be said to be the first cause of all things. For if by the succession of causes we could trace out the being of God, there would have been an eternity preceding his existence; inasmuch as all possible calculations on the succession of causes would only constitute a limitted duration of time, and fall as much short of the eternity of God, as our calculations of time may be supposed to do. But although God cannot with propriety be said to be the first cause, yet he is the efficient cause of all things, viz. a

cause

cause uncaused and eternally self-existent, gave being and order to nature, co-eval with his own existence, and creation regulated (which is the same as nature) being eternal, is the reason why we cannot trace the footsteps of the creator by a succession of causes up to the eternal cause (for that the series is also eternal) any more than we can trace an endless line by the motion of a cannon ball before alluded to. For existence without a beginning, a line without end, or an eternal series of natural causes (which on the position of the eternity of nature must be admitted) are each and every of them beyond our calculations of succession, motion or progression, which are predicated on the fleeting moments of time.

To suppose that an eternal series of natural causes begins with a first cause, is the same as supposing a beginning to the existence of God, and consequently that the series is not eternal, but that there was a previous eternity, which is a downright contradiction to the eternity of God. According to the rules of chronology, a first always implies a particular æra; thus Moses represents God to be under six thousand years old at present, his words are these, " In the beginning God created the heavens and the earth." This Epocha is calculated from the Jewish chronology, which wants but few figures to comprize. The Chinese ascribe an æra of of about forty thousand years existence to their God; but these are only different beginnings and do neither of them explain the eternal, self-existent cause. It may be said that Moses spake only with respect to the creation of the "Heavens and the earth;" be it so, yet if in any part of space there had been any previous display of creation, that which Moses was speaking of could not have been the beginning.

Yet it may be objected, that God might have been eternal, though creation might have had a beginning; but this would include the same sort of absurdity as to suppose a king without any subjects: because that previous to creation there could be nothing to govern or provide for, and consequently there could not have been any display of Providence, which is essential to the being of a God. Therefore creation and providence or nature, are as eternal as God. So that with respect to God and his works of nature there could be no first or last, for they are eternal: as will be fully evinced in the succeeding chapter.

We proceed next to enquire into the infinity of God. And first, we will premise, that there is no medium between infinite and finite as applied to God, or to his works of nature (which are the same

same as his creation and providence) or as applied to mere space. (God displays his providence in the series of nature's operations.) Infinity is boundless and unlimited, but finitude is circumscribed and limitted, between which there is no comparison or proportion. A supposed infinite nature or space would be as unlimitted all possible ways as that of an eternal line may be supposed to be two ways, and every part of its immensity would be void of a centre.

CIRCUMFERENCE necessarily admits of a centre, and though ever so extensive, comes within the description of finitude; but immensity having no circumference is also without a centre, so that the rapid motion of a cannon ball forever, could not extend itself through immensity, for that which is boundless, cannot be explored and comprehended by the succession of motion, or any progressive operation, or by the addition of numerical parts though they should be supposed to be ever so large and numerous: inasmuch as every of them is supposed to be local, they would therefore make but a local whole; and finally bear no proportion to infinite nature (which comprehends all things) or to infinite space: so with respect to an infinite mind, it is not included in any place, or excluded from any place, but fills immensity with cogitation, and perfectly understands all things, and is

possest

possest of all possible powers, perfections and excellencies without addition or dimunition.

This is a summary of the infinity of God, consisting of wisdom, power, justice, goodness and truth, with their eternally connected and almighty operations, co-extensive with the immense fullness of things.

SECTION V.

The Cause of IDOLATRY *and the Remedy of it.*

Inasmuch as God is not corpoeral, and consequently does not and cannot come within the notice of our bodily sensations; we are therefore obliged to deduce inferences from his providence, and particularly from our own rational nature, in order to form our conceptions of the divine character, which through inattention, want of learning, or through the natural imbecility of mankind, or through the artifice of designing men, or all together, they have been greatly divided and subdivided in their notions of a God. Many have so groped in the dark, as wholly to mistake the proper object of divine worship, and not distinguishing the creator from his creation, have paid adoration to "four footed beasts and creeping things." And some have ascribed divine honors to the sun, moon, or stars; while others have been infatuated to worship dumb, senseless and unintelligent idols, which derived their existence as Gods, partly from mechanics, who gave them their figure, proportion and beauty, and partly from their priests, who gave them their attributes; whose believers, it appears, were so wrought upon, that they cried out in the extacy of their deluded zeal "Great is Diana." Whatever delusions have taken place in the world relative to the object of divine worship, or respecting the indecencies or immoralities of the respective superstitions themselves, or by what means soever introduced or perpetuated, whether by designing men whose interest it has always been to impose on the weakness of the great mass of the vulgar; or as it is probable, that part of those delusions took place in consequence of the weakness of uncultivated reason, in deducing a visible instead of an invisible God from the works of nature. Be that as it will, mankind are generally possessed of an idea, that there is a God; however they may have been mistaken or misled as to the object. This notion of a God, as has been before observed, must have originated from a universal sense of dependence, which mankind have on something that is more wise, powerful and beneficent than themselves, or they could have had no apprehension of any superintending principle in the universe, and consequently would never have sought after a God, or have had any conception of his existence, nor could designing

men

men have imposed on their credulity by obtruding false Gods upon them: but taking advantage of the common belief that there is a God, they artfully deceive their adherents with regard to the object to be adored. There are other sorts of idols which have no existence but in the mere imagination of the human mind; and these are vastly the most numerous, and universally (either in a greater or less degree) interspersed over the world; the wisest of mankind are not and cannot be wholly exempt from them, inasmuch as every wrong conception of God is (as far as the error takes place in the mind) idolatrous. To give a sample, an idea of a jealous God is of this sort. Jealousy is the offspring of finite minds, proceeding from the want of knowledge, which in dubious matters makes us suspicious and distrustful; but in matters which we clearly understand there can be no jealousy, for knowledge excludes it, so that to ascribe it to God is a manifest infringement of his omniscience.*

The idea of a revengeful God is likewise one of that sort, but this idea of divinity being borrowed from a savage nature, needs no further confutation. The representation of a God, who, (as

---

* "The Lord thy God is a JEALOUS GOD."

we are told by certain divines) from all eternity, elected an inconsiderable part of mankind to eternal life, and reprobated the rest to eternal damnation, merely from his own sovereignty, adds another to the number; this representation of the Deity undoubtedly took its rise from that which we discover in great, powerful and wicked tyrants among men, however tradition may since have contributed to its support, though I am apprehensive, that a belief in those who adhere to that doctrine, that they themselves constitute that blessed elect number, has been a greater inducement to them to close with it, than all other motives added together. It is a selfish and inferior notion of a God void of justice, goodness and truth, and has a natural tendency to impede the cause of true religion and morality in the world, and diametrically repugnant to the truth of the divine character, and which, if admitted to be true, overturns all religion, wholly precluding the agency of mankind in either their salvation or damnation, resolving the whole into the sovereign disposal of a tyrannical and unjust being, which is offensive to reason and common sense, and subversive of moral rectitude in general. But as it was not my design so much to confute the multiplicity of false representations of a God, as to represent just and consistent ideas of the true God, I shall therefore omit any further obfervations on them in this place with this remark, that all unjuft reprefentations, or ideas of God, are fo many detractions from his character among mankind. To remedy thefe idolatrous notions of a God, it is requifite to form right and confiftent ideas in their ftead.

THE difcovery of truth neceffarily excludes error from the mind, which nothing elfe can poffibly do; for fome fort of God or other will crowd itfelf into the conceptions of dependent creatures, and if they are not fo happy as to form juft ones, they will fubftitute erroneous and delufive ones in their ftead; fo that it ferves no valuable purpofe to mankind, to confute their idolatrous opinions concerning God, without communicating to them juft notions concerning the true one, for if this is not effected, nothing is done to purpofe. For, as has been before obferved, mankind will form to themfelves, or receive from others, an idea of Divinity either right or wrong: this is the univerfal voice of intelligent nature, from whence a weighty and conclufive argument may be drawn of the reality of a God, however inconfiftent moft of their conceptions of him may be. The fact is, mankind readily perceive that there is a God, by feeling their dependence on him, and as they explore his works, and observe his providence, which is too sublime for finite capacities to understand but in part, they have been more or less confounded in their discoveries of a just idea of a God, and of his moral government. Therefore we should exercise great application and care, whenever we assay to speculate upon the Divine character, accompanied with a sincere desire after truth, and not ascribe any thing to his perfections or government, which is inconsistent with reason or the best information which we are able to apprehend of moral rectitude, and be at least wise enough not to charge God with injustice and contradictions, which we should scorn to be charged with ourselves. No king, governor or parent would like to be accused with partiality in their respective governments, *" Is it fit to say unto Princes, ye are ungodly, how much less to him that regardeth not the persons of princes, or the rich more than the poor, for they are all the work of his hands."*

CHAPTER

Chapter II.

SECTION I.

Of the ETERNITY of CREATION.

As Creation was the result of eternal and infinite wisdom, justice, goodness and truth, and effected by infinite power, it is like its great author, misterious to us. How it could be accomplished, or in what manner performed, can never be comprehended by any capacity, but that by whose almighty fiat it was executed. Yet from the necessary attributes, perfections, eternity and infinity of God, we may demonstrate that creation must also have been eternal and infinite. Had it not been eternal there could not have been an eternal display of those divine attributes and perfections, which necessarily constitute a God.

To suppose God to have been self-existent and eternal, but inactive till some certain æra or period of time, when he may have been said to have commenced the work of creation, would imply a contradiction to his nature as GOD: as on this thesis there would have been an eternity previous to the æra of the creation, for time or duration without beginning, to any certain epocha, is equally eternal, as time from such epocha without end; the one repects the preceding and the other the succeeding eternity; consequently if creation was commenced in time, the eternity preceding it must be supposed to be possessed by an inactive being, if by any at all. But if GOD be admitted to have been eternal, he may as well be supposed to have been eternally active, or in other words eternal exertion would have been inseperably connected with his existence as God, and if eternally active, why not as well eternally create? viz. co-eval with the preceding eternity. As there could be but one simple and uncompounded exertion in the act of creation, and immensity being perfectly replete with it, the exertion need not and could not be repeated. Though providence, which is the exertion or operation of nature, is continued in an eternal series, eternal creation is no more than eternal exertion or action, the one is as mysterious as the other, and disputing against them is neither more nor less than disputing against the eternity of God.

God. Eternal whether applied to duration, existence, action or creation, is incomprehensible to us, but implies no contradiction in either of them; for that which is above our comprehension we cannot perceive to be contradictory, nor on the other hand can we perceive its rationallity or confiftency. We are certain that God is a rational, wife, underftanding Being, becaufe he has in degree made us fo, and his wifdom, power and goodnefs is vifible to us in his creation and government of the world: From thefe facts we are rationally induced to acknowledge him, and not becaufe we can comprehend his being, perfections, creation or providence: could we comprehend God he would ceafe to be what he is. The ignorant among men cannot comprehend the underftanding of the wife among their own fpecies, much lefs the perfection of a GOD. Neverthelefs, in our raciocination upon the works and harmony of nature, we are obliged to concede to a felf-exiftent and eternal caufe of all things, as has been fufficiently argued, though at the fame time it is mifterious to us, that there fhould be fuch a being as a felf-exiftent and eternally independent one. Thus we believe in God, although we cannot comprehend any thing of the how, why, or wherefore it was poffible for him to be; and as creation was

the

the exertion of such an incomprehensible and perfect being, it must of necessary consequence be, in a great measure, misterious to us; we can nevertheless be certain, that it has been of an equal eternity and infinitude of extension with God.

None will dispute the reality of creation, inasmuch as none can go amiss of the evidence of the certainty of it. This being premised, it necessarily follows that it was either eternal, or in time, as there can be no third way or mean between these two; for that which is not eternal must have had a beginging, which is the same as an existence in time.

With respect to us, we cannot effect or do any thing but in time; we have a dependent existence, and after a series of succeeding parts of time we arrive to a capacity of manhood, and every action of our lives is performed in the order of time: and as one part of time succeeds another, so our actions succeed each other, and every of our individual actions are progressive in themselves, simply considered, and are measured by time, whose fleeting moments pass swiftly on towards their never ending stage, eternity. But when we speak of the act, exertion or creation of God, we should conceive of them, as not being confined or limitted

limitted to the order of time, or successively connected with its fleeting moments like ours; for such conceptions circumscribe and limit the power of God, and are ideally subversive of his eternity, infinity and absolute perfection, subjecting him to a capacity or condition, which is manifestly finite. But creation is nothing short of an infinite exertion of God, who being eternally omnipresent, the operation or exertion of the act of creation was eternally every where; as omniscient it was perfectly consistent and best; as omnipotent it was perfected without succession of time; and being eternally and infinitely compleat, the almighty act of creation could never be repeated.

IMMENSITY being replete with creation, the omniscient, omnipresent, omnipotent, eternal and infinite exertion of God in creation, is incomprehensible to the understanding or the weakness of man, and will eternally remain the prerogative of infinite penetration, sagacity and uncreated intelligence to understand.

SECTION II.

The NATURAL IMPOSSIBILITY *of a* SUCCESSIVE CREATION *evinces the* ETERNITY *of it.*

NEVERTHELESS, for arguments sake, and further to illustrate the doctrine of eternal creation, we will examine into the merits of any supposed successive creation; and first, it will not be disputed but that time is compounded of parts, viz. a succession of years, months, days, minutes, and seconds of duration. That time cannot extend its succession or retrospection co-eval with eternity, hath been already fully evinced; so that it necessarily follows, that whatever is done in time, or according to the order of time cannot be eternal, or infinite, as it may respect the preceding or succeeding eternity: and consequently such things or acts which are done in those confined and limitted parts of duration are the exertions and productions of finite beings: so that if in our raciocination on creation, we evince that in the very nature of things it could not have been perfected according to the order of time, then the doctrine of eternal creation will of necessary consequence be established.

Thus having stated and opened the argument, we proceed to enquire into the merits of it. Provided the act of creation had been continued ever so many days, months or years in a successive or progressive manner, it would still be a bounded work; for the addition of ever so many local parts, could make but a local whole, which is as certain as that two and two make four, and is that which is

called

called a mathematical certainty, so that immensity could not have been repleted by a successive creation, had it been continued from any given time, forever, and that with the greatest progressive velocity. The motion of a cannon ball to be continued with the utmost rapidity from this time forever, would be as inadequate to measure immensity, as the motion of a snail may be supposed to be. For infinitude cannot be compounded of parts, or measured by time, nor repleted by any thing which pertains to, or operates by succession; for it hath no bounds, terms or limits, but is boundless and endless, swallows up our calculations of time with all its productions, and drowns the utmost stretch of all finite thoughts and comparisons.

From the foregoing arguments the inference necessarily follows, that as creation has a real existence, and could not have been perfected in time, it is therefore eternal.

SECTION III.

The ETERNITY *and* INFINITY *of* GOD, *demonstrative of the* ETERNITY *and* INFINITY *of his* CREATION *and* PROVIDENCE.

THE eternity and infinity of God necessarily imply the eternity and infinity of creation and providence

providence. That an infinite being should be local in his government, or display of his providence, is a downright contradiction both to the infinity of his power and goodness, the same as a supposed creation in time would be to his eternity. The complex idea of a God contains in it an idea of his providence, as much as the complex idea of a king includes that of subjects, or the idea of parents that of an offspring: to suppose a king without subjects, parents without issue, or a God without a providence, is equally chimerical, and to suppose a providence previous to creation, is as romantic a supposition as either of the former; for on this position there could have been no existencies or creatures to govern or provide for, and consequently there could have been no display of wisdom, power and goodness (which is the same as a providence) previous to creation, which would preclude an eternal providence, and consequently the eternal existence of a God. For nothing can be more evident than that the eternal display of those divine perfections, is absolutely essential to the being of a God, as it makes him to be what he is, viz. an eternally active, providential, and good being. Therefore, as certain as God is eternal and infinite, creation is so likewise.

It may be objected that God was eternally happy in himself, and needed none of the services of of his creatures, and therefore passed the previous eternity in the fruition of those attributes, which, in the succeeding eternity, he saw fit to exercise; but it should be considered, that if there had been a sufficient reason in the divine mind not to have displayed his perfections or providence in the preceding eternity, if God had acted consistently, then he would have made no display of them in the succeeding eternity: for if there may be a supposed reason for inactivity in God, in the previous eternity, it must have held good as applied to the latter, inasmuch as eternal and infinite reason must have been eternally the same. Among men it is said that contrivance is half, but an infinite mind, which can receive no enlargement by thinking or by experiments, and whose perfections are eternally the same, cannot fail of eternally acting uniformly from the same reasons: and as a supposed creation in time must have had the divine approbation; and the reason as well as the power to have effected it must have been eternal with God, it consequently could not have failed to have eternally produced the same effect, viz. eternal creation and providence.

FURTHERMORE, if creation and providence, although they may be supposed to have commenced in time, yet if complexly considered, they contain or

imply

imply any real perfection or excellence, then it necessarily follows, that previous to the æra of creation, God was imperfect; for if there be any display of perfection in a supposed creation and providence in time, God must be supposed to have been deficient of it in the preceding eternity, and as a deficiency or want of perfection in God would be a downright contradiction to his being, and equally so in the previous as in the subsequent eternity, we therefore infer that creation and providence must have been eternal. Finally, if we admit that creation had a beginning, there was a beginning to the moral government and display of the divine perfections, which must have been exerted co-eval with God, and from hence it follows that there was also a beginning to the being and existence of God, which would render him dependent on some pre-existent cause, and be subversive of his eternity, self-existency and independency; as has been before argued. We are therefore obliged to admit the eternity of creation and providence, which is the same as eternal exertion or action: and as the act was not and could not be progressive, or according to the order of time, but as one simple or uncompounded exertion of eternal and immense perfection, repleted the boundless work, it opened an eternal and infinitely ample field for the display of divine providence.

SECTION

SECTION IV.

Of the INFINITUDE *and* ETERNITY *of* PROVIDENCE *in the* CREATION *and* FORMATION *of* FINITE BEINGS.

THAT the succession of time, according to our calculations of it, is not eternal, has been fully evinced, whether applied to creation, formation, or providence, or to any thing else, provided it be supposed to have a beginning, which is always supposed, when we speak of time or its division. But by premising a self-existent and consequently an eternal cause, we may then suppose an eternal succession of causes, which in nature to us would be incomprehensible, and consequently incapable of being numerated by us; inasmuch as the efficient and self-existent cause is eternal and the creation and regulation of things without the beginning of numbers or period of existence, or vicissitude: and thus the succession would be without beginning or end, which is as eternal as an infinite line may be supposed to be; and may be denominated an eternal series, as they are the harmonious revolutions of nature in which the providence of God consists, and in which it may be truly said to be eternal, and we may as well suppose an eternal formation, as an eternal creation or action

tion, for if we but admit the eternity and infinity of God, that of the eternity and infinity of his creation and providence (which may as well include formation) follows of consequence, as there could be no providence or government before there were creatures to govern or provide for; so that we are obliged to admit, that creatures were either eternally created, or eternally formed, or both; which doctrine may be objected to from this consideration, that creation and dependent creatures on such a position, would, as to their eternity, be co-eval with God, how then could they be dependent on him? I answer as well as the act of God, which may be eternal and yet dependent on the being or essence of God, or as there may be eternal emanations eternally flowing from an eternal cause. The eternal existence or succession of finite beings in the preceding eternity, is as reconcilable to the attributes, perfections and providence of God, as that they should be immortal or capable of a subsequent eternal duration, which we believe with respect to the souls of mankind.

This doctrine of eternal creation and providence, as also the infinitude of it, may give offence to such persons who may read this book, and who have habituated themselves to trace their genealogy from Adam as the first rational finite being.

They

They may be surprised at an apprehension of an eternal infinitude of creation, finite beings and providence. But this must eternally have been the case as before argued; so that we should conceive that as God was eternal, and eternally active, he might, and has eternally created and formed intelligent accountable agents; nor is the eternal creation or eternal formation, and consequently the eternal existence or succession of finite beings, as they may respect the antecedent eternity, at all more contradictory or impossible with God than the immortality of the human soul, or the eternal perpetuation or succession of finite beings, as they may respect the subsequent eternity. Inasmuch as self-existent, eternal and infinite perfection is eternally the same, and may and must have been equally exerted eternally: alluding to one entire eternity, without beginning or end.

Though we cannot comprehend the self-existency eternity and infinity of God, or the eternity and infinitude of his creation and providence; yet we can comprehend, that a being that is not self-existent, is necessarily dependent upon a being that is by nature self-existent and self-sufficient, or it could not have existed; for that a dependent being cannot exist independently, any more than it could exist and not exist at the same time.

THEREFORE

THEREFORE the self-sufficiency, independency and self-existency of the efficient cause of all things, is demonstrable from the dependent intelligent beings, and the things of nature now existing and with which our external senses, internal reflections and understandings are conversant; and from the self-sufficiency and existency of the efficient cause of all things we infer, that that cause has all possible power, or in other words, that it is omnipotent, or it could not have self-sufficiently existed and given being to the universality of things, and having thus established the omnipotency of the efficient cause of all things, we infer its eternity and infinity, for that a being of all power, self-sufficiency, existency or omnipotency, could not have existed in time, or at any certain æra; inasmuch as it would be a contradiction to his self-sufficiency or omnipotency, that he had not existed before such æra or any other period of time; for a self-existent and omnipotent being could not have waited on the will, pleasure or power of any other being or cause for his existence, and all-sufficiency, and therefore must have self-sufficiently, omnipotently, and eternally existed, for otherwise he could not be self-sufficient, all-sufficient or omnipotent, since the power of existence is essential to omnipotency, for without the existence of it there could be no such power in the universe, and as an existent omnipotent

nipotent power includes all power, it necessarily, among others includes the power of an eternal existence, for any power, short of an eternal one, could not be truly and absolutely omnipotent, as it would be deficient in the article of its eternity; therefore omnipotent power is eternal.

THE eternal creation and providence of God is the necessary result of his eternal existence and activity. If God has been eternally existent and active he has done something, for he could not have been active in doing nothing; and if something, we quere whether it is not something worthy of a God. To ascribe trifles to him is unworthy of him; to suppose, for instance, that he worked by the day, or rested from labour, or carried on the work of creation according to our notions of the succession of time, or progressively, are suggestions inadequate to an infinite being, or to answer the design of perfecting an immense creation, and extending or displaying an unlimitted providence, which could never have been perfected by a progressive or finite exertion, had it been continued *ad infinitum*. But on the contrary, let us but premise that God is eternal and infinite, and the consequence must unavoidably follow that his creation and providence are likewise eternal and infinite, which necessarily implies the eternal creation,

I   formation

formation and existence, or succession of finite intelligent beings: For a creation and regulation of things (which we call nature) abstractly considered from intelligences, could not have constituted a providence, as there could have been, on such a position, no display of the divine goodness or character, in the creation and government of mere incogitative and stupid matter, incapable of sensation, reflection, or enjoyment; for such a creation & harmony of mere natural things could not have displayed any apprehension of the being, attributes and perfections of a God, whose divinity could no otherwise have been discerned but by the exercise of reason. Therefore intelligent finite beings must have been interspersed co-eternal and co-extensive with the being, creation and providence of God; and disputing against the eternal existence or succession of finite intelligencies, or against the eternity and infinity of creation and providence, is neither more or less in the final consequences of it, than disputing against the reality of a God. For as certain as there is a God, he is eternally and infinitely perfect, and if so, his creation and providence is also eternally and infinitely perfect and compleat, whatever our ignorant apprehensions and reasonings on this divine subject may be:

THERE

THERE may perhaps arise some queries in the mind of the reader, relative to the several parts of the arguments in this treatise, concerning succession in the exertion of God in creation, wherein it is argued that a successive creation had it been continued forever, could not have extended the amplitude of it beyond a limitted or local one, and yet in this and other sections of this work, it is argued that there must have been an eternal succession or series in the productions and vicissitudes of natural things and particularly in finite intelligent beings, as they may respect the antecedent and subsequent eternity.

THESE arguments at first sight appear to clash. That there should have been an eternal succession in the order of nature, and yet that we cannot by our successive admeasurements comprehend the immensity of things, seems to be contradictory, but it should be considered that the successions of nature are eternal and therefore without beginning or end, but that our calculations are finite, as they have a beginning and end, and therefore cannot comprehend the eternal succession of things, or the eternity of God, or the infinitude of his creation or providence. It has been already argued that by tracing the order of the

the succession of causes retrospectively, we cannot arrive at the eternal or self-existent cause; for that the succession is eternal, and therefore exceeds our numerical calculations, which are governed by the addition of units or regulated by the order of time. Though from the present order of nature we argue its eternal succession and vicissitude, which exceeds our numeration, because there is no first in the series, as they are infinite and eternal, the same as a premised endless (extended) chain, in which there could be no first link, so in an eternal or infinite succession, there could not be a first in the succession, as it would be a contradiction to infinite extension, or to an eternal duration of the existence of God.

Those things which have a beginning and end we can trace by our calculations to their respective æras, but are lost in our attempts to compute an eternal duration or existence, or an infinite extension or creation, for that which is endless or boundless exceeds all our mathematics, and swallows up all our thoughts and comparisons. To preambulate a premised mathematical eternal line, or an infinite circle, or to calculate an eternal series or succession of causes, or the mere eternal existence of a God, or of duration, are to us equally impossible, nevertheless we are as certain of an eternal duration, as we are of the eternal existence of God, for if God has been eternal, the duration of his existence must have been also eternal, whether we are able to calculate it or not, and the same may be truly affirmed of an eternal creation, or of an eternal providence, or of the eternal existence and succession or generation of intelligent finite beings. An eternal series or succession in nature is as reconcileable to our understandings, as the eternal existence of nature, or the eternal existence of a God, so that we may as well dispute against any mere eternal existence whatever, as against an eternal succession. For if one may be the other is possible, whether we can comprehend them or not. The manner of these infinite calculations are to us incomprehensible, but not contradictory; for we cannot understand that to be a contradiction, which to us is incomprehensible.

FINALLY, as there could be no God without a providence, and no providence without intelligent beings on whom only it could be exercised, therefore, inasmuch as there is a God, finite intelligences have been interspersed through the creation and providence of God co-eval with his existence. But as to a premised successive creation, or a progressive one consisting of local parts, which collectively considered, could make but a local whole, it could not be of the creation and providence of God, for this very reason, that by our mathematical calculations we could comprize it, and therefore it could be but finite, which would be infinitely inadequate for the territorial providence of an absolutely perfect and infinite being.

SECTION V.

The Distinction between Creation and Formation.

IT is proper to make a concise distinction between creation and formation, to prevent any confusion in our minds, in applying the one to the other. Formation belongs to that, which we call the eternal series of causes and effects, which we have been frequently describing as surpassing our calculations by numbers, and though it is eternal, it is in the eternal order of nature dependent on creation, and creation as eternally dependent on the eternal self-existent cause. Creation affords the materials of formation or modification, and that power of nature called production, gives birth to the vast variety of them; but production could not be from nothing; formation and modification are therefore the production of creation. Creation, as has been before observed, having been eternal and without succession, could not be repeated ed, inasmuch as there was an eternal and immense fulness; yet acts of natural production by formation, may and have been carried on in an eternal series, as the productions of vegetable and animal life, may exhibit a sample; in fine productions (which are the same as growths) in general are nothing else but formation. Nor is death, decay and dissolution any thing else but a dissolution of forms, and not annihilation or a dissolution of creation, which is infinitely *complete* and independent of any particular form; though it must exist in some form or other, and is necessarily united with all possible forms: and thus it is, that all forms in general are indebted to creation for their existence. And the immense creation, consisting of elements, possesses its various forms and is endowed with all necessary properties, qualities, dispositions and aptitudes that we denominate by the term *nature*, which must have been *co-eval* with the eternity of God, and must necessarily remain to all duration *co-extensive* and *co-existent* with the divine nature.

SECTION

SECTION VI.

Observations on Moses's Account of Creation.

The foregoing theory of creation and providence will probably be rejected by most people in this country, inasmuch as they are prepossessed with the theology of Moses, which represents creation to have had a beginning, "In the beginning God created the heavens and the earth." In the preceeding part of this chapter it has been evinced that creation and providence could not have had a beginning, and that they are not circumscribed but unlimited; yet it seems, that Moses limited creation by a prospective view of the heavens, or firmament, from this globe, and if creation was thus limitted, it would consequently have circumscribed the dominion and display of the divine providence or perfection; but if Moses's idea of the creation of " the heavens and the earth," was immense, ever so many days of progressive work could never have finished such a boundless creation; for a progressive creation is the same as a limitted one; as each progressive days work would be bounded by a successive admeasurement, and the whole six days work added together, could be but local and bear no manner of proportion to infinitude, but would limi

the

the dominion and consequently the display of the divine perfections or providence, which is incompatible with a just idea of the eternity and infinity of God, as has been argued in the foregoing pages.

It may be objected, that immensity, all around the terraqueous ball to the verge of Moses's "heavens and earth," had been eternally replete with creation, providence and goodness, but that the part of space comprized in his representation of the "heavens and the earth" was, till the æra of its beginning (which according to the chronology of the Jews, was, till less than six thousand years ago) an empty chasm in the creation, and consequently in the providence of God, which so far would be subversive of a just conception of his infinity. Inasmuch as on this position, creation and providence must have been incomplete till the epocha of the supposed creation of the "heavens and the earth," at which time it may be supposed to have been compleated, and which supposes an addition to the creation, and consequently to the providence of God. But had they been previously infinitely extended, they could not have admitted an enlargement. For immensity, as it may respect creation, providence, or mere space, is incapable of progression or addition, inasmuch as immensity forecloses it. From hence we infer, that as certain as the creation and providence of God was eternally and infinitely complete, Moses's story of the creation of the "heaven's and the earth," is inadmissible, as it militates against the perfection of God; for as the work of creation is, so is its author, whether perfect or imperfect, local or infinite.

There are a variety of other blunders in Moses's description of creation, one of which I shall mention, which is to be found in his history of the first and fourth days work of God: "*And God said let there be light and there was light, and God called the light day and the darkness he called night, and the evening and the morning was the first day.*" Then he proceeds to the second and third day's work, and so on to the sixth; but in his chronicle of the fourth days work, he says that "*God made two great lights, the greater light to rule the day, and the lesser light to rule the night.*" This appears to be an inconsistent history of the original of light; day and night were ordained the first day, and on the fourth day the greater and less lights were made to serve the same purposes; but it is likely that many errors have crept into his writings, through the vicissitudes of learning, and particularly from the corruptions of translations, of his as well as the writings of other ancient authors, besides, it must be acknowledged, that those ancient writers laboured under great difficulties in writing to posterity, merely from the
consideration

consideration of the infant state of learning and knowledge, then in the world, and consequently we should not act the part of severe critics with their writings, any further than to prevent their obtrusion on the world as being infallible.

SECTION VII.
Of the ETERNITY and INFINITUDE of DIVINE PROVIDENCE.

WHEN we consider our solar system, attracted by its fiery centre, and moving in its several orbits with regular, majestic and periodical revolutions; we are charmed at the prospect and contemplation of those worlds of motion, and adore the wisdom and the power by which they are attracted, and their velocity regulated and perpetuated. And when we reflect that the blessings of life are derived from and dependent on the properties, qualities, constructions, proportions and movements of that stupendous machine, we gratefully acknowledge the divine beneficence. When we extend our thoughts (through our external sensations) to the vast regions of the starry heavens, we are lost in the immensity of God's works; some stars appear fair and luminous and others scarcely discernable to the eye, which by the help of glasses make a brilliant appearance, bringing the knowledge of others far remote within the verge of our feeble discoveries

discoveries, which merely by the eye could not have been discerned or distinguished. These discoveries of the works of God, naturally prompt the inquisitive mind to conclude that the author of this astonishing part of creation, which is displayed to our view, has still extended his creation; so that if it were possible that any of us could be transported to the farthest extended star, which is perceptible to us here, we should from thence survey worlds as distant from that as that is from this, and so on *ad infinitum*.

FURTHERMORE, it is altogether reasonable to conclude, that the heavenly bodies, *alias* worlds, which move or are situate within the circle of our knowledge, as well as all others throughout immensity, are each and every of them possessed or inhabited by some intelligent agents or other, however different their sensations or manner of receiving or communicating their ideas may be from our's, or however different from each other. For why would it not have been as wise or as consistent with the perfections which we adore in God, to have neglected giving being to intelligences in this world as in those other worlds, interspersed with æther of various qualities in his immense creation? And inasmuch as this world is thus replenished, we may with the highest rational certainty infer, that as God has given us to rejoice, and adore

him

him for our being, he has acted consistent with his goodness, in the display of his providence, throughout the universality of worlds.

To suppose that God Almighty has confined his goodness to this world, to the exclusion of all others, is much similar to the idle fancies of some individuals in this world, that they, and those of their communion or faith, are the favorites of heaven, exclusively; but these are narrow and bigotted conceptions, which are degrading to a rational nature, and utterly unworthy of God, of whom we should form the most exalted ideas.

FURTHERMORE, there could be no display of goodness, or of any of the moral perfections of God, merely in repleting immensity with a stupid creation of elements, or sluggish senseless and incogitative matter, which by nature may be supposed to be incapable of sensation, reflection and enjoyment: undoubtedly elements and material compositions were designed by God to subserve rational beings, by constituting or supporting them in their respective modes of existence, in this or those other numerous worlds.

THERE may be in God's boundless empire of nature and providence, as many different sorts of modified sensation, as there are different worlds and temperatures

temperatures in immensity; or at least sensation may more or less vary; but whether their sensations agree in any or many respects, or not, or whether they agree with ours, or, if in any part, how far, are matters unknown to us; but that there are intelligent orders of beings, interspersed through the creation of God, is a matter of the highest degree of rational certainty of any thing that falls short of mathematical demonstration, or of proofs which come within the reach of our outward sensations, called sensible demonstration. For if this is the only world that is replenished with life and reason, it includes the whole circumference of God's providence; for there would be no display of wisdom or goodness, merely in governing rude elements and senseless matter, nor could there be any valuable end proposed by such a supposed government, or any happiness, instruction or subserviency to being in general, or any reason assigned, why such a creation (for it cannot be a providence) should have had the divine approbation, and consequently we may be morally certain that rational beings are interspersed co-extensive with the creation of God.

Although the various orders of intelligences, throughout infinitude, differ ever so much in their manner of sensation, and consequently in their manner of communication, or of receiving ideas,

yet

yet reason and consciousness, must be the same in all; but not the same with respect to the various objects of the several worlds, though in nature the same. For instance, a person born blind cannot possibly have an idea of colours, though his sensibility of sound and feeling may be as acute as ours; and since there are such a variety of modes of sensation in this world, how vastly numerous may we apprehend them to be in immensity? We shall soon by pondering on these things feel the insufficiency of our imagination, to conceive of the immense possibility of the variety of their modes of sensation and the manner of intercourse of cogitative beings. It may be objected that a man cannot subsist in the sun; but does it follow from thence, that God cannot or has not constituted a nature peculiar to that fiery region, and caused it to be as natural and necessary for it to suck in and breathe out flames of fire, as it is for us to do the like in air. Numerous are the kinds of fishy animals, which can no other ways subsist but in the water, in which other animals would perish, (amphibious ones excepted;) while other animals, in a variety of forms, either swifter or slower move on the surface of the earth, or wing the air: of these there are sundry kinds, which during the seasons of winter live without food; and many of the insects which are really possessed of animal life, remain frozen, and as soon as they are let loose by the kind influence of the sun, they again assume their wonted animal life; and if animal life may differ so much in the same world, what inconceivable variety may be possible in worlds innumerable, as applicable to mental, cogitative and organized beings. Certain it is, that any supposed obstructions, concerning the quality or temperature of any or every of those worlds, could not have been any bar in the way of God Almighty, with regard to his replenishing his universal creation with moral agents. The unlimited perfection of God, could perfectly well adapt every part of his creation to the design of whatever rank or species of constituted beings, his God-like wisdom and goodness saw fit to impart existence to; so that as there is no deficiency of absolute perfection in God, it is rationally demonstrative that the immense creation is replenished with rational agents, and that it has been eternally so, and that the display of divine goodness must have been as perfect and complete, in the antecedent, as it is possible to be in the subsequent eternity.

From this theological way of arguing on the creation and providence of God, it appears that the whole, which we denominate by the term *nature*, which is the same as creation perfectly regulated, was eternally connected together by the creator

ator to answer the same all glorious purpose, *to wit*; the display of the divine nature, the consequences of which are existence and happiness to being in general, so that creation with all its productions operates according to the laws of nature, and is sustained by the self-existent eternal cause in perfect order and decorum, agreeable to the eternal wisdom, unalterable rectitude, impartial justice and immense goodness of the divine nature, which is a summary of God's providence. It is from the established ordinances of nature that summer and winter, rainy and fair seasons, monsoons, refreshing breezes, seed time and harvest, day and night interchangeably succeed each other, and diffuse their extensive blessings to man. Every enjoyment and support of life is from God, delivered to his creatures in and by the tendency, aptitude, disposition and operation of those laws. Nature is the medium, or intermediate instrument, through which God dispenses his benignity to mankind. The air we breathe in, the light of the sun, and the waters of the murmuring rills, evince his providence: and well it is that they are given in so great profusion that they cannot by the monopoly of the rich be engrossed from the poor.

WHEN we copiously pursue the study of nature, we are certain to be lost in the immensity of the works and wisdom of God; we may nevertheless, in a variety of things discern their fitness, happifying tendency and sustaining quality to us ward, from all which, as rational and contemplative beings we are prompted to infer, that God is universally uniform and consistent in his infinitude of creation and providence, although we cannot comprehend all that consistency, by reason of infirmity, yet we are morally sure, that of all possible plans, infinite wisdom must have eternally adopted the best, and infinite goodness have approved it, and infinite power have perfected it. And as the good of being in general, must have been the ultimate end of God in his creation and government of his creatures, his omniscience could not fail to have it always present in his view. Universal nature must therefore be ultimately attracted to this single point, and infinite perfection must have eternally displayed itself in creation and providence. From hence we infer, that God is as eternal and infinite in his goodness, as his self-existent and perfect nature is omnipotently great.

SECTION.

SECTION VIII.

The PROVIDENCE *of* GOD *does not interfere with the* AGENCY *of* MAN.

MANKIND are more or less apt to confound their ideas of divine providence, with the actions or agency of man, which ought to be considered distinctly, inasmuch as they are not one and the same; the former is the agency of God, by the intervention of the operations of nature, and the latter the agency of man. The providence of God supports the universe, and enables rational agents to act in certain limited spheres with a derived freedom, for otherwise it could not be denominated the agency of man, but of God. So likewise in our notions of the infinity of God, we ought to make a distinction between his essence and his creation. The infinity of the divine nature does not include all things, though it includes all possible perfection; it it included all things, it would include all imperfections also, which is inadmissible, nor does the providence of God include all manner of actions or agencies, it does not include the actions of free and accountable agents, for that they are more or less imperfect and sinful; though his providence sustains their power of agency, for God cannot controul the actions of free beings, since, if he did, it would be a contradiction to their being

being free. Necessity and freedom are in the diversity of their natures diametrically opposed to each other, for which reason we cannot in truth be said to act necessarily and freely in the same actions, and at the same time, any more than we can exist and not exist at the same time: nor is it possible for omnipotence itself to effect these or such like contradictions, as they are attended with impossibilities in their own nature, for that if one part of a contradiction is true the other cannot be so.

Some have deduced arguments for a proof of the fatality of the actions of mankind from a supposed prescience of the knowledge of God, but there is not and cannot be any prescience or foreknowledge in the omniscient mind, for there is no first or last, beginning or end to the divine knowledge, but with him it is one eternal *now*, and cannot be divided into tenses, epochas or succession like ours. Succession in knowledge is the distinguishing characteristick of a finite mind, it is knowing things by degrees or progressively, which method of attaining knowledge could never extend to the comprehension of the infinitude of things. But eternal and infinite knowledge is always the same, and always present with God, which necessarily precludes the notion of *before*, or *after*, in the divine knowledge, as much as unbounded space

space excludes the notion of a centre, which can have no existence without a circumference. Suppose a chain to be extended without end, which is the same as an eternal or infinite extension, none but the divine mind could comprehend its links, as a finite numeration could not ascertain their number, nor would there be any first or last link to such a premised chain: the comparison will be the same, when we suppose an eternal series of causes and events, in which there could not be a first cause, though there must have been an eternal one, so that God cannot be the first cause of all things, as argued in the fourth section of the first chapter. And as the eternal cause was not a first cause, so there can be no first or last knowledge to an omniscient eternal mind. But it may be objected, that though the knowledge of God be admitted to be always the same, without addition, diminution, or succession, yet his omniscience of the actions of mankind (in time) as well as that of things in general, was eternal, and therefore in the divine mind had a previous existence to the actions themselves, and consequently human actions must necessarily have taken place exactly as they have done, or God would have been imperfect in knowledge, which by some is thought to militate against the liberty of man. But it should be considered that though the knowledge of the actions of mankind, existed in the divine mind, previous to the actions themselves having been acted in time; nevertheless those actions of man were not necessarily produced from that knowledge in God, but on the contrary the actions of mankind necessitate his knowledge. For had it not been for the reality of those actions in time, the eternal mind could not have had the knowledge of them, inasmuch as God could not have known falsehood to have been truth; the eternal knowledge of God was therefore predicated, or grounded, on the facts of those actions; so that instead of the actions of mankind being necessitated, they necessitate the knowledge of God: as for example, I will premise that the reader sees me move my hand, the motion in this case necessitated him to know it; and inasmuch as God is eternally omniscient, it necessitated him to know it eternally, as much as it did the reader in time.

God is eternally and infinitely capacious, and therefore necessarily knows all things, and his omniscience is as much necessitated by the truth of facts, as the knowledge of man. From hence we infer that the actions of mankind may be free, but that the omniscience of God is necessary, as it is a necessary perfection of the divine nature to know all things, but that which never exists cannot be known by God or man. It is therefore facts,
which

which constitute truth, and necessarily produce all knowledge both divine and human; and as the omniscience of God is predicated on truth, it must respect the natural and moral worlds with that intrinsic difference, which truly subsists between them.

It is manifest that natural bodies gravitate and are governed by fate, but that rational beings are not. But whether mankind act necessarily or freely, can never be inferred merely from the eternal omniscience of God, for if so be that the actions of mankind be admitted to be either necessary or free, it could not be the knowledge of God, which makes them to be as they are; nor does the knowledge of God alter them; but they have their intrinsic nature independent of the omniscience of God; and upon which his omniscience was eternally predicated: so that was it possible, that they could not be known, or that they were not known by God, their actions would nevertheless be either necessary or free, as in truth they are in their own nature, nor does the knowing or not knowing of them, either by God or man, alter their nature, whether necessary or free: for truth is uniform, and the omniscience of God cannot fail to be predicated thereon, for otherwise God could not be omniscient: so that in very deed God knows the actions of
mankind

mankind to be what in truth they are, the divine prescience being necessitated by reality. To suppose the conduct or demeanour of mankind to have been predetermined by God, and effected merely by his providence, is a manifest infringement of his justice and goodness in the constitution of our mental powers, in giving us a false and erroneous consciousness of guilt, thereby making us mentally miserable through deception, or mere imaginary apprehension of vicious actions, in which we are wholly passive, being actuated by the superintending power of the universe, and consequently not at all blameable for what we do, and in no other sense guilty but from the fallacious representations of a deluded conscience; which according to the premised truth of things wholly exculpates us from it, and which if we knew to be true, the notion of sin would set as easy on our minds as a glove on our hand. Therefore a predetermination of the actions or conduct of mankind, is inadmissible, for it is injurious to the divine character (among men) to suppose it, as it would make God the author of moral evil to the exclusion of his offending creatures, or exclude moral evil from the universe; and if so, there need no farther dispute about it.

MANKIND in general, in their notions or writings on the freedom of their actions, blend it with mechanism,

mechanism, which is not strange, for it is almost impossible to describe human liberty in its intrinsic genuine nature, free from a compulsive alloy of one kind or other; the universe all around us being subjected to the laws of fate, our bodily sensorium not excepted, so that there is not any thing in the universe analagous to, or any ways resembling intelligent nature with which we can with any propriety compare it: and as the principle of intelligence itself, is diverse from all other sort of existencies with which we are conversant, so the nature and manner of its action or exertion of its powers, is specifically different from all other things, which renders analogy impertinent.—All matter, which we have any conception of, is governed by the almighty influence of fate in its various and extensive operations, and well it is that it is thus regulated and made subservient to rational nature. The natural palpitation of the heart, the beating of the pulse and gravitation of our bodies, with the other laws of our animal nature, are as mechanical as the movements of our solar system; every thing therefore in the universe is subject to the laws of fate, except the actions or exertions of moral beings only, which are by nature free, and which by intuition we know to be so, without argumentative demonstration to prove it, the knowledge of it being essential to all intelligent natures; and all the difficulties, which ever have been started against its reality, have been owing to the weakness of our reasonings. It is in consequence of this intuitive certainty, that we are free, that our consciences acquit or condemn us in all our actions and deportment of life, and from this consciousness of liberty results all our mental happiness and misery, praise or blame, and from which we deduce all our notions of virtue or vice, or of accountability. But when we assay to investigate the liberty of the will, or the intrinsic nature of freedom, or wherein it consists, we are apt to be more or less confounded or embarrassed with the laws of fate, with which we are closely surrounded, and for want of skill to distinguish liberty from compulsion, involve it (in our mistaken notions) with the operations of those mechanical laws; and to finally draw irregular inferences against the reality of it; concluding that mind as well as matter, is under the compulsive influence of the laws of fate; though at the same time, such a conclusion is diametrically opposite to our intuitive certainty of the contrary. And after all, we cannot but feel ourselves guilty, or not guilty, according to the prescriptions of our own consciences, and are mentally happy or miserable on the presumption of our intuitive knowledge of the

freedom

freedom of our agency, which never fails to frustrate all our unphilosophical theory, which militates against it. For the consciousness of liberty, with which our understandings are impressed by intuition, is natural and true, and will have its effects on our consciences, in spite of our theorical speculations of the destiny of our actions. The freedom of our actions, from which virtue and vice became possible in the nature of man, was implanted in our minds coeval with the exercise of reason; or the knowledge of moral good and evil; and though our reasonings on this important subject may be too much tinctured with the fatality of things about us, and our conclusions more or less faulty and erroneous, yet our intuition of the reality of our liberty cannot be a deception, for it is the invariable voice of all rational nature, that must have had the sanction of divinity, intuitively promulgated to rational nature universally, which lays the foundation of agency, and consequently of accountability, at the supreme bar of God, or the vicegerency of our own consciences: for it is disgustfully absurd to common sense to suppose, that necessary beings should be commended or discommended, punished or rewarded, for their destined or passive actions. Had it been in the nature of things possible for God to have made

moral

moral agents act necessarily, undoubtedly they would have been restrained from wickedness, and mechanically moved to the practice of that which we now call virtue, (though it would lose its nature if subjected to the laws of fate,) and have been made mechanically happy, which would have prevented the confusions and disorders of the moral world, and the miseries which have ensued in consequence thereof. But it was in the nature and fitness of things impossible, for God to have constituted a rational nature exclusive of liberty; for that it naturally and necessarily results from such a nature, or is congenial with it, so that the one cannot exist without the other; in consequence whereof moral evil became possible, and has had access to this world, merely through the vicious agency of man, which has been the destruction not only of individuals, but of families, republics, kingdoms and empires, whatever effects it may produce in the succeeding stage of our existence.

It has been a great dispute in the schools, whether an ass would not starve to death between two mows, or parcels of choice hay, equally good, and equidistant from him, and but just out of his reach, merely for want of a preponderating motive to chuse to which of the two to apply himself, to satisfy his hunger. However, it is more than probable that the sagacity of the ass in such circumstances, would exceed the theory of those, who in such a case, devote him to death in their speculation. The same sort of speculation has, by some, been thought to hold good, as applied to the motives of human actions and conduct in general; arguing that we cannot act without motives, and that among a plurality of them, a preponderating one is requisite, to determine the act of choice, or of the will; that if the motives or inducements are supposed to be equal, they would counterballance each other; for the illustration of the argument, they allude to mechanical similies, as that of scales and steelyards, which may be ballanced with equal weights to the suspension of their motion, and which by preponderating weights turn their beam; and thus, by erroneously making application of mechanical comparisons to actions of a moral nature, lose sight of their liberty. Or as water is said to run freely or without constraint, in like manner some suppose, that man acts freely from the strongest motives, which motives in the order of nature, extrinsically and necessarily determine all their actions, and which are nevertheless as free as the running of water in its natural course,

course, or as the preponderation of the beam of the scales or steelyards, by the preponderating inducement of a heavier weight. But it should be considered, that the essence of intelligent nature does not occupy space as material beings do; nor is it corporeal, or composed of matter; it is not heavy or light, round or square, long or short, black or white: What then is it like? Why it is like itself, or as Doctor Watts expresseth it,

"*There's nothing like it round the pole,*
"*Nothing can describe the soul.*"

Nor can the motion of water, which is governed by gravitation, or the preponderation of the beam of steelyards or scales, which are necessarily acted upon by the same law, or any other movements or operations of nature or art, be analogous to the acts of the mind, or admit of any just comparison, which has been the cause of confusion, in all writers who have attempted it.

For the essence of thinking beings, and their manner of acting, is essentially distinct from all and every part of the universe besides, and every simile or comparison, which we draw from thence, serves only to confound or perplex a just arrangement of ideas of our exalted intelligent nature, and the superlative manner of its exertions or operations

rations, which we depreciate (ideally) by deducing its character of nature or action, from matter, figure and motion, with their various modifications, effects or combinations, either animate or inanimate; though it is very natural to represent the liberty of the mind by external analogies. One of the Indians of this country being asked, what his soul was? gave for answer "It is my think." This was both laconic and pertinent; and with respect to our liberty, it is impossible for us to obtain a greater certainty that we are free agents, than that which we naturally derive from the intuition of it. So that the greatest philosopher, and the humble and unlearned peasant, are in this respect on a level, being each of them conscious that they are free; from which sentiment it is, that we blame ourselves and our species, when we or they depart from the conduct of reason.

As long as the human conscience will be a source of mental happiness or misery to the species, it avails nothing to teach the doctrine of the necessity of our actions, as nature will make us approve or disapprove of ourselves, according to our proficiencies in moral good or evil. If nature is in the fault (which is inadmissible) and gives us an erroneous consciousness concerning our liberty, and consequently of moral good and evil; yet

as

as long as nature (or conscience) remain the same, our intelligent reflections and apprehensions of merit, or demerit, will also remain the same; which cannot fail to be attended with the like consequences of tranquility and happiness, or of guilt and misery; so that if nature has deceived us in those matters, we can have no remedy to appease a guilty conscience, unless our calvinistical clergy could in good earnest beat it into our heads, that our consciousness of guilt or blame is a mere delusion, and that in truth God Almighty eternally designed and predestinated all our actions: such a faith as this, was it possible, might cure a guilty conscience; but I believe, that the God of nature, has so strongly implanted his law in the human soul, that the teachers of fatalism can never erase it, but that conscience will forever give such teachers the lye, though a part of mankind may, and have given a tacit and traditional assent to that unreasonable doctrine:

The doctrine of fate has been made use of in armies as a policy to induce soldiers to face danger. Mahomet taught his army that the " term of every man's life was fixed by God, and that none could shorten it, by any hazard that he might seem to be exposed to in battle or otherwise," but that it should be introduced into

peaceable

peaceable and civil life, and be patronized by any teachers of religion, is quite strange, as it subverts religion in general, and renders the teaching of it unnecessary: except among other necessary events it may be premised, that it is necessary that they teach that doctrine, and that I oppose it from the influence of the same law of fate, upon which thesis we are all disputing and acting in certain necessary circles, and if so, I make another necessary movement, which is, to discharge the public teachers of this doctrine, and expend their salaries in an œconomical manner, which might better answer the purposes of our happiness, or lay it out in good wine or old spirits to make the heart glad, and laugh at the stupidity or cunning of those who would have made us mere machines.

Some advocates for the doctrine of fate will also maintain that we are free agents, notwithstanding they tell us there has been a concatenation of causes and events, which has reached from God down to this time, and which will eternally be continued; that has and will controul and bring about every action of our lives, though there is not any thing in nature more certain than that we cannot act necessarily and freely, in the same action, and at the same time, yet it is hard for such persons, who have verily believed that they are elected (and thus by a predetermination of God become his special favorites) to give up their notions of a predetermination of all events, upon which system their election and everlasting happiness is nonsensically founded; and on the other hand, it is also hard for them to go so evidently against the law of nature (or dictates of conscience) which intuitively evinces the certainty of human liberty, as to reject such evidence; and therefore hold to both parts of the contradiction, *to wit*, that they act necessarily, and freely, upon which contradictory principle, they endeavour to maintain the dictates of natural conscience, and also, their darling folly of being electedly and exclusively favorites of God.

Such persons, very commonly argue, that the prescience, predetermination, or decrees of God, are by necessary consequences the same in result; and that they equally effect human agency; and as it is generally admitted, that God has an eternal omniscience of human agency, therefore they infer, that the conduct or actions of mankind are necessary; as say they, it must be conformable to the divine prescience, for otherwise, God would be imperfect in knowledge: not considering that God cannot know that a free agent acts necessarily

ly, or that a necessary agent acts freely, but that he knows things, or facts, to be as in truth they are; so that provided we act freely, God knows we act freely, but if necessarily, he knows we act necessarily. Yet it may be further argued, on the principles of fate, that there was a certainty in human actions, or they could not have been known. True, but this certainty did not proceed from the divine prescience, but from human agency, therefore if our agency is free, it is certain that it is free, but if necessary, it is certain that it is necessary; so that the certainty of our actions, or the divine prescience of them, are both resolved into the nature or reality of them; nor is there any other prescience or certainty, relative to human agency, but what results from its intrinsic nature. Therefore the argument deducible from eternal prescience, or certainty, will as well apply to the liberty of human agency, as to the destiny thereof. Upon the whole, we may rationally conclude, that instead of our actions being necessitated by the divine prescience, they necessitate it; inasmuch, as the knowledge of God or man, must be predicated on truth, and truth cannot fail of being predicated on nature: nature is therefore our polar star, to direct us relative to the question of the liberty or destiny of our actions in life, for though it be admitted, that our deportment in

life

life be either neceffary or free, yet it is not the knowledge of God, or of any other intelligencies that makes it to be as it is; but our agency muft be refolved into the nature of it, this it is that will determine whether it is free or not, and this it is which neceffitates the divine prefcience. For God not only knows the particular conduct or actions of his creatures, but alfo the manner of their actions, and it is the manner of their actions, which muft determine whether they are neceffary or free, and it is the nature of their actions which muft afcertain the manner of them, and the divine prefcience is predicated thereon.

From the foregoing arguments we infer, that it is from the intrinfic nature of our actions we muft deduce the important conclufion of their freedom or fatality, and not from the prefcience or mere knowledge of God.

A predetermination of human actions, by God, would truly amount to the fame as his decree of them, thefe phrafes are fynonimous, and both of them include the exertion of the divine will, in all the particular actions of mankind, inafmuch as whatever God wills, by a predetermination of events, is as abfolutely binding and neceffary in its confequences, as his decreeing thofe events could poffibly be. But the divine prefcience amounts to

nothing

nothing more than a mere knowledge of human actions, in which the will or determination of God may have had no manner of influence, cause or concernment, and which may be resolved wholly into the free agency of man.

From what has been remarked on this subject, it appears, that a divine decree or predetermination of the agency of mankind, would involve them in fatal necessity, but that the prescience of God does not determine whether their actions are necessary or free.

The subject of human agency, is in many respects intricate, difficult and perplexed, and has been made more so, in consequence of the artifice and sophistry of party writers, and would need a volumn to clearly investigate it, which at a future period I purpose to do, and therefore in this concise system have only touched the great outlines of the subject and argued thereon as far as my system required, which is to exclude human agency from the providence of God: for if a certain concatenation of causes and events, relative to human actions, have been by the author of nature extended to mankind, which has actuated them, then it would follow that God only has been an active being in this world, and that by his arrangement of of causes and events, he has actuated mankind, or been the efficient cause of their agency; which would involve the Deity in guilt, or exclude moral evil from the world.

This consideration alone, is abundantly sufficient to establish the *reality of man's freedom* for ever; which at the same time coincides with our *consciousness of it*, and upon which all our notions of *right and wrong*, or of *moral good and evil*, are founded.

We shall conclude this section and chapter with a few cursory observations on St. Paul's disquisition of the subject of election or predestination, which is to be found in his ninth chapter of Romans. *But when Rebecca also had conceived by one, even by our father Isaac, for the children not being yet born, neither having done any good or evil, that the purpose of God according to election might stand not of works but of him that calleth, it was said unto her the elder shall serve the younger, as it is written; Jacob have I loved, but Esau have I hated. What shall we say then, is there unrighteousness with God? God forbid, for he saith unto Moses, I will have mercy on whom I will have mercy; and I will have compassion on whom I will have compassion; so that it is not of him that willeth, or of him that*

runneth

runneth, but of God that sheweth mercy; for the scripture saith unto Pharoah, even for this same purpose have I raised thee up, that I might shew my power in thee, and that my name might be declared throughout all the earth. Therefore hath he mercy on whom he will have mercy, and whom he will he hardeneth. Thou wilt say then unto me why doth he yet find fault for who hath resisted his will?" To this objection the Apostle attempts to argue, " *Nay, but O man, who art thou that repliest against God! shall the thing formed say of him that formed it why hast thou made me thus? hath not the potter power over the clay of the same lump to make one vessel unto honor and another unto dishonor? what if God, willing to shew his wrath and to make his power known, endured with much long suffering, the vessels of wrath fitted to destruction.*"

FROM the foregoing quotation, as well as from the reading of St. Paul's epistles in general, it is manifest that he held strenuously to the doctrine of predestination, or election, of a certain part of mankind to the favour and salvation of God, and excluded the residue of them, as in the instance of Jacob and Esau, " *Jacob have I loved, but Esau have I hated,*" and the cause (not the reason) given for God's love of the one and hatred of the other is " *That the purpose of God, according to election*

tion, might stand not of works but of him that calleth;" and to more fully exclude the agency, or works of Jacob and Esau, from having any influence or concern in the election of Jacob and hatred of Esau, it is said, "*The children not having yet been born, or having done any good or evil.*" From this example the Apostle proceeds to Moses's history of Pharoah, "*Even for this same purpose have I raised thee up, that I might shew my power in thee, and that my name might be declared throughout all the earth;*" and the cause assigned for the destruction of Pharoah, is, "*Therefore hath he mercy on whom he will have mercy, and whom he will he hardeneth;*" again, "*it is not of him that willeth, or of him that runneth, but of God that sheweth mercy;*" and again, "*I will have mercy on whom I will have mercy, and I will have compassion on whom I will have compassion.*"

When I was a boy, by one means or other, I had conceived a very bad opinion of Pharoah, he seem'd to me to be a cruel despotic Prince, he would not give the Israelites straw, but nevertheless demanded of them the full tale of brick; for a time he opposed God Almighty, but was at last luckily drowned in the red sea, at which event, with other good christians, I rejoiced, and even exulted at the overthrow of the base and wicked

Tyrant

Tyrant; but after a few years of maturity, and examination of the history of that monarch, given by Moses, with the before recited remarks of the Apostle, I conceived a more favorable opinion of him, inasmuch as we are told that God raised him up, and hardened his heart, and predestinated his reign, his wickedness and overthrow. But to return to the Apostle's doctrine of fate, with his objection against it, "*Thou wilt then say unto me, why doth he, (viz. God) yet find fault, for who hath resisted his will?*" This is a home objection to the doctrine of predestination, which the Apostle never answered; it will apply in all possible cases of human agency, as well as in those relative to Jacob and Esau, or Pharoah; why did God hate Esau, or punish Pharoah, was not their actions and death perfectly agreeable to his predestination, or will? and if so, "*Why doth he yet find fault, for who hath resisted his will?*" And on the position of the destiny or preordination of human agency, who can resist the divine will? surely such dependent weak creatures as men cannot frustrate or make void the predestination or design of God: human art or power, is, in every sense, very inadequate to such an undertaking; for omnipotence can and will affect the decrees of a God, and if the agency of moral beings is included in the divine decrees, or in the predestination of all

events

events, then the conduct of Esau, Pharoah, and every individual of the human race, must have had the divine approbation; and if so, the Apostle's objection is conclusive, to wit; "*Why doth he yet find fault, for who hath resisted his will?*" We will nevertheless advert to the Apostle's discussion of this objection, who says, "*Nay, but O man, who art thou that repliest against God? shall the thing formed say of him that formed it, why hast thou made me thus?*" We readily grant, that any intelligent being, who by the condition of nature, or God's providence, is better than not to be, can have no just complaint against God's providence: but on the position that God has given being to any of his creatures, which, under the direction of his providence, is worse than not to be; (which on the position of eternal damnation must be admitted) such creatuers would have just ground of complaint, that God had (to them involuntarily) given them a being which was worse than non-existence.

THE Apostle proceeds to argue against his objection, "*Hath not the potter power over the clay, of the same lump to make one vessel to honor and another to dishonor.*" This is a comparison brought from incogitative matter, which is destitute of sensation, reflection,

flection, or of honor, or dishonor, happiness or misery, and therefore makes nothing for or against the solution of the Apostle's argument, as not being applicable to the government of rational beings; for it is of no consequence to a lump of clay, whether it be moulded into the figure of a wine glass or a chamber utensil. *"What if God willing to shew his wrath and make his power known,"* Still the objection comes with full force, why is God wrath at the conduct of any of his creatures? *"Who hath resisted his will?"* There is no finite being that ever has or could resist it, therefore, according to the Apostle's doctrine, every thing terminates agreeable to the divine predestination; *ergo,* there is no fault or blame lays the objection, for, *"Who hath resisted his will?"* The conduct of creatures is all perfectly right on this stating of the case. *"And makes his power known."* That the Creator and upholder of the universe, should make his power known, by necessitating his creatures to rebel against and disobey him, and then punish them for it, is diametrically repugnant to our ideas of justice, and of the divine character. The power of creating and sustaining the universe is infinite, and thus God makes his power known; but the power of doing injustice should never be ascribed to him. Nor is there any propriety in ascribing the passion of an-

ger

ger or wrath to God (though it be admitted that mankind are free agents, and consequently justly blameable for their violations of the law of reason): for any being, who is capable of the passion of anger, or wrath, must be admitted to be mutable; which is incompatible with the divine perfection; but for God to be wrath with his creatures, on the Apostle's position of his predestinating their actions, would be in reality the same as to be wrath with himself, since on the thesis of destiny, God must have been the efficient cause of the actions, or conduct of his creatures. "*Endured with much long suffering, the vessels of wrath fitted to destruction.*" This long suffering is unintelligible upon the Apostle's theme of predestination; for if we can understand any thing from it, it supposes that we are free agents, and that God, in his "*long sufferings,*" gives his creatures an opportunity to repent and reform; but such a supposition would be giving his doctrine the lye, for there could be no "*long*" (nor short) "*suffering,*" to the final advantage of creatures predestinated and fitted "*to destruction,*" in this case there could be no remedy, forbearance, or "*long suffering.*" Finally, St. Paul did not in the least, confute his objection "*Who hath resisted his will?*" The substance of all he said to justify divine providence in electing part of the human race and rejecting the rest, or of

his

his loving Jacob, hating Esau, and drowning Pharoah, was only this "*For I will have mercy, on whom I will have mercy, and I will have compassion, on whom I will have compassion,*" that is, *I will because I will.*

CHAPTER

Chapter III.

SECTION I.

The DOCTRINE *of the* INFINITE EVIL *of* SIN *considered.*

THAT God is infinitely good in the eternal displays of his providence has been argued in the seventh section of the second chapter, from which we infer, that there cannot be an infinite evil in the universe, inasmuch as it would be incompatible with infinite good; yet there are many who imbibe the doctrine of the infinite evil of sin, and the maxim on which they predicate their arguments in its support, are, that the greatness of sin, or adequateness of its punishment, is not to be measured, or its viciousness ascertained by the capacity and circumstances of the offender, but by the capacity and dignity of the being against whom the offence is committed; and as every transgression is against the authority and law of God, it is therefore against God; and as God is infinite, therefore sin is an infinite evil; and from hence infer the infinite and vindictive wrath of God against sinners, and of his justice in dooming them, as some say, to infinite, and as others say, to eternal misery; the one without degree or measure, and the other without end of duration.

Admitting this maxim for truth, that the transgressions or sins of mankind are to be estimated, as to their heinousness, by the dignity and infinity of the divine nature, then it will follow, that all sins would be equal; which would confound all our notions of the degrees or aggravations of sin; so that the sin would be the same to kill my neighbour as it would be to kill his horse: For the divine nature, by this maxim, being the rule by which man's sin is to be estimated, and always the same, there could therefore be no degrees in sin or guilt, any more than there are degrees of perfection in God, whom we all admit to be infinite, and who for that reason only cannot admit of any degrees or enlargement. Therefore as certain as there are degrees in sin, the infinity of the divine nature cannot be the standard whereby it is to be ascertained; which single consideration is a sufficient confutation of the doctrine of the infinite evil of sin, as predicated on that maxim; inasmuch

much as none are so stupid as not to discern that there are degrees and aggravations in sin.

I RECOLLECT a discourse of a learned Ecclesiastic, who was labouring in support of this doctrine, his first proposition was: "*That moral rectitude was infinitely pleasing to God.*" From which he deduced this inference, viz; "*That a contrariety to moral rectitude was consequently infinitely displeasing to God, and infinitely evil.*" That the absolute moral rectitude of the divine nature is infinitely well pleasing to God, will not be disputed, for this is none other but perfect and infinite rectitude; but there cannot in nature be an infinite contrariety thereto, or any being infinitely evil, or infinite in any respect whatever; except we admit a self-existent and infinite diabolical nature, which is too absurd to deserve argumentative confutation. Therefore, as all possible moral evil must result from the agency of finite beings, consisting in their sinful deviations from the rules of eternal unerring order and reason, which is moral rectitude in the abstract; we infer, that, provided *all finite beings in the universe*, had not done any thing else but sin and rebel against God, reason and moral rectitude in general; all possible moral evil would fall as much short of being infinite, as all finite capacities, complexly considered, would fail of being infinite;

which

which would bear no proportion at all. For tho' *finite minds*, as has been before argued, bear a *resemblance to God*, yet they bear *no proportion* to his *infinity*; and therefore there is not and cannot be any being, beings, or agency of being or beings, complexly considered or otherwise, which are infinite in capacity, or which are infinitely evil and detestable in the sight of God, in that unlimited sense; for the *actions* or *agency* of *limited beings* are also *limited*, which is the same as *finite*: so that both the virtues and vices of man are finite; they are not virtuous or vicious but in degree; therefore moral evil is finite and bounded.

Though there is one and but one infinite good, which is God, and there can be no dispute, but that God judges, and approves or disapproves of all things and beings, and agencies of beings, as in truth they are, or in other words judges of every thing as being what it is; but to judge a *finite evil to be infinite*, would be *infinitely erroneous* and disproportionable: for so certain as there is a distinction between *infinity* and *finitude*, so certain finite *sinful agency* cannot be *infinitely evil*: or in other words *finite offences* cannot be *infinite*. Nor is it possible that the greatest of sinners should in justice deserve infinite punishment, or their nature sustain it; *finite beings* may as well be supposed

P

posed to be capable of *infinite happiness* as of *infinite misery*, but the rank which they hold in the universe exempts them from either: it nevertheless admits them to a state of agency, probation or trial, consequently to interchangeable progressions in moral good and evil, and of course to alternate happiness or misery. We will dismiss the doctrine of the *infinite evil of sin* with this observation, that as no *mere creature* can suffer an *infinitude* of misery or of punishment, it is therefore incompatible with the wisdom of God, so far to capacitate creatures to sin, as in his constitution of things to foreclose himself from *adequately* punishing them for it.

SECTION II.

The Moral GOVERNMENT *of* GOD *incompatible with eternal* PUNISHMENT.

HAVING considered the doctrine of the infinite evil of sin, we proceed to the consideration of that of eternal damnation. Though it is in the nature of things impossible, that an infinite weight of punishment should be inflicted on the wicked, nevertheless, admitting a never ending punishment on them to be just and consistent with the moral government of God, it would be in itself possible. Therefore in order to determine the question concerning

cerning eternal punishment, (which cannot be eternal with respect to the preceeding eternity, though it may be possible with respect to that which succeeds the æra of the existence of the wicked,) we must advert to the providence of God, as it respects the moral world particularly. That God in his creation and providence ultimately designed the good of being in general, has been clearly evinced in the preceeding pages; nor can this doctrine of the divine munificence be objected to, except it is disputed whether God be a good and gracious being or not, which to do would be highly criminal: for a good being would have good purposes the ultimate end of its conduct, though it be supposed to be a mere creature, but perfectly so as applicable to the œconomy of God, who must be supposed to have had the good and happiness of his creation, the ultimate end and design of his providence.

The wisest and best of men may not succeed in their benevolent purposes to serve mankind, for want of wisdom, opportunity or power; but this is no ways applicable to God, who can and will effect the ultimate purposes of his providence. Such expressions as these may be thought to militate against the agency of man; but it ought to be considered, that though God has implanted a principle

ple of liberty in our minds, it is in some respects limited; he has not put it in our power eternally to ruin ourselves, for our agency is as eternal as our existence; so that the agency of this life cannot constitute an eternal happiness or misery for us in this world or worlds to come, but our agency in its particular periods is temporary, and so are its rewards and punishments. For as our minds cannot comprehend eternity, so neither can the consequences of our agency, which is happiness or misery extend to it; for we are limited beings and act in certain circumferences in all and every respect, except as to existence without end; and this it is which renders our agency eternal as it respects the succeeding eternity: God's government of the natural and moral worlds is the same as his providence, so that when we speak of the moral government of God, we mean that display of his providence which respects moral beings: The former is governed by fate, but the latter by rewards and punishments.

It is from the knowledge of right and wrong, good and evil that we are capable of moral government; and it is from the deficiency of this principle of knowledge, in the natural world, that it is subjected to mechanical laws, so that the natural world includes every part of the creation,

which

which is below the dignity of a rational nature, which cannot be subject to mechanical operations, but is in the order of things more exalted than gross creation, consisting of elements or matter variously compounded, tempered and modified, with its cohesion, attraction and all other of its qualities, properties, proportions, motions and harmony of the whole. And as the natural world is made subservient to the moral, the government of it may therefore be truly and properly said to belong to the providence of God, which it otherwise could not, inasmuch as rational beings are benefited thereby; but the government of mere material, inanimate and unintelligent beings, abstractly considered from moral beings, could not have been an object of divine providence, nor would such a supposed government constitute a providence; inasmuch as it would be void of sensibility, happiness and goodness. This being premised, we proceed more particularly to the consideration of the moral government of God, in the exercise whereof it is not to be supposed, that he would counteract his eternal plan of doing good to, and happifying being in general; and in afmuch as eternal punishment is incompatible with this great and fundamental principle of wisdom and goodness, we may for certain conclude, that such a punishment will never have the divine approbation

probation, or be inflicted on any intelligent being or beings in the infinitude of the government of God. For an endless punishment defeats the very end of its institution, which in all wife and good governments is as well to reclaim offenders, as to be examples to others; but a government, which does not admit of reformation, and repentance, must unavoidably involve its subjects in misery; for the weakness of creatures will always be a source of error and inconstancy, and a wise governor, as we must admit God to be, would suit his government to the capacity and all other circumstances of the governed; and instead of inflicting eternal damnation on his offending children, would rather interchangeably extend his benificience with his vindictive punishments, so as to alienate them from sin and wickedness, and incline them to morality; convincing them from experimental suffering, that sin and vanity are their greatest enemies, and that in GOD and *moral rectitude* their *dependence* and *true happiness* consists, and by reclaiming them from *wickedness and error*, to the *truth*, and to *the love and practice of virtue*, give them occasion to *glorify* GOD *for the wisdom and goodness of his government*, and to be ultimately happy under it. But we are told that the eternal damnation of a part of mankind greatly augments the happiness of the elect, who are repre-

sented

sented as being vastly the less numerous, (a diabolical temper of mind in the elect:) Besides, how narrow and contracted must such notions of infinite justice and goodness be? Who would imagine that the Deity conducts his providence similar to the detestable despots of this world? *O horrible most horrible impeachment* of DIVINE GOODNESS! I rather too us exaltedly suppose that God eternally had the ultimate best good of being, generally and individually in his view, with the reward of the virtuous and the punishment of the vicious, and that no other punishment will ever be inflicted, merely *by the divine administration,* but what will *finally* terminate in the BEST GOOD of the PUNISHED, and thereby subserve the great and important ends of the divine government, and be productive of *the restoration and felicity of all finite rational nature.*

MANKIND in general seems to be evidently impressed with a sense and strong expectation of judgment to come, after animal life is ended; wherein the disorders, injustice and wickedness, which have been acted by rational agents, shall be fully and righteously adjusted, and the delinquents punished; and that such, who obey the laws of reason, or moral rectitude, may be rewarded according to their works: this apprehension is so general
with

with all denominations and sectaries of men, that it is rather the intuition of nature than mere tradition. It is nevertheless to be considered, that this notion of accountability, and judgment to come, has not gone so far as to determine, whether the incorrigible sinner, from the close of human life, shall be everlastingly debarred from reformation and repentance, and precluded from the favour of God or not; but having taught a just and righteous judgment, left it as the prerogative of God to proportion the rewards of the virtuous and the punishments of the wicked, with their respective durations, which we find by reasoning cannot be eternal, and consequently must be temporary; but in what degrees, manner or proportions of intenseness, or of duration, we cannot comprehend, but must wait the decission of the righteous judge, whose omniscience takes cognizance of the thoughts, designs and actions of his creatures; and whose impartial justice will hold the balance and extend interchangeable happiness or misery to them, according to their respective merits or demerits, or the virtues or vices of their minds, in certain temporary periods co-extensive with our immortality: and though the judgments of God may be vastly more severe and terrible to incorrigible sinners beyond the grave, than such as can be inflicted, or conceived of in this life,

yet

yet we may by reasoning from the wisdom and goodness of God and the nature and capacity of the human mind determine, that its happiness or misery cannot be perpetual and eternal.

The most weighty arguments deducible from the divine nature have been already offered, *to wit*, the ultimate end of God, in creation and providence, to do the greatest possible good and benignity to being in general, and consequently, that the great end and design of punishment, in the divine government, must be to reclaim, restore, and bring revolters from moral rectitude back to embrace it, and to be ultimately happy; as also, that an eternal punishment, would defeat the very end and design of punishment itself; and that no good consequences to the punished could arise out of a never ending destruction; but that a total, everlasting, and irreparable evil would take place on such part of the moral creation, as may be thus sentenced to eternal and remediless perdition; which would argue imperfection either in the creation, or moral government of God, or in both.

Furthermore, provided there was, in the nature of things, a liability of eternal destruction to any one intelligent being, there must consequently ly have been the same liability in all, or the justice and goodness of God would not be equal or uniform. But if there could have been, in the nature and fitness of things, a possibility of perpetually and eternally happifying the moral world, without agency, probation or trial, there can be no dispute, but that the God of nature would have adopted such a measure, and have made it needless and impossible for us to have speculated on the causes of our misery: and inasmuch as such a plan has not taken place, we may infer, that it was not possible, in the reason and fitness of things, that it should; and as imperfection opened the door to error and wickedness, or to a deviation from moral rectitude; which has actually taken place in the system of rational beings, and punishment also as a necessary consequence of it; it therefore follows, that if eternal punishment was possible, to any one of the rational creation, it must hold equally so to the whole, or the divine system of fitness would be unequal. From which we infer, that though God in his creation and providence, designed the ultimate best good and felicity of the moral world, he had nevertheless so far departed from his eternal plan, or intention, that it was liable to be frustrated, and that universal misery and eternal damnation was possible to overspread the whole; all this necessarily follows on the position

tion, that any rational natures are liable to eternal destruction; and therefore the doctrine of the possibility, or liability, of eternal punishment, is inadmissible.

FURTHERMORE, accountability, probation or trial, are in nature inseperably connected with the existence of moral beings, and must eternally remain so to be, for weakness and imperfection is that which subjects all finite rational beings to trial, and is the only ground of the possibility of it. All intelligent agents therefore, except the most high God, are probationers. A state of improvement is necessarily connected with that of trial and proficiency. What reason can be given to make it appear, that the immortal souls of mankind, in their succeeding state of existence, may not err, and more or less deviate from the rules of eternal, unerring order and reason; they must be admitted to be capable of moral action, for it is essential to their existence; and though the next state of being may be ever so much dissimilar from this, in the mode or manner of it, yet we shall be but creatures in that state, and why not liable to error, transgression and blame, and also to punishment for the same; for as finiteness or imperfection are the grounds of the liability of our present offences, that liability will eternally continue, and that

that in proportion to our future imperfection. Could God have established any creature, or race of creatures, in a confirmed and perpetual happiness, by a sovereign act of omnipotence, consistent with his moral perfections, and the nature of intelligent agents themselves, we should have experienced such a confirmation in this life. But a confirmed and perpetual state of blessedness, will agree to no character short of God's: this is therefore his prerogative, and it is the absolute perfection of his nature, which confirms him in that state. But as to finite cogitative beings, they cannot in the nature of things, be any more confirmed in happiness, than they can in moral rectitude, which is the ground and source of it; nor is it possible for an imperfect nature to attain to perfection, though they may be eternally improving; nor can they be perpetually morally good, for perpetual uniformity is perfection itself; but they are always liable to change, to error and sin, and consequently to misery, which is inseperably connected with it, as the only certain means of repentance, reformation and restoration.

Moral good is the only source from whence a rational mind can be supplied with a happiness agreeable to the dignity of its nature. It would be impossible for omnipotence itself to make a vicious

cious mind taste the ecstatic felicity of a moral happiness, so long as it may be supposed to be vicious, inasmuch as morality, in the nature of the thing itself, is prerequisite to such a happiness, without the possession and actual enjoyment of which the mind cannot be mentally happy, or enjoy itself agreeable to its discerning, conscious and sentimental nature; but must disapprove of the erroneous departure (or its vicious pursuits) from the amiable rules of moral fitness, and feel proportionably guilty and miserable. Nor could pardon or atonement alter the condition of a vicious mind, for miserable it must be, as long as it remains vicious, whether God be supposed to forgive the wickedness of it or not; for it is the conscious exercise of moral goodness only, which is capable of happifying the rational mind, therefore such reflections, pursuits and habits, which are comprised in our agency, as will in their own nature admit of a rational happiness, make us happy; and such agency of man as is inadequate and improper to constitute such happiness, and which naturally tends to misery will involve us therein; and miserable we must be, until the bias and disposition of the mind is turned from moral evil to moral good, which is the same as repentance and restoration. This is the eternal law of nature, respecting the agency and the happiness or misery of imperfect rational

nature

nature, throughout its never ending agency and trial; and consequently, our eternity, will be as much diversified with happiness and misery, as our agency may be supposed to alternately partake of moral good and evil. So certain as we retain our rational nature, in our succeeding state of existence, we shall be capable of moral actions, which admit of proficiency, agency and trial; and not only so, but subjects us to agency and accountability, as much as in this life, or in any condition of finite reason whatever; and every improvement of a rational mind, alters the consciousness of it, and consequently the happiness or the misery of it. Absolute power may inflict physical evils, but is utterly incapable of inflicting those of a moral nature; nor can mere positive injunction by law affect the consciences of rational beings, who must be either happy or miserable on the basis of their own agency, and consciousness of merit or demerit.

It has been owing to improvement that we have progressively advanced from the knowledge and capacity of childhood to that of manhood, and to our improvement, which is the same as agency, in moral good and evil, that has alternately made us happy or unhappy in a mental sense; from hence we infer, that if rational nature, in the

world

world to come, is essentially anologous to what it is in this life, agency and probation will be continued with the immortality of the soul, be the manner of its existence, or of its communicating or receiving ideas as it will.

FURTHERMORE, the doctrine of a future improvement, or agency, may be argued from the death of infants and children. None will pretend that they have an opportunity of proficiency in this life, therefore we infer, that if such a state be requisite to fit and improve their feeble minds for the enjoyment of a rational happiness, agency must be continued to the future state; and admitting that they are immortal, and that agency is precluded from the world to come, they would remain children in knowledge eternally; nor could any departed soul, on such a position, expand its rational functions beyond its size of understanding at the time of departing this life; which would make immortality to man a cypher, except as to the perpetuation of their powers of cogitation in a limited circumference; the reflection whereof would be more or less rude and incoherent; which at best would be but a small fund for an eternal contemplation.

BUT if it be admitted, that the souls of mankind, of every age and denomination, will in their
futurity

futurity be progressive in knowledge, (which must be the case with cogitative beings) then it necessarily follows, that agency and trial proceed hand in hand with it. Therefore it is impossible, that there should be a particular day of judgment, in which mankind, or any, or either of them, shall receive their eternal sentence of happiness or misery; for such a sentence is inconsistent with any further trial or agency, and therefore is inadmissible.

FURTHERMORE, proficiency or agency, is inconsistent with a confirmed state of happiness or of misery; for in the same proportion as our ideas, pursuits, intentions and habits vary, so does our happiness or misery.

FINITE minds cannot be confirmedly happy or miserable, any more than they can be absolutely identical which is the prerogative of the divine mind: finite intelligences gain ideas by a succession of thinking, and are happy or miserable in proportion as the succession of ideas will admit; and every succession in the multiplicity of thinking, is incompatible with a proper identity of mind, (except as to the principle of thinking itself) was it to be perfectly identical, it could not admit of a succession of ideas, which is the same as addition, nor of a dimunition of them, but would be confined to one perception only, and in this case, the

happiness

happiness or misery, resulting from it, would be as identical as the perception itself may be supposed to be, and incapable of enlargement or diminution; which might be denominated a confirmed state. But a confirmed state is utterly incompatible with a state of improvement, and is applicable to the divine perfection only. Inasmuch as succession of thinking cannot be ascribed to God, he is therefore identically the same, but progressive agents, are always capable of additional knowledge, which lays them under additional obligations to moral government, and thus duty is always co-extensive with the improvement of rational agents; and inasmuch as agency, proficiency and accountability, are in nature co-existent, or concomitant with intelligent finite beings, we infer, that the doctrine of eternal damnation is without foundation, for that it would, if true, put a final end to any further agency, trial or accountability; therefore, so certain as our agency is eternal our condemnation cannot be so.

SECTION.

SECTION III.

Human Liberty, Agency and Accountability, cannot be attended with Eternal Consequences, either good or evil.

FROM what has been argued in the foregoing section, it appears, that mankind in this life are not agents of trial for eternity, but that they will eternally remain agents of trial. To suppose that our eternal circumstances will be unalterably fixed in happiness or misery, in consequence of the agency or transactions of this temporary life, is inconsistent with the moral government of God, and the progressive and retrospective knowledge of the human mind. God has not put it into our power to plunge ourselves into eternal woe and perdition; human liberty is not so extensive, for the term of human life bears no proportion to eternity succeeding it; so that there could be no proportion between a momentary agency, (which is liberty of action,) or probation, and any supposed eternal consequences of happiness or misery resulting from it. Our liberty consists in our power of agency, and cannot fall short of, or exceed it, for liberty is agency itself; or is that by which agency or action is exerted; it may be, that the curious would define it, that agency is the effect of liberty, and that liberty is the cause, which
produces

produces it; making a distinction between action and the power of action: be it so, yet agency cannot surpass its liberty; to suppose otherwise, would be the same as to suppose agency without the power of agency, or an effect without a cause; therefore as our agency does not extend to consequences of eternal happiness or misery, the power of that agency, which is liberty, does not. Sufficient it is for virtuous minds, while in this life, that they keep " *Consciences void of offence towards God and toward man.*" And that in their commencement in the succeeding state, they have a retrospective knowledge of their agency in this, and retain a consciousness of a well spent life. Beings thus possessed of a habit of virtue, would enjoy a rational felicity beyond the reach of physical evils, which terminate with life; and in all rational probability would be advanced in the order of nature to a more exalted and sublime manner of being, knowledge and action, than at present we can conceive of, where no joys or pains can approach, but of the mental kind; in which elevated state, virtuous minds will be able, in a clearer and more copious manner than in this life, to contemplate the superlative beauties of moral fitness; and with extatic satisfaction enjoy it, notwithstanding imperfection and consequently agency, proficiency and

trial

trial, of some kind or other, must everlastingly continue with finite minds.

And as to the vicious, who have violated the laws of reason and morality, lived a life of sin and wickedness, and are at as great a remove from a rational happiness as from moral rectitude; such incorigible sinners, at their commencing existence in the world of spirits, will undoubtedly have opened to them a tremendous scene of horror, self-condemnation and guilt, with anguish of mind; the more so, as no sensual delights can there (as in this world) divert the mind from its conscious guilt; the clear sense of which will be the more pungent, as the mind in that state will be greatly enlarged, and consequently more capaciously susceptible of sorrow, grief and conscious woe, from a retrospective reflection of a wicked life, yet we have reason to hope and believe through the wisdom of the divine government, they may in some limited period of duration have a contrition for and detestation of sin and vanity, the procuring cause of their punishment, and be reclaimed from viciousness and restored to virtue and happiness; but liable to transgression, and future misery, in consequence of an imperfect nature, eternally subjected to agency and trial, and consequently to alternate happiness and misery, which must be the case with al
intelligent

intelligent probationary beings. But after all our researches, the insufficiency of the human understanding, to discover the œconomy of the divine government, over the moral world, is so great, that we can determine but very little about the manner of its rewards and punishments, or of the extent of them; except that they cannot be perpetual or eternal; but on the other hand will be as temporary and interchangeable as the virtue and vice of moral agents. Nevertheless, from the arguments which we have deduced from the wisdom and goodness of God in his creation and providence, we may with rational certainty conclude, that moral goodness and happiness will ultimately be victorious over sin and misery, which will undoubtedly be more conspicuously so in the future stages of our immortality; so that there will be a far greater plentitude of the former than of the latter; to which the latter finally is made subservient, for otherwise we could not account for the wisdom and goodness of God in his creation, providence or moral government.

The endless disproportion between the cogitations and agency of the human mind, in this momentary life, may, with great propriety, be urged against an everlasting fixedness of the condition of happiness or misery, after this life is ended;

merely

merely in consequence of the agency of this. Our conceptions themselves are progressive, we think by succession, and our ideas, in their operations, are numerical, and by nature subject to number; each individual idea has its circumscription, and the whole, collectively considered, would make but a limited knowledge; and the more inconsiderably so, as it is most probable, that not one hundredth part of our reflections, from infancy to old age, are worthy to be denominated knowledge; by reason of their fictitious and incoherent rudeness; so that when we contemplate on the endlessness of eternity, our cogitations are lost in its infinitude; for neither numbers, quantity, admeasurement, or any possible motion, or comparison of cogitations, or of things, can possibly co-extend with it; and consequently human liberty, or agency and accountability, in their progressive exertions, can bear no manner of proportion or connection with an eternity of rewards or punishments; for the nature of our liberty, agency and accountability is but finite, and therefore can no otherwise operate but by succession, and cannot be attended with eternal consequences, any more than succession itself can comprize eternity. We may therefore with a well grounded judgment determine, that neither the virtues or vices of human

man life, can be attended with eternal consequences of good or evil; inasmuch as such endless consequences, necessarily imply an infinite disproportion between them and human agency: but the truth of the matter is, our liberty, and therefore our accountability, cannot exceed the limits of our cogitations and knowledge; this is the circumference in which our liberty can exercise itself, and this is the boundary of its agency; and although eternal probation is necessarily connected with the eternal existence of finite minds, yet the merits or demerits of an everlasting probation, has its various operations forever on the mind, existing in the conscience, and causing it to be alternately happy or miserable, in such proportions, and periods, as conformity or nonconformity to moral rectitude, in our eternal probation, will admit.

The policy of human governments has demanded, that corporeal punishments should be inflicted on the violaters of their laws, *to wit*, the whip, the halter, the gibbit, and the like; from these and from the ideas of physical evils, which are common to us in this life, it seems, that most of mankind form to themselves an arrangement of ideas of the manner of God's punishing incorrigible sinners in the world to come. The idea of
fire

fire and brimstone is, in this part of the world, their main apprehension, to which they unite the evils of a guilty conscience, in as much as mental, as well as physical evils, with their divers modes of sufferings, are common to them in this life: but it should be considered, that death puts a final end to physical evils, except these our mortal bodies are to be raised and re-united to their respective souls; which if admitted, they must unavoidably suffer death a second time, and such as may be supposed to be cast into hell-fire (in the vulgar sense) would suffer a second dissolution instantly, unless their resurrection bodies are supposed to be of the salamander kind. And thus a physical suffering, instead of being eternal, would be but for a moment, or at most but temporary; and if we suppose those resurrection bodies will be able to endure fire, it must be likewise supposed, that it would be their proper element, and consequently that they would be happy in it; as so intense a heat would destroy such bodies, whose qualities may be supposed to be opposed it.

SECTION.

SECTION IV.

Of Physical Evils.

PHYSICAL evils are in nature inseperable from animal life, they commenced existence with it, and are its concomitants through life; so that the same nature, which gives being to the one, gives birth to the other also; the one is not before or after the other, but they are co-existent together, and cotemporaries; and as they began existence in a necessary dependence on each other, so they terminate together in death and dissolution. This is the original order to which animal nature is subjected, as applied to every species of it; the beasts of the field, the fowls of the air, the fish of the sea, with reptiles and all manner of beings, which are possessed of animal life; nor is pain, sickness or mortality any part of God's punishment for sin.

On the other hand sensual happiness is no part of the reward of virtue: to reward moral actions with a glass of wine or a shoulder of mutton, would be as inadequate, as to measure a triangle with sound, for virtue and vice pertain to the mind, and their merits or demerits have their just effects on the conscience, as has been before evinced: but animal gratifications are common to the human race indiscriminately, and also to the beasts of the field; and physical evils as promiscuously and universally extend to the whole, so that "*There is no knowing good or evil by all that is before us, for all is vanity.*" It was not among the number of possibles, that animal life should be exempted from mortality: omnipotence itself could not have made it capable of eternalization and indissolubility; for the self same nature which constitutes animal life, subjects it to decay and dissolution; so that the one cannot be without the other, any more than there could be a compact number of mountains without vallies, or that I could exist and not exist at the same time, or that God should effect any other contradiction in nature: all contradictions being equally impossible, inasmuch as they imply an absolute incompatibility with nature and truth; for nature is predicated on truth, and the same truth which constitutes mountains, made the vallies at the same time; nor is it possible that they could have a seperate existence. And the same truth which affirms my existence, denies its negative; so also the same law of nature, which in truth produceth an animal life and supports it for a season, wears it out, and in its natural course reduces it to its original elements again. The vegetable world also presents us with a constant aspect of productions and dissolutions; and the bustle of elements is beyond all conception; but the dissolution of forms is not the dissolution of matter, or

the

the annihilation of it, or of the creation, which exists in all possible forms and fluxilities; and it is from such physical alterations of the particles of matter, that animal or vegetable life is produced and destroyed: elements afford them nutrition, and time brings them to maturity, decay and dissolution; and in all the prolific production of animal life or the productions of those of a vegetative nature, throughout all their growth, decay and dissolution, make no addition or diminution of creation; but eternal nature continues its never-ceasing operations (which in most respects are mysterious to us) under the unerring guidance of the providence of God.

Animal nature consists of a regular constitution of a variety of organic parts, which have a particular and necessary dependence on each other, by the mutual assistance whereof the whole are animated. Blood seems to be the source of life, and it is requisite, that it have a proper circulation from the heart to the extreme parts of the body, and from thence to the heart again, that it may repeat its temporary rounds through certain arteries and veins, which replenish every minute part with blood and vital heat; but the brain is evidently the seat of sensation, which through the nervous system conveys the animal spirits to every

part

part of the body, imparting to it sensation and motion, constituting it a living machine, which could never have been produced, or exercised its respective functions in any other sort of world but this; which is in a constant series of fluxilities, and which causeth it to produce food for its inhabitants. An unchangeable world could not admit of production or dissolution, but would be identically the same, which would preclude the existence and nutriment of such sensitive creatures as we are. The nutrition extracted from food by the secret aptitudes of the digesting powers (by which mysterious operation it becomes incorparated with the circulating juices, supplying the animal functions with vital heat, strength and vigour) demands a constant flux and reflux of the particles of matter, which is perpetually incorporating with the body, and supplying the place of the superfluous particles, that are constantly discharging themselves by insensible perspiration; supporting, and at the same time, in its ultimate tendency, destroying animal life. Thus it manifestly appears, that the laws of the world in which we live, and the constitution of the animal nature of man, are all but one uniform arrangement of causes and effects; and as by the course of those laws, animal life is propagated and sustained for a season, so by the operation of the same laws, decay and mortality are the necessary consequences.

Chapter IV.

Treating on the Immortality *of the* Human Soul.

SECTION I.

Of the Aptitudes *of* Sensation, *and of their* Subserviency *to the* Mind.

HAVING considered the providence of God, as it respects the mortality of the body, we proceed to the consideration of the immortality of the soul; and in order for a clear understanding of this important subject, it is requisite that we first speculate on the powers, use and end of our external sensations, and point out their particular subserviency to the mind; and secondly, explain the intrinsic difference between them whereby the

latter

latter may exist independent of the former: and thirdly, deduce arguments from the necessary attributes and moral perfections of God, as also from his creation and providence, of the moral certainty of the soul's immortality, or natural eternalization. Human nature is compounded of sensation and reflection. Sensation comprehends the body with its five senses, *viz.* those of feeling, tasting and smelling (the two latter of which are only a diversity of the modes of feeling) as also the more extensive senses of seeing and hearing. Reflection, comprehends the operations of the mind, and is that which is commonly denominated the soul, with its various manner of exertions; as that of memory, reason, judgment, determination, contrivance, invention, and the like, which will be particularly explained and illustrated in its order.

THE senses are exquisitely well calculated to make discoveries of external objects to the mind, they are the medium through which the mind receives its first notices of things, or mere apprehension of them, without denying or affirming any thing concerning them, and it is in, by, or through the instrumentality of the senses only, that the mind of man, in this life, is enabled to form any idea of external objects, or to exert its thinking, conscious nature. The instances of persons born

deficient

deficient in part, as to their senses, will serve to illustrate the subject matter of our enquiry; those who are born blind, can never be taught what colours are, or what we mean by seeing: an idea of colours, or the knowledge of occular perception, is to them supernatural and impossible; so also respecting those who are born deaf, an idea of sound would to them be equally supernatural; the most harmonious music would to them be as imperceptible, as nonentity is to us, of which they could not form any conception. This we know to be true in fact.

The sense of feeling, upon which those of taste and smell are erected, or from which they are produced, which (strictly speaking) are only so many diverse modes of feeling, are essential to an animal body; without which they could not be denominated animate, but inanimate; but seeing and hearing are not essential to animation, as it is often destitute of those sensations; so that it is impossible in nature, that we should have an instance, wherein the mind can possibly be ignorant of the idea of feeling, it is nevertheless as certain that we are beholden to the sense of feeling for our apprehension of it, as to that of seeing for our apprehension of colours; or to our hearing for the apprehension of sound---In consequence of

palsies

palsies and such like disorders, our sense of feeling has been in part impaired. In some instances human bodies on one side have been so benumbed, that on that side they have been wholly incapable of feeling; such instances have been common in every age and country of the world; which together with those other experiments of blindness and deafness, evinces the dependency of the mind on its sensorium, while in this life.

Whatever external object presents itself to the senses, gives the mind an apprehension of it. To enumerate the diversity and multiplicity of the objects of sense would be endless, and also needless. The notices or apprehensions of things, which are communicated to the mind by the mere aptitude of sensation itself, abstracted from a succession of reflection, or thinking, are what I denominate simple ideas; which are excited by the intervention of the senses between external objects and the mind, and are much the same helps to the mind, as glasses are to the senses, by assisting the natural eye to discover such object, which without them the eye could not perceive, and the mind by that means obtains an apprehension of such extended objects by looking through two mediums, *to wit*, the eye and the glass; the eye is in this case the first medium, without which the mind

could

could not discern the glass; and the glass the second medium, which enables the eye, and consequently the mind, to discover worlds in the expansion of the heavens, which the mind through its first medium only, could not explore. It is on simple ideas, which the mind thus mediately obtains through the instrumentality of its senses, that all our proficiency in knowledge and science is predicated. There is not one individual apprehension or original simple idea but what the mind receives through its sensory, so that sensation in the order of nature, discloses the way and manner of the exertions of cogitative nature. Common conversation, learning, business and whatever pertains to the social life, is manifestly dependent on it. Those, who are taught the art of reading and writing, can hold correspondence with each other though in different quarters of the globe, by which means we are also enabled to maintain a correspondence of ideas with writers who have been long dead; twenty four characters or letters arranged together, according to certain rules prescribed, are capable of making such an impression on the sense of seeing, that by and through that sense, the mind of those who read can understand the ideas of those who have written intelligibly. "*It is not by any concomitant act of ratiocination*

ocination that we come to be apprized of the existence and difference of the common objects of sense; but we find them to be existent and different in and by the pure act of sensation itself; we have in and by this act such a representation of things made to us, that we apprehend, that this is not that, nor one the other: It is true by reason and reflection, we come to a more compleat and particular knowledge of the differences; but we have not our first apprehensions of those differences from thence." Though reason and experience, in a variety of instances, may correct sense; yet independent of it, there could have been no such thing as reasoning or experience among mankind, or any such creature as man, sensation being a part of his nature. There are many modes and customs arbitrarily introduced into learning and arts. It was neither sensation or reason that pointed out any particular shape, sound or name to the twenty-four letters; but it was the effect of contrivance and invention, which are faculties of the mind: nevertheless the mind must have been previously notified, through the medium of its senses, of shapes and sounds in general, or else it had not been able to have conceived of, or to have invented shapes or sounds in particular, which might be adapted to answer the design of communicating or receiving ideas; and thus it is, that sensation in all cases, lays the foundation of the exercise of thought and reflection: judgment is no further concerned in such like cases, than that the figure and size of the letters, and their particular sounds, be uniform and distinct, that the characters might be handily written and printed; and any supposed figure or sound of letters, which are equally well adapted to the design of giving and receiving ideas, and holding intercourse between intelligent beings, are equally approvable by reason, provided they may have obtained common consent and use. The same may be observed of the rules of spelling and many other parts of learning. Language itself is absolutely artificial and arbitrary; for though natural sensation taught all nations to apprehend the common objects of sense alike, yet neither sensation nor reason taught any particular language, and consequently the nations and tribes of the world differ in their speech, though they agree in their sensible apprehensions of external things; but we arbitrarily affix certain ideas to words or sounds, and those, who are acquainted with, and understand their connection, are linguists, and are able to correspond together.

WORDS or sounds have no particular ideas naturally connected with them; common consent and use, in applying certain ideas uniformly to them

them, is that which furnishes them with intelligence, (some particular sounds which betoken distress or gladness, excepted,) so that in conversation, when certain sound, which from common use have the approbation of any language, and such sounds with their connective ideas move the subtil expanded air, that it vibrates on the drum of the ear, it immediately communicates to the mind the intelligence which by art is connected with such sounds: so when I feel myself hungry and faint, I think of food; and when thirsty of drink: I smell the fragrancy of a rose, and my mind forms an idea of that flower; I hear it thunder, and it represents to my mind the complex idea of a thunder-storm; I see a vessel, which excites in my mind an idea of its figure; in fine, every of the multiplicity of simple ideas, which ever have or can be excited in the mind of man, has been and must be communicated by the instrumentality of the senses, and are distinguished from every of our other ideas by the manner of their perception; which is merely from the pure aptitude of sensation itself, abstractly considered from reasoning, collecting or infering one thing from another, and which are common to animal nature in general as well as to the human kind. Simple ideas, of themselves, considered abstractly from reasoning, could not comprehend any thing of a

moral

moral nature, nor confer any moral obligation; inasmuch as the knowledge of moral good and evil does not result merely from them; both man and beast enjoy them promiscuously as they are the productions of animation, and do not pertain to the exalted essence of reason.

SECTION II.

The intrinsic difference between SENSATION *and the* PRINCIPLE *of the* SOUL, *and of their distinct* FUNCTIONS.

THE human mind is capable of understanding the moral fitness of things in a limited sense. It is capable of reasoning on simple ideas, by compounding them and considering them complexly; it is capable of seperating and considering them abstractly or complicatedly, and examining into their connection, proportion and other properties, and to make experiments and essays on many things, and search into the natural causes of things, and discover their tendency and subserviency. Our moral notions of things are the result of reasoning on the works of nature, and examining into the consequences of things, thereby discerning their ultimate tendency and rational fitness, as it affects being in general. But these extended parts of

scientifical

scientifical knowledge, do not so readily come within the circle of our understanding as the common notions of morality, which respect society in its various relations and connections in life. It is not my design to enter into an explanation of these social duties, which are evident to mankind in general, but only to observe, that though they are ever so apparent, yet the knowledge of right and wrong, truth and falsehood, with their respective consequences, are discovered by reason only, sensation being altogether inadequate to such discoveries. Invention, contrivance and arts of various kinds, which have contributed to subserve mankind, *such as* the liberal arts, sciences, mechanism, manufactures and the like, are from the exertion of the mind. The display of these noble faculties evinces, that there is a principle in the nature of man, superior to any thing which could be the offspring of mere sensation.

WHATEVER improvement the mind makes in its reflection, invention and reasoning, upon simple ideas, are the proficiences of intelligence; for sensation is one entire and simple exertion, which does not admit of improvement; but it is the mind which improves upon those original images. The ideas thus deducible from those which we denominate simple, are vastly more numerous than those

those original images themselves; inasmuch as they admit of all manner of diversification and refinement. The ideas of natural things are in their several kinds, capable of being associated together by the mind, as those pertaining to music by themselves, and those which pertain to military discipline, or to any art, science or manufactory, should have their seperate assemblages; likewise ideas pertaining to moral fitness are in their nature incapable of association with mere natural ones; *for instance*, justice cannot compare with sound, nor wisdom with beauty, nor a good conscience with a good coat, or with any unthinking or unconscious being. For as ideas of natural things in their respective classes, are capable of, and naturally associate together by reason of their natural fitness and utility; so ideas of moral fitness, naturally associate and connect together. When from a deduction of reasoning on the works of nature, or from any particular part thereof, we draw an inference of God's goodness to man, by reasoning on the ultimate tendency of the natural world to subserve the moral, we deduce a moral inference from elementary and material things, which is that which we denominate to be the progressive act of raciocination; and inasmuch as in and by the providence of God "*We live, move and have our being,*" as some of our "*Own poets have said, for we are also his offspring,*" the

the inferences of divine goodness would be as numerous as the mind of man could conceive of, nor could but a very small part of the divine benignity be comprehended by our finite understandings. The mind being thus able to deduce moral ideas from external things, which we denominate simple ideas, is capable of compounding or forming a complex idea of a number of them; can add to or substract from such complex idea, can form propositions, make deductions and final consequences, and thus proceed in argumentation on moral as well as other subjects, to the extent of the mind's capaciousness. Was it not for memory, which is a faculty of the soul, mankind must have remained children in knowledge to this day, inasmuch as without it they could gain nothing by experience, which on such a position would reduce human nature so low, that a man would as likely burn his fingers in a candle as a child; as in this case, experiments could not be instructive, nor could we on this position of the debility of memory retain so much as one simple idea, but that which may be supposed to be in the present tense: what we could comprehend for the time being, would comprize the sum total of our knowledge, for without memory it would be impossible for us to argue and infer one thing from another

another, or to exercise reason; so also, if the mind had the exercise of memory, but no judgment, it could not draw any consequences, or come to any conclusion in those things, which may be supposed to be retained in the memory; so that to remember in such circumstances as this, would be to no purpose, nor answer any wise or valuable end; and to suppose the mind to have the faculty of memory and judgment, yet, if it had no will or power, to put the resolutions of the judgment into execution or action, the mind in such a condition would be able to reflect, remember, reason and judge of things, but all to no wise end, or to serve any purpose of agency or design worthy of a rational creature, being under an invincible confinement and restraint, for want of a power to execute the decrees of the judgment: but experience assures us that we are free, and that it is through the medium of the senses, that the mind is made apprehensive of its first notices of things, *alias* simple ideas; and that is it able to reflect, remember and judge of things, and has a power of willing, or of agency, and in fact is able to exert itself in a great variety of actions and conduct. The mind is but one entire, pure or simple essence; it is the same intelligent principle which apprehends simple ideas, that retains those perceptions in memory; it is the same principle, which reflects and reasons upon those ideas thus retained in itself, that exerts its powers of ratiocination to the extent of the minds capaciousness, and which wills or controuls its own actions. All the different operations, agencies or exertions of the mind, be they what they will, are only the various exertions of the same principle; it is therefore the same soul that receives the perception of external objects or simple ideas, which reflects upon them, and which remembers, reasons and infers one thing from another, draws conclusions, judges and exerts itself, actuates the body, and does every thing which belongs to thinking: liberty therefore is essential to intelligent beings, notwithstanding the many metaphysical arguments which have been advanced to overthrow it.

To point out the exact boundaries between sensation and reflection, or the precise functions of the one and of the other, and clearly to discern where the aptitude of sensation ends, and reflection begins, in the apprehension of mere simple ideas, is curiously nice or impossible, but it does not follow from hence that there is no distinction between them, or, which is the same thing, between the body and the mind, any more than that there is no such thing as day and night, because we differ in our opinions often times concerning the discovery of the precise dawn of day-light, or because we more or less are at a loss to prefix in our minds the exact moment when it becomes visible, or that there is no distinction between truth and falsehood; because that in intricate and perplexed matters, we do not comprehend their respective limitations. When the dawn of the day becomes apparent, we clearly distinguish the day from the night, though we may have been at a loss about the exact moment when it dawned; and truth and falsehood are distinguishable by us in plain cases; so also concerning sensation, and the reflections or mere cogitations of the mind, in the production of simple ideas (for none will pretend that the aptitudes of sensation extend to rationality,) it may be difficult or impossible for us to understand the exact proportion, which sensation and reflection in the order of nature, have contributed towards the production of those simple images, from which all our knowledge of things in general is predicated. We may nevertheless for certain, determine that sensation is not reflection, but that they are essentially and intrinsically different from each other. It is as natural for the mind to reflect, reason or phylosophise upon the works of nature, as it is for sensation to represent to the mind the first and simple perception of them. All sorts of rationation, contrivance, invention and arts, are

intrinsically

intrinsically distinct exertions from the aptitude of sensation, and pertain to a more exalted principle.

The terraqueous globe with its productions, is evidently designed by the creator to subserve animal life, and the body to subserve the soul, or in fine that all matter, variously endowed, was made subservient to rational beings; and as sensation is the production of matter, it is subjected to physical evils, which have been considered in the fourth section of the third chapter.

Sensation, abstractedly considered from a superior principle, could never have given us any possible apprehensions of the being and providence of God, which could never have been known but by reasoning from effects to their cause: for the eternal cause of all things is not corporeal, and therefore cannot come within the notice of our senses, but must be sought out by reasoning; for it is as much out of the power of sensation to make that discovery, as it would be out of the power of the mind to form ideas of colours, or sound, in the instances of persons born blind or deaf. Nor could mere sensation have taught us the distinction between truth and falsehood, right and wrong, good and evil; to understand those distinctions would require the exercise of reason, nor could sensation, abstractly considered, give us

the

the least apprehension of a state of immortality; for sensation terminates at death, and if there was not an intrinsic and essential difference between soul and body, both would be destroyed by death; and for want of making a just distinction between soul and body, some have been misled into an apprehension of the gloomy prospect of an annihilation at death.

SECTION III.

Of the PROVIDENCE *of* GOD, *as it respects the important Subject of the* IMMORTALITY *of the* SOUL.

DEATH is rightly called the king of terrors, it is a solemn change, and to visible appearance the destruction of the whole man; but it should be considered, that it is not at all beyond the power or goodness of God, to invest the soul at the death of the body, with new modes of sensation, entirely diverse from those we are at present united to; and which, while we are in this life, we cannot conceive of; provided it be requisite, in order to our immortality or mode of future existence: but we are so imperfect with respect to our speculations on the manner of existence of unembodied souls, that we know not whether it will be necessary or requisite, that departed souls should be united to any sort of sensorium at all, when they are seperated from the body by death; they may, for what we know, be suited without any sensitive vehicle to their immortal state, and manner of existence; in the same predicament, which their disunion from the body may unfold to them. All possible power and goodness belongs to God, so that there can be no rational doubt or disbelief, but that the God who made us, has constituted our souls, so that they will survive their bodies, and exist in such a manner, as is of all others the best for them, (consistent with that of the scale of being in general) and most worthy of the perfection of God; although at present he has not seen fit to indulge us with the knowledge of it. The providence of God has been abundantly and conspicuously displayed towards us in this life, on which we may with great assurance, predicate our darling and important hope of immortality. Ungrateful and foolish it must be for rational beings in the possession of existence, and surrounded with a kind and almighty providence, to distrust the author thereof concerning their futurity, because they cannot comprehend the mode or manner of their succeeding and progressive existence:

WHEN we consider the eternity and infinity of God, and of his creation and providence, and that his

his ultimate design in the whole, must have been to exalt and happify the moral world, that human life is but a presage and pre-requisite existence for an introduction into another more dignified in the order of being: those vain and idle distrusts of our immortality will vanish, and our minds will be established in a firm reliance on God, that in the order of nature and course of his providence, (however inconceiveable to us) he has secured our immortality. It is in vain for us, while in this life, to expect to understand the manner of our future existence, or how mental beings (devoid of sensitive vehicles, or of such sort of sensations as ours) exert thought and reflection on new subjects in a new world, or how they interchangeably communicate intelligence to one another. These matters cannot be known to us, so long as we are dependent on our present senses for the predication of our knowledge; for our present organized sensations are inadequate to such discoveries; they were calculated for this world only, in which they admirably well answer their design, use and end, but are unequal to the task of giving our minds any images or representations of things beyond the grave, their common repository.

INCONSIDERATE it is for mankind to object against the doctrine of immortality, because they

cannot

cannot conceive of such a state, or how it will be, (neither do I pretend to communicate the knowledge of the manner of it) this is deducing an objection, not from reason or argument, but from mere ignorance. I shall therefore proceed to collect rational arguments, from the perfections, creation and providence of God, and particularly from the intrinsic nature of the soul, to evince its immortality. But objecters to this doctrine demand sensible or occular demonstrations for it, which cannot be had, " *For eye hath not seen, nor ear heard, nor hath it entered into the* " mind " *of man to conceive* " an idea of the manner of it. A man born blind might with the same propriety, or rather impropriety, object against the reality of colours or of sight, (and pledge his ignorance for the proof of it, as the predicate of his objection,) as we may object against the doctrine of immortality, because we cannot in this life, and thro' the medium of our sensorium, apprehend the manner of our succeeding existence; the reality of which depends not on the weakness of our reasonings, or the inadequateness or impropriety of our present sensations, to discover the state, condition, or manner of it; but it depends altogether on God, and on his eternalizing the nature of cogitative and understanding beings, or not. While we

are

are in this life we should adore God, and with gratitude confide in the ultimate goodness of his providence to disclose to our minds the mysterious objects and manner of the world to come at death, for then, and not till then, shall we need that knowledge. Undoubtedly our creator wisely limited the objects of our perception to the world wherein we live, and restricted our simple ideas to the objects of sense, from which we are necessitated to superstruct all our knowledge of things in general. Thus it is, that our creator in the order of the succession of causes has made use of those mere simple images of external things, to disclose to our understanding, whatever he sees fit to gratify us with the knowledge or perception of, while in this life; therefore all our knowledge of things universally, while in this life, must be deduced from the present order of human nature, and the world in which we are citizens, from which we attempt to illustrate the doctrine of immortality.

IDEAS once taken or conceived by the mind through the medium of its senses, and retained in memory, are capable of being reviewed, revised, corrected, improved, and diversified in all possible methods of thinking and argumentation, although the external objects, which excited those simple images from whence those argumentative arrangements originated, may have been absent for a succession of years; for instance, I may have retained the ideas or arguments of an author, whom I had read twenty years ago, though I may not have read the book, or heard of it since; so I may retain a remembrance of sounds, which I heard as long since, and be able to make new observations or argumentations thereon; so likewise in instances wherein persons have been deprived, or have lost their senses of seeing or hearing, or both, yet the mind having once received simple ideas through those senses, in the time of their usefulness, is able to reflect and reason on those original images, the same as though it had never been deprived of those sensations, but could never, after the deprivation of its senses of seeing or hearing, receive any new simple ideas of either seeing or hearing in consequence of the loss of them, but would be restricted to those simple images of seeing or hearing, which were apprehended by the mind, previous to its loss of those senses for its new and progressive compositions, or modifications of those original simple ideas, and retain the knowledge and consciousness of the state of things made perceptible to them through the medium of those senses of seeing and hearing, for ever after the loss of them, or at least during

he

the period of life; which we know to be true in fact. From all which we may with great propriety infer, that the human soul admitting it a seperate state of existence, must necessarily retain a remembrance or consciousness of this world, and of its agency or conduct in it, though the body, *the instrument of sensation,* (through which medium the soul, during the period of life, was enabled to apprehend its simple ideas,) be totally destroyed by death.

ADMITTING that the soul survives death, and is by nature immortal; and also that the mode of its existance is different from this world, and its manner of existence and converse in it; and that death is a release from carnallity and physical evil, and raise departed spirits to a superior rank or condition in the order of being, to their survivers in life; it will follow of necessary consequence, that those, who are survivors, could form no manner of conception of such an elevated kind of existence, as it would be supernatural to human conception in this compounded nature, consisting of sensation and reflection.

TO SUPPOSE, while we are in this state, we could retain a representation or understanding of the manner of that which is beyond death, would be be the same as to suppose that both states are alike; and that after death we shall exist in the same manner as we do here; and thus inadvertently (ideally) carry our mortality with us into the next state, and conceive of acting over much the same scene as at present, which mode of existance would be obnoxious to a second death, and is incompatible with our darling hope of immortality: therefore as certain as our souls are immortal, the manner of our immortality, cannot be understood by us in this life. Was it possible for us in this life to break in upon the order of being, and perceive and understand the felicities and glorious manner of existence in the world to come, it could not fail to imbitter all our present enjoyments, and make us discontented and miserable from the anticipation of a felicity beyond our condition in the order of being, and wholly disqualify us to act and conduct in our several stations and relations in the present life: from hence we may learn the wisdom and goodness of God, in concealing from us, in this state, the extatic blessedness which virtuous souls will be qualified for, and be admitted to partake of in the next.

It is not rational to expect that any new law of nature will take place upon our commencing existence in a future state; though the manner of that

that state, and of our existence in it, will be new to us; inasmuch as the eternal order of nature has not as yet brought us into those future circumstances, and as our first perceptions of things in this world are new to us, so in the same sense, the manner of our future state, and of our existence in it, will be new; there will be an entire change of the mode of our perception, and likewise in the objects of our perception, but the identity of our souls never can be changed; for the principle of the mind of A, and its individual consciousness, can never be the individual or identical principle of the mind and consciousness of B; the same will hold equally true with respect to all rational beings; for that there are as many individual souls, as there are seperate or distinct cogitative principles or essences.

Were we to admit that two individual and distinct minds were conscious of the same consciousness (except as to their individuality of essence, which is not possible) they would not be, in consequence thereof, the same mind, any more than as though their whole consciousnesses were dissimilar; for likeness is not sameness, any more than unlikeness is so; but reason and consciousness will eternally remain the same, as to nature and kind, in all possible modes of existence; tho'
the

the manner of perception, or the objects of it, may be liable to inconceiveable alterations and diversity; notwithstanding thinking beings are essentially the same: For if they reflect and reason, they are conscious they do so, be they in what state or manner of existence they will; or be the objects of reflection and consciousness what they will. Our present five senses are diverse in their manner of communicating the notices of external objects to the mind; so that in this life we experience the advantage of a diversity in the mode of sensation, as seeing is not hearing. We may from hence infer the possibility of our minds forming ideas in the succeeding state of being, through such a medium, as at present we can have no manner of conception of; for reasoning, which is essential to the exercise of a rational soul, is but a succession of thinking, and comparing ideas together, and drawing conclusions from certain premises, previously laid down in the mind; nor is the manner or the objects of perception, particularly essential to reasoning; for if so be the mind has an apprehension of things, it can reason thereon, be the manner of those apprehensions as it will, or in what world it will; for as it is not essential to mere creation to occupy any particular form, tho' it must exist in some form or other, so any particular mode of existence or apprehension is not essential

sential to the soul, though it must likewise exist in some state or other, and be supplied with some sort of apprehension or other, on which it may predicate its reasonings, and superstruct its knowledge and happiness.

From the foregoing discourse, it does not appear any ways contradictory to the order of nature, as far as we are acquainted with it, that our souls may survive our bodies, and that they are by nature immortal and capable of existing in a mode and manner very different from this world; and our manner of existence and conversation in it, and which at present we can form no right conception of; and that in our premised and progressive state, or condition of being and action, we may retain a remembrance, and consequently a consciousness, that we are the same individual intelligent beings, who inhabited and actuated our respective bodies, while in this life; and also retain a memory and consciousness of our manner of existence, and of our deportment or agency in moral good and evil; For if this is not the case, our respective proficiencies in moral good and evil in this stage of action, cannot be attended with consequences of conscious mental happiness or misery, in our commencing a premised succeeding existence. For that to be intelligently or mentally happy or miserable without a conſciouſneſs of it is contradictory and impoſſible. So that provided in our progreſſive ſtate of being and action, we are not conſcious of what we have done and tranſacted in this world, God in his order of nature (which is the ſame as his providence) could not reward or puniſh mankind, in a future ſtate, for their virtuous or vicious agencies in this; which would be incompatible with the divine adminiſtration of juſtice and goodneſs.

We muſt therefore admit, that if our ſouls have a future exiſtence, we muſt then have a conſciouſneſs, not only of our identity of being, but alſo of our demeanour in this life; and thus by a retroſpective conſciouſneſs, begin a condition of mental felicity, or mental pungent woe, according to our works; which an awakened conſcience, and the juſtice of God will diſcloſe, at that important and dreadful criſis of our unbodied and incomprehenſible exiſtence.

Animal nature, as has been before obſerved, conſiſts of a regular conſtitution of a variety of organic parts, every of which has a neceſſary dependence on each other. Blood is the ſource of life, and in order to preſerve the machine, and perpetuate its functions, it is requiſite that it ſhould have a due circulation from the heart to the ſurface of the

the body, to replenish it with homogeneous particles, vital heat and vigour; and that it should have a retrograde motion from thence to the heart that it may repeat its temporary rounds; certain arteries and veins have been wisely constructed for that purpose. But the brain is evidently the seat of sensation, which through the nerves conveys the animal spirits to every part of the body, qualifying it with sensation and elastic motion, which is of an exquisite, subtil, ethereal and electrical quality, and almost (and some say quite) instantaneous in its operation, in which the mind takes its residence in this life. This sensorium, through which we form ideas of external objects, can form no conception of other minds, or of mere mental beings, except by the application of their external sensations to ours, or by language either oral or written, of which we understand the signs; nor can our gross sensations represent the perception of our own minds to ourselves. The knowledge therefore of our cogitative nature is not compounded of simple ideas, which are deduced mediately from material beings; but the knowledge which mental beings have of their own existence is from their consciousness of being, reflection, and ratiocination, together with other mental exertions; which are invisible, as well to our own sensations as to our neighbour's; inasmuch as intellectual

lectual beings are imperceptible to the aptitudes of sensation; for they are neither long or short; round or square; black or white; nor do they occupy space as material beings do; or consist of such a quality, on which our sensations can operate; but, as has been observed, the mind is conscious of itself, and of its own agency, though it could not have had any apprehension of external objects independent of sensation. As sensation is compounded of matter, its aptitudes are restricted to material existences; and therefore can make no discoveries of mere cogitative beings, whether that of our own souls, or of the souls of others: for our own minds, are as invisible to our own sensations, as that of a pure angel may be supposed to be; which I presume will be conceded to by the contemplative, who examine into matters of fact collectable from their own experience.

THAT our minds reflect, remember, reason and judge of things, and are able to reconsider them, and make refinements and proficiencies upon their own reasonings, is a fact which every day's experience will confirm. The soul has a power, not only to exert its mental faculties, but to actuate its organized body into spontaneous motion, to answer the purposes of wisdom, contrivance and design; which are effects too stupendous to arise out of mere matter, figure and motion, with their effects and combinations; and which must therefore be afcribed to a fuperior principle, that is intrinfically diftinct from matter, and which may continue to exift when the body is deftroyed by death, and is no longer a fuitable habitation or receptacle for it.

The body itfelf, notwithftanding its fluctuating and perifhable nature, does not prefent us with any idea of annihilation; its final diffolution and return to its original elements again, is no more than a diffolution of the form, and conftruction of the particles, with their cohefive and animal aptitudes and combinations, and by no means a diffolution or annihilation of matter: for no particular form is effential to the exiftence of matter, though it is effential to the exiftence of animal life; but mere matter does exift in all poffible forms and fluxilities.

And, as in nature there is no annihilation of matter, as fuch, it is a ftrong argument in favor of the immortality of rational beings; inafmuch as they are not liable to fuch phyfical changes, as animal bodies are obnoxious to. Thought and reflection, memory, and judgment, invention and defign, derive not their effence from the mafs of

incogitative

incogitative elements, but are in their own nature immortal; for that which is immaterial is exempted from physical evils, and inasmuch as matter universally, was created and variously endowed, tempered and qualified, regulated and governed, (more especially such a part as composes human bodies,) wholly to subserve thinking and rational beings; (as has been in the preceeding discourse fully evinced) and inasmuch as the ultimate end of creation, and the principle design of providence, must have been to subserve the moral world, by displaying the wisdom, power and goodness of God to cogitative and understanding beings, we may be morally certain, that in the order of nature, and course of God's providence, he has secured to us a never ending existence, and that mind as well as matter will be eternal; for human life, abstractly considered from the reality of immortality, would hardly be desired by the generality of mankind, could they have but a clear understanding of the physical evils of it, and also of the oppressions, abuses and injustice, which is "*Done under the Sun.*" From the consideration whereof the reputed wise man, "*Praised the dead more than the living, which are yet alive.*" Should we admit that death extinguisheth the being of man, what narrow and contracted notions must we consequently entertain of God and of his creation?

We

We should be necessitated to deduce an inference of injustice against his providence, from the unequal distribution of justice in this life, which, on a supposition of a future state of being, may be remedied. As true as mankind now exist, and are endowed with reason and understanding, and have the power of agency and proficiency in moral good and evil, so true it is, that they must be ultimately rewarded, or punished, according to their respective merits or demerits; and it is as true, as this world exists, and rational and accountable beings inhabit it, that the distribution of justice therein is partial, unequal and uncertain, and consequently it is as true, as that there is a God, that there must be a future state of existence, in which the disorder, injustice, oppression and viciousness, which are acted and transacted by mankind in this life, shall be righteously adjusted, and the delinquents suitably punished; and that the virtuous who obey the laws of reason or moral fitness, which are the laws of God, shall receive a just and rational enjoyment of happiness, according to their works: for God may as well cease to be, as cease to be ultimately just.

THE natural hope and strong expectation of immortality, which mankind in all ages, countries, and nations, have entertained, is a presage and earnest

earnest of that eternal inheritance, for it could not be from the invention and tradition of man, in as much as it has taken place among every of the traditions and sectaries in the world, except the Sadducees (who rejected it, because it was not to be met with in the theology of Moses, their law-giver, who, they supposed, was immediately dictated by God and could not have failed of promulgating the doctrine of immortality, had it been in fact true:) but none of the human race, who have not been prepossessed by traditions to the contrary, have failed of hoping and believing in the reality of a future existence, the barbarous and uncultivated nations of the earth not excepted, and inasmuch as this expectation hath made such deep and universal impression on the human mind, we must conclude it to be the voice of nature powerfully and universally evincing the immortality of man;

ADMITTING that it was in the power of God to have imparted the quality or nature of endless existence to cogitative and understanding beings, we may be morally certain, that human souls are by nature thus eternalized, for otherwise it would follow, that God had not done that, for the immortality, and consequently the blessedness of man, which he might have done for them, but that instead of

making

making them immortal, he had made them mere perishable and worthless animals, and deluded them with vain and empty hopes and strong expectations of surviving the grave, to no purpose, except, to impose on them by frustrating the natural hope of immortality, by the stroke of death which he had originally implanted in them. But as there can be no dispute concerning the perfection of power in God, to eternize mental, cogitative and understanding beings, so there can be no dispute, but that his perfection of goodness, has induced him in his order of providence, to accomplish so great, benevolent and God-like a work, to his eternal glory, and the everlasting best good, of a whole world of intelligent rational beings.

WHEREFORE let us persevere in the practice of virtue, habitually conforming ourselves to the moral rectitude of things, and wait patiently the few days, that God sees fit to continue us in this life, remembering, that at death, the mysterious state of immortality will be unfolded unto us, and that until then, it will be best for us not to understand the superior manner and extatic felicities thereof. Sufficient it is for us at present, for the encouragement of morality, that we believe, from the highest moral certainty, that there is such a state, leaving it to the God who made us, to unfold the

manner

manner of it, at such time as his order of nature shall bring us into the fruition of it.

Chapter

Chapter V.

SECTION I.

Speculations on the DOCTRINE *of the Depravity of* HUMAN REASON.

IN the course of our speculations on divine providence we proceed next to the consideration of the doctrine of the depravity of human reason; a doctrine derogatory to the nature of man, and the rank and character of being which he holds in the universe, and which, if admitted to be true, overturns knowledge and science and renders learning, instruction and books useless and impertinent; inasmuch as reason, depraved or spoiled, would cease to be reason; as much as the mind of a raving madman would of course cease to be rational: admitting the depravity of reason, the consequence would unavoidably follow, that as far as it may be supposed to have taken place in the minds of mankind, they could be no judges of it, in consequence of their supposed depravity; for without the exercise of reason, we could not understand what reason is, which would be necessary for us previously to understand, in order to understand what it is not; or to distinguish it from that which is its reverse. But for us to have the knowledge of what reason is, and the ability to distinguish it from that which is depraved, or is irrational, is incompatible with the doctrine of the depravity of our reason. Inasmuch as to understand what reason is, and to distinguish it from that which is marred or spoiled, is the same to all intents and purposes, as to have, exercise and enjoy, the principle of reason itself, which precludes its supposed depravity: so that it is impossible for us to understand what reason is, and at the same time determine that our reason is depraved; for this would be the same as when we know that we are in possession and exercise of reason, to determine that we are not in possession or exercise of it.

It may be, that some, who embrace the doctrine of the depravity of human reason, will not admit, that it is wholly and totally depraved, but
that

that it is in a great measure marred or spoiled. But the foregoing arguments are equally applicable to a supposed depravity in part, as in the whole; for in order to judge whether reason be depraved in part, or not, it would be requisite to have an understanding, of what reason may be supposed to have been, previous to its premised depravity; and to have such a knowledge of it, would be the same as to exercise and enjoy it in its lustre and purity; which would preclude the notion of a depravity in part, as well as in the whole; for it would be utterly impossible for us to judge of reason undepraved and depraved, but by comparing them together. But for depraved reason to make such a comparison, is contradictory and impossible; so that, if our reason had been depraved, we could not have had any conception of it any more than a beast. Men of small faculties in reasoning cannot comprehend the extensive reasonings of their superiors, how then can a supposed depraved reason, comprehend that reason which is uncorrupted and pure? to suppose that it could, is the same as to suppose that depraved and undepraved reason is alike, and if so there needs no further dispute about it.

THERE is a manifest contradiction in applying the term *depraved*, to that of reason, the ideas contained

contained in their respective difinitions will not admit of their association together, as the terms convey heterogeneous ideas; for reason spoiled, marred, or robbed of its perfection, ceaseth to be rational, and should not be called reason; inasmuch as it is premised to be depraved, or degenerated from a rational nature; and in consequence of the deprivation of its nature, should also be deprived of its name, and called subterfuge, or some such-like name, which might better define its real character.

Those who invalidate reason, ought seriously to consider, "*Whether they argue against reason with or without reason; if with reason, then they establish the principle, that they are labouring to dethrone:*" but if they argue without reason, (which, in order to be consistent with themselves, they must do) they are out of the reach of rational conviction, nor do they deserve a rational argument.

We are told that the knowledge of the depravity of reason, was first communicated to mankind by the immediate inspiration of God. But inasmuch as reason is supposed to be depraved, what principle could there be in the human irrational soul, which could receive or understand the inspiration, or on which it could operate, so as to represent, to those whom it may be supposed were

inspired

inspired, the knowledge of the depravity of (their own and mankind's) reason (in general:) For a rational inspiration must consist of rational ideas; which pre-supposes, that the minds of those who were inspired, were rational, previous to such their inspiration; which would be a downright contradiction to the inspiration itself; the import of which was to teach the knowledge of the depravity of human reason, which without reason could not be understood, and with reason it would be understood, that the inspiration was false.

WILL any advocates for the depravity of reason suppose, that inspiration ingrafts or superadds the essence of reason itself, to the human mind? admitting it to be so, yet such inspired persons could not understand any thing of reason, before the reception of such supposed inspiration; nor would such a premised inspiration, prove to its possessors, or receivers, that their reason had ever been depraved. All that such premised inspired persons could understand, or be conscious of, respecting reason, would be after the inspiration may be supposed to have taken effect, and made them rational beings, and then instead of being taught by inspiration, that their reason had been previously depraved, they could have had no manner of consciousness of the existence or exercise of it,

'till

'till the imparting the principle of it by the supposed energy of inspiration; nor could such supposed inspired persons communicate the knowledge of such a premised revelation to others of the species, who for want of a rational nature, could not be supposed, *on this position,* to be able to receive the impressions of reason.

That there are degrees in the knowledge of rational beings, and also in their capacities to acquire it, cannot be disputed, as it is so very obvious among mankind. But in all the retrospect gradations from the exalted reasonings of a Locke or a Newton, down to the lowest exercise of it among the species, still it is reason, and not depraved; for a less degree of reason by no means implies a depravity of it, nor does the imparing of reason argue its depravity, for what remains of reason, or rather of the exercise of it, is reason still. But there is not, and cannot be such a thing as depraved reason, for that which is rational is so, and for that reason cannot be depraved, whatever its degree of exercise may be supposed to be.

A blow on the head, or fracture of the perecranium, as also palsies and many other casualties that await our sensorium; retard, and in some cases wholly prevent the exercise of reason, for a longer, or shorter period; and sometimes through

the

the stage of human life; but in such instances as these, reason is not depraved, but ceases in a greater or less degree, or perhaps wholly ceases its rational exertions or operations; by reason of the breaches, or disorders of the organs of sense, but in such instances, wherein the organs become rectified, and the senses recover their usefulness, the exercise of reason returns; free from any blemish or depravity. For the cessation of the exercise of reason, by no means depraves it.

There is in God's infinite plentitude of creation and providence, such an infinite display of reason, that the most exalted finite rational beings, fall infinitely short of the comprehension thereof. For though the most inconsiderable rational beings, who can discern any truth at all, bear a resemblance or likeness to God, as well as every rational nature of whatever degree in the scale of beings; yet neither the greatest or least of them can bear any manner of proportion to God; inasmuch as no possible degree of reason or knowledge, can bear any proportion to that reason and knowledge, which is eternal and infinite, as has been before argued. And though human reason cannot understand every thing, yet in such things, which it does understand, its knowledge which is acquired by reasoning, is as true and certain, as

the

the divine knowledge may be supposed to be: for to more than understand a thing, speaking of that particular, is impossible even to omniscience itself. For knowledge is but knowledge, and that only whether it is in the divine mind, or ours, or in any other intelligencies; therefore knowledge is not imperfect; for a knowledge of any thing is the same as to have right ideas of it, or ideas according to truth, and as all knowledge of things in general must be predicated on truth, it will agree in the divine or human mind.

From what has been argued on this subject, in this and the preceeding chapters, it appears, that reason is not, and cannot be depraved, but that it bears a likeness to divine reason, is of the same kind, and in its own nature as uniform as truth, which is the test of it; though in the divine essence, it is eternal and infinite, but in man it is eternal only, as it respects their immortality, and finite, as it respects capaciousness. Such people, as can be prevailed upon to believe, that their reason is depraved, may easily be led by the nose, and duped into superstition at the pleasure of those, in whom they confide, and there remain from generation to generation: for when they throw by the law of reason, *the only one* which God gave them to direct them in their speculations and
duty,

duty, they are expofed to ignorant or infiduous teachers, and alfo to their own irregular paffions, and to the folly and enthufiafm of thofe about them, which nothing but reafon can prevent or reftrain: Nor is it a rational fuppofition that the commonality of mankind would ever have miftrufted, that their reafon was depraved, had they not been told fo, and it is whifpered about, that the firft infinuation of it was from the Priefts; (though the Arminian Clergymen in the circle of my acquaintance have exploded the doctrine.) Should we admit the depravity of reafon, it would equally affect the priefthood, or any other teachers of that doctrine, with the reft of mankind; but for depraved creatures to receive and give credit to a depraved doctrine, ftarted and taught by depraved creatures, is the greateft weaknefs and folly imaginable, and comes nearer a proof of the doctrine of a total depravity, than any arguments which have ever been advanced in fupport of it.

SECTION

Z

SECTION II.

Containing a Disquisition of the LAW *of* NATURE, *as it respects the* MORAL SYSTEM, *interspersed with* OBSERVATIONS *on subsequent* RELIGIONS.

THAT mankind are by nature endowed with sensation and reflection, from which results the powers of reason and understanding, will not be disputed. The senses are well calculated to make discoveries of external objects, and to communicate those notices, or simple images of things to the mind, with all the magnificent simplicity of nature, which opens an extensive field of contemplation to the understanding, enabling the mind to examine into the natural causes and consequences of things, and to investigate the knowledge of moral good and evil, from which, together with the power of agency, results the human conscience. This is the original of moral obligation and accountability, which is called natural religion; for without the understanding of truth from falsehood, and right from wrong, which is the same as justice from injustice, and a liberty of agency, which is the same as a power of proficiency in either moral good or evil; mankind would not be rational or accountable creatures. Undoubtedly it was the ultimate design of our creator, in giving us being, and furnishing us with

with those noble compositions of mental powers and sensitive aptitudes, that we should, in, by, and with that nature, serve and honor him: and with those united capacities search out and understand our duty to him, and to one another, with the ability of practising the same, as far as may be necessary for us, in this life. To object against the sufficiency of natural religion, to effect the ultimate best good of mankind, would be derogating from the wisdom, justice and goodness of God, who in the course of his providence to us has adopted it: besides, if natural religion may be supposed to be deficient, what security can we have that any subsequent revealed religion should not be so also? For why might not a second religion from God, be as insufficient or defective as a first religion from him may be supposed to be? From hence we infer, that if natural religion is insufficient to dictate mankind in the way of their duty, and make them ultimately happy, there is an end to religion in general. But as certain as God is perfect, in wisdom and goodness, natural religion is sufficient and complete; and having had the divine approbation, and naturally resulting from a rational nature, is as universally promulgated to mankind as reason itself. But to the disadvantage of the claim of all subsequent religions, *called revelations, whether denominated*

inspired

inspired, external, supernatural, or what not, they came too late into the world to be essential to the well being of mankind, or to point out to them the only way to heaven and everlasting blessedness: Inasmuch as far the greatest part of mankind, who have ever lived in this world, had departed this life previous to the æras and promulgations of such revelations. Besides, those subsequent revelations to the law of nature, began the same as human traditions have ever done, in very small circumferences, in the respective parts of the world where they have been inculcated, and made their progress as time, chance and opportunity presented. Does this look like the contrivance of heaven and the only way of salvation? or is it not more like this world and the device of man? Undoubtedly the great parent of mankind laid a just and sufficient foundation of salvation for every of them, for otherwise such of them, who may be supposed not to be thus provided for, would not have whereof to glorify God for their being, but on the contrary would have just matter of complaint against his providence or moral government, for involuntarily necessitating them into a wretched and miserable existence, and that without end or remedy; which would be ascribing to God a more extensive injustice than is possible to be charged on the most barbarous despots that ever were among mankind. But

But to return to our speculations upon the law of nature. That this divine law surpasses all positive institutions, that have been ushered into the world since its creation, as much as the wisdom and goodness of God exceeds that of man, is beautifully illustrated in the following quotation; " But it may be said, what is virtue? it is the faithful discharge of those obligations which reason dictates. And what is wisdom itself? but a portion of intelligence" with which the creator has furnished us," " in order to direct us in our duty. It may be further asked, what is this duty? whence does it result? and by what law it is prescribed? I answer, that the law which prescribed it is the immutable will of God; to which right reason obliges us to conform ourselves, and in this conformity virtue consists. No law which has commenced since the creation, or which may ever cease to be in force, can constitute virtue; for before the existence of such a law, mankind could not be bound to observe it, but they were certainly under an obligation to be virtuous from the beginning. Princes may make laws and repeal them, but they can neither make nor destroy virtue, and how indeed should they be able to do what is impossible to the Deity himself: virtue being as immutable in its nature as the divine
will

will, which is the ground of it.* A Prince may command his subjects to pay certain taxes or subsidies, may forbid them to export certain commodities, or to introduce those of a foreign country. The faithful observance of these laws makes obedient subjects, but does not make virtuous men: and would any one seriously think himself possessed of a virtue the more for not having dealt in painted callicoe; or if the Prince should by his authority abrogate these laws, would any one say he had abrogated virtue. It is thus with all positive laws: they all had a beginning, are all liable to exceptions, and may be dispensed with, and even abolished. That law alone, which is ingraven on our hearts by the hand of the creator, is unchangeable and of universal and eternal obligation. The law, says Cicero, is not a human invention,

---

* Virtue, did not derive its nature merely from the omnipotent will of God, but also from the eternal truth and moral fitness of things; which was the eternal reason, why they were eternally approved of by God, and immutably established by him, to be what they are; and so far as our duty is connected with those eternal measures of moral fitness, or we are able to act upon them, we give such actions, or habits, the name of virtue or morality. But when we in writing or conversation say, that virtue is grounded on the divine will, we should at the same time include in the complex idea of it, that the divine will, which constituted virtue, was eternally and infinitely reasonable.

tion, nor an arbitrary political institution, it is in its nature eternal and of universal obligation. The violence Tarquin offered to Lucretia, was breach of that eternal law, and though the Romans at that time might have no written law which condemned such kind of crimes, his offence was not the less heineous; for this law of reason did not then begin, when it was first committed to writing: its original is as antient as the divine mind. For the true, primitive and supreme law, in no other than the unerring reason of the great Jupiter. And in another place he says; this law is founded in nature, it is universal, immutable and eternal, it is subject to no change from any difference of place, or time, it extends invariably to all ages and nations, like the sovereign dominion of that being, who is the author of it."

The promulgation of this supreme law to creatures, is co extensive and co-existent with reason, and binding on all intelligent beings in the universe; and is that eternal rule of fitness, as applicable to God, by which the creator of all things conducts his infinitude of providence, and by which he governs the moral system of being, according to the absolute perfection of his nature. From hence we infer, that admitting those subsequent

quent revelations, which have more or less obtained credit in the world, as the inspired laws of God, to be consonant to the laws of nature, yet they could be considered as none other but mere transcripts therefrom, promulgated to certain favorite nations, when at the same time all mankind was favoured with the original. The moral precepts contained in Moses's decalogue to the people of Israel, were previously known to every nation under heaven, and in all probability by them as much practised as by the tribes of Israel. Their keeping the seventh day of the week as a sabbath, was an arbitrary imposition of Moses (as many other of his edicts were) and not included in the law of nature. But as to such laws of his, or those of any other legislator, which are morally fit, agree with, and are a part of the natural law, as for instance; " Thou shalt not covet," or " Kill." These positive injunctions cannot add any thing to the law of nature, inasmuch as it contains an entire and perfect system of morality; nor can any positive injunctions or commands enforce the authority of it, or confer any additional moral obligation on those to whom they are given to obey; the previous obligation of natural religion, having ever been as binding as reason can possibly conceive of, or the order and constitution of the moral rectitude of things, as resulting from God, can make it to be:

To

To illustrate the argument of the obligatory nature of the natural law, let us reverse the commandments of the decalogue, by premising that Moses had said thou shalt covet; thou shalt steal and murder; would any one conclude, that the injunctions would have been obligatory, surely they would not, for a positive command to violate the law of nature could not be binding on any rational being, how then came the injunctions of Moses, or any others, to be binding in such cases, in which they coincide with the law of nature? We answer, merely in consequence of the obligatory sanctions of the natural law, which does not at all depend on the authority of Moses or of any other Legislator, short of him who is eternal and infinite: nor is it possible that the Jews, who adhere to the law of Moses, should be under greater obligation to the moral law, than the Japannese; or the Christians than the Chinese; for the same God extends the same moral government over universal rational nature, independent of Popes, Priests and Levites. But with respect to all mere positive institutions, injunctions, rites and ceremonies, that do not come within the jurisdiction of the law of nature, they are political matters, and may be enacted, perpetuated, dispensed with, abolished, re-enacted, compounded or diversified, as conveniency, power, opportunity, inclination, or interest, or all

together

together may dictate; inasmuch as they are not founded on any stable or universal principle of reason, but change with the customs, fashions, traditions and revolutions of the world; having no centre of attraction, but interest, power and advantages of a tempory nature.

When we reflect on the state and circumstances of mankind in this world, their various languages and interchangeable methods of communicating intelligence to each other, (which are subject to perpetual alterations and refinements; the insuperable difficulties in translating antient writings, with any considerable degree of perfection; as also our being exposed to the villainous practices of impostors, with a variety of other deceptions, blunders and inaccuracies, which unavoidably attend written and diverse or variously translated revelations; we cannot too much admire the wisdom and goodness of God in imparting his law to us in the constitution of our rational nature, to point out our duty in all circumstances and vicissitudes of human life; which a written revelation would not be able to do, admitting, that it had sustained no spurious alterations from its first composure, which we will premise to have been perfect: for human affairs are so constantly changing and varying

rying, that the same action, or conduct, would, under different circumstances, be alternately good and evil; and to have our duty in every of the multiplicity of incidental circumstances and changes of life, pointed out to us by a written revelation, would compose a Bible of a monstrous size. Furthermore, as every individual of the human race is attended with more or less diversity of circumstances of action in life, therefore in order for us to be taught our duty by a written revelation, it would be requisite, that each individual of mankind should have their particular, and diverse revelation; in which their particular duty might be known in all cases: so that we should suspend our actions, until we may be supposed to have turned to the particular paragraph of our respective revelations, and consulted them, in order to conduct our agency thereby (in which case printing would be in great demand.) Still there would be a difficulty in understanding an external printed revelation, or which paragraph of the bulky volume would be applicable to the various parts of the conduct of human agency; so that we should be obliged finally to make use of (depraved) reason, to understand it, or, in other words, should be obliged to make use of the deistical Bible to explain and understand our own, which brings us back again to the religion of nature or reason.

Was

Was it not that we were rational creatures, it would have been as ridiculous to have pretended to have given us a Bible, for our instruction in matters of religion or morality, as it would to a stable of horses. And on the other hand, admitting that we naturally understand moral good and evil, it renders such a book no ways essential to us, though if it be admitted to be argumentative and instructive, it might, like other sensible writings, subserve mankind; but if it is supposed to be in part defective in reason, and intersperfed with superstition, it would, under the sanction of divine authority, be vastly more prejudicial to mankind, than as though it was stamped merely by the authority of man; for an error in that which is received as infallible, can never be confuted or rectified; inasmuch as it usurps the authority of human reason. Furthermore, admitting that the copies of written revelation, which are now extant in the world, perfectly accord with their several original manuscripts (which is impossible to be true) yet they could not be equally instructive to mankind with the productions of a variety of modern authors, who have written since their epocha, inasmuch as the world has ever since been improving in learning and science; and as those written revelations must necessarily have

been

been (as to their subject matter and all and every other particular) accommodated to the state, circumstances and degrees of learning and knowledge, of those, to whom the revelations were first supposed to have been communicated, and also to those to whom it was afterwards taught, and it would reduce it below the understanding of this age. For it appears from the scripture accounts, that shepherds, fishermen, and the illiterate of those early ages of the world, were principally made use of as the promulgators thereof to the rest of mankind, and that " Not many wife or noble," were " Called," or embraced their revelations in the early times. " But the weak things of this world" were " Chosen," for which reason they were called " Babes:". Though after such religion became popular, princes and politicians of several parts of the world promoted it as an instrument of state-policy. Be this as it will, the first promulgators of written revelations could not reveal to the world more than they knew themselves; nor could they be made to know any more than their capacity (under their then circumstances) was capable of receiving: any external written revelation is therefore utterly incompatible with a progressive or increasing state of knowledge. We will premise, that the world's dissolution will be postponed one hundred thou-

sand

sand million of years from this epocha, or that it will eternally remain. What an idle conceit would it be for us to suppose, that the succeeding generations of mankind, in their religious knowledge, will be chained down to the theology of those positive written revelations, which were introduced into the world, in its early, illiterate, and superstitious age; this would be utterly subversive of a state of proficiency, much the same as for a man to consult his nonage for rules of knowledge, and instruction to govern his manhood.

Was the creator and Governor of the universe to erect a particular academy of arts and sciences in this world, under his immediate inspection, with tutors rightly organized, and intellectually qualified to carry on the business of teaching, it might, like other colleges (and possibly in a superior manner,) instruct its scholars. But that God should have given a revelation of his will to mankind, as his law, and to be continued to the latest posterity as such, which is premised to be above the capacity of their understanding; is contradictory and in its own nature impossible. Nor could a revelation to mankind, which comes within the circle of their knowledge, be edifying or instructive to them, for it is a contradiction to call that which is above

my

my comprehension, or that which I already, (from natural capacity) understand, a revelation to me: to tell me, or inspire me, with the knowledge of that which I knew before, would reveal nothing to me; and to reveal that to me which is supernatural or above my comprehension, is contradictory and impossible. But the truth of the matter is, that mankind are restricted by the law of nature to acquire knowledge or science progressively, as before argued. From which we infer the impropriety, and consequently the impossibility, of God's having ever given us any manuscript copy of his eternal law: for that to reveal it at first would bring it on a level with the infancy of knowledge then in the world, or (fishermen shepherds, and illiterate people could not have understood it) which would have brought it so low, that it could not be instructive or beneficial to after generations in their progressive advances in science and wisdom.

Chapter.

ORACLES

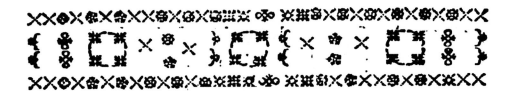

Chapter VI.

SECTION I.

Argumentative Reflections on SUPERNATURAL *and* MYSTERIOUS REVELATION *in general.*

THERE is not any thing, which has contributed so much to delude mankind in religious matters, as mistaken apprehensions concerning supernatural inspiration or revelation; not considering, that all true religion originates from reason, and can no otherwise be understood, but by the exercise and improvement of it; therefore they are apt to confuse their minds with such inconsistencies. In the subsequent reasonings on this subject, we shall argue against supernatural revelation in general, which will comprehend the doctrine of inspiration or immediate illumination of the mind. And first; we will premise, that a revelation consists of an assemblage of rational ideas, in-

telligibly

telligibly arranged and underſtood by thoſe to whom it may be ſuppoſed to be revealed; for otherwiſe, it could not exiſt in their minds as ſuch. To ſuppoſe a revelation, void of rationality or underſtanding, or of communicating rational intelligence to thoſe, to whom it may be ſuppoſed to be given, would be a contradiction; for that it would contain nothing except it were unintelligibleneſs which would be the ſame as to reveal and not to reveal; therefore, a revelation muſt conſiſt of an aſſemblage of rational ideas, intelligibly communicated to thoſe who are ſuppoſed to have been the partakers or receivers of it; from the firſt ſuppoſed inſpiration, down to this or any other period of time. But ſuch a revelation as this, could be nothing more or leſs than a tranſcript of the law of nature, predicated on reaſon, and would be no more ſupernatural, than the reaſon of man may be ſuppoſed to be. The ſimple definition of ſupernatural is, that which is " Beyond or above the powers of nature," which never was or can be underſtood by mankind; the firſt promulgators of revelation not excepted; for ſuch revelation, doctrine, precept or inſtruction only, as comes within the powers of our nature, is capable of being apprehended, contemplated or underſtood by us, and ſuch, as does not, is to us incomprehenſible

incomprehensible and unknown, and consequently cannot for us compose any part of revelation.

The author of human nature impressed it with certain sensitive aptitudes and mental powers, so that apprehension, reflection or understanding could no otherwise be exerted or produced in the compound nature of man, but in the order prescribed by the creator. It would therefore be a contradiction in nature, and consequently impossible for God to inspire, infuse, or communicate the apprehension, reflection or understanding of any thing whatever into human nature, out of, above, or beyond the natural aptitudes, and mental powers of that nature, which was of his own production and constitution; for it would be the same as to inspire, infuse, or reveal apprehension, reflection or understanding, to that which is not; inasmuch as out of, beyond or above the powers of nature, there could be nothing to operate upon, as a prerequisite principle to receive the inspiration or infusion of the revelation, which might therefore as well be inspired into, or revealed to nonentity, as to man. For the essence of man is that, which we denominate to be his nature, out of or above which he is as void of sensation, apprehension, reflection or understanding, as nonentity may be supposed to be; therefore such revelation as is adapted to the nature and capacity of man, and

comes

comes within his powers of perception and understanding, is the only revelation, which he is able to receive from God or man. Supernatural revelation, is as applicable to beasts, birds and fishes, as it is to us; for neither we, nor they are capable of being acted upon supernaturally, as all the possible exertions and operations of nature, which respect the natural or moral world, are truly natural. Nor does God deviate from his rectitude of nature in matters of inspiration, revelation or instruction to the moral world, any more than in that of his government of the natural. Man is a species of being who belongs in part to both worlds, therefore, was God to reveal any particular thing to us, he must of course adapt his revelation to our bodies, as well as to our souls; or to our senses as well as to our reason: but a revelation so adapted would be natural instead of supernatural. Which truly is the case respecting all our sensations, reflections and understandings. We will premise that at a future time God should superadd a sixth sense to our sensorium, and that inconceivably diverse from our present five senses, and as misterious to us at present, as the idea of colours are to persons born blind, by which, when superadded to the other senses, we might perceive and understand such things, as at present are mysterious or

supernatural

supernatural to us, and which without the beforementioned sixth sense would have eternally remained so, but that sense being once added to the sensorium, would become as natural as the other senses, and the premised additional knowledge acquired by it, would be as natural as that which is produced by the instrumentality of the other five senses; so that superaddition to nature, was it possible, and a fact, would not at all contribute to evince the possibility of a supernatural revelation; so likewise admitting that God should superadd mental ability to the principle of the human soul, by which, with the five senses only, it could form simple ideas, and extend its reasonings to a far greater progression than previous to or without such additional mental ability it could have done; still the extensiveness of such supposed reasonings would be as natural, as that which may be supposed to be acquired by the previous mental powers, or that which was supposed to be acquired by the instrumentality of the sixth sense before mentioned. For if it be supposed, that either sensation or reason, or both, be ever so much enlarged by a superaddition, or the mind ever so much improved and enlarged by any and all possible methods, still progression in knowledge would not be supernatural, whether in consequence of a supposed superaddition to nature, or by the improvement

provement of our present compounded natural powers, of sensation or reason or both. Should the perception or knowledge of colours or of sound be communicated to those who are born blind or deaf, or both, and who ever after continue to be so, such discoveries would be supernatural; as, on this position, there could have been no pre-requisite sensitive power or aptitude, which the minds of those who were supposed to be born blind or deaf, could have made use of, in acquiring the premised knowledge of colours or of sound. Therefore, when such discoveries as these are made, we must admit them to be " beyond or above the powers of nature," which is the same as supernatural; so likewise should we extend our knowledge beyond the limits of our mental capacity, or, which is the same, to understand more than we do or can understand, it would be supernatural: and when such facts as these take place in the world, it will be time enough to credit supernatural revelation. The infinitude of the wisdom of God's creation, providence and moral government will eternally remain supernatural to all finite capacities, and for that very reason we can never arrive to the comprehension of it, in any state of being and improvement whatever: inasmuch as progression can never attain to that which is infinite, so that an eternal

nal proficiency in knowledge could not be supernatural, but on the other hand would come within the limits and powers of our nature, for otherwise such proficiency would be impossible to us; nor is the infinite knowledge of God supernatural to him, for that his perfection is also infinite. But if we could break over the limits of our capacity, so as to understand any one supernatural thing, which is above or beyond the power of our natures, we might by that rule as well understand all things, and thus by breaking over the confines of finite nature and the rank of being which we hold in the universe, comprehend the knowledge of infinity. From hence we infer, that every kind and degree of apprehension, reflection and understanding, which we can attain to in any state of improvement whatever, is no more supernatural than the nature of man, from whence perception and understanding is produced, may be supposed to be so: nor has or could God Almighty ever have revealed himself to mankind in any other way or manner, but what is truly natural.

All manner of inspiration, revelation, instruction or understanding must unavoidably be denominated to be natural or supernatural, as there is no third way or medium between these two; so that if instead of the word supernatural, we adopt the

words

words immediate, special, instantaneous, or any other phrases, yet we must be careful to affix the same definition or ideas to those several words or phraseology, as we do to the word supernatural, when applied to revelation, viz. "that which is beyond or above the powers of nature." So that when we make use of any terms whatever to define revelation, we must be sure to mean supernatural, for otherwise we should define revelation to be no more than natural, which in the opinion of some people would spoil it, and divest it of all its charms; as most believers are fond of a revelation, which they unintelligibly imagine to be supernatural, though neither they nor any body else know any thing what it is. The word *mystery*, as applied to revelation, has the same impropriety as the word supernatural. To reveal, is to make known, but for a mystery to compose any part of a revelation, is absurd; for it is the same as to reveal and not reveal at the same time; for was it revealed, it would cease to be mysterious or supernatural, but together with other parts of our knowledge would become natural. Was a revelation, like other writings, adapted to our capacity, it might like them be instructive to us; but a mysterious or supernatural one would not. For such doctrine, precept or injunction, which is unintelligible to us, the terms, positions and inferences whereof exceed our comprehension, or "concerning which our ideas are inadequate," (which is the very definition of a miſtery) cannot be ſo much as examined into, or contemplated upon by us, nor could a ſtate of improvement unfold thoſe myſterious things, for which our ideas are altogether inadequate. Such knowledge as we acquire by improvement, is that to which our capacity is adequate, or we could not attain it. But admitting that the knowledge of a miſterious revelation may be arrived at merely by improvement, ſtill ſuch a revelation, (though it is improper to call it ſo) could not be inſtructive, which muſt be the end and deſign of a ſuppoſed revelation, for ſuch a premiſed improvement would have comprehended it as well without it as with it. For if reaſon has to advance its progreſſion of knowledge, independent of any aſſiſtance from the ſuppoſed myſterious revelation, untill it is ſuppoſed to comprehend it, it would render it altogether uninſtructive and uſeleſs; inaſmuch as the comprehenſion or underſtanding of it is ſuppoſed to be obtained by the exerciſe and improvement of reaſon, without any aſſiſtance from the hidden myſtery itſelf, which could not be revealed until reaſon, by natural improvement, came upſides with it, and by thus exploring the knowledge of a myſterious revelation, would at the ſame time nullify the unfulneſs of it.

And

And as reason is naturally progressive in its operations, having once rivaled such revelation, would still advance its improvement beyond it, which, when reason had once surpassed, could gain no instruction therefrom, any more than it did in its previous progression in rivalling it.

SECTION II.

Containing OBSERVATIONS *on the* PROVIDENCE *and* AGENCY *of* GOD, *as it respects the Natural and Moral World, with* STRICTURES *on* REVELATION *in general.*

ALTHOUGH the apprehensions, cogitations, reasonings and agency of mankind are perfectly comprehended in the divine Omniscience, nevertheless our nature is not susceptible of immediate revelation from God, or mere spirits or mental beings, on which our senses cannot operate; on account of the dissimilarity of their natures to ours, they are incapable of making any impression on our organs of sense, or so much as to represent one simple idea to the mind, much less to correspond with us on the sublime topics of religion, philosophy or science, inasmuch as in this life we are absolutely indebted to our external senses for our first apprehensions of the objects of sense, which we denominate to be pure simple ideas, without which we cannot exert our minds in any manner at all), as argued in the first and second Sections of the fourth Chapter, to which I refer. Sensation in the order of nature is the predicate of simple ideas, and simple ideas the predicate of reflection, and reflection continued is a succession of thinking, and by comparing two or more ideas (whether they are mere simple ones, or such as are derived therefrom) together, we perceive their agreement, or disagreement which adds still to the train of a complex reflection, that under the guidance of reason is formed into premises and argumentative deductions, and so on to the extent of the mind's capacity, so that the whole superstructure of our reasoning is demonstratively predicated on simple ideas, which result mediately from the instrumentality of the senses, through the medium whereof the mind is enabled to display its rational nature. This then is the established order of the compound nature of man, wherein the perceptions of sense are prerequisitely essential to the exertions and discoveries of the mind, by which only we are capable of receiving intelligence or revelation from God or man, or from any other intelligencies. God is invisible to us, and does not come within the notice of our gross sensations. The idea of a God we infer from our experimental dependence on something superior to ourselves in

wisdom

wisdom, power and goodness, which we call God; our senses discover to us the works of God which we call nature, and which is a manifest demonstration of his invisible essence. Thus it is from the works of nature that we deduce the knowledge of a God, and not because we have, or can have any immediate knowledge of, or revelation from him. But on the other hand, all our understanding of, or intelligence from God, is communicated to us by the intervention of natural causes, (which is not of the divine essence) this we denominate to be natural revelation, for that it is mediately made known to us by our senses, and from our sensations of external objects in general, so that all and every part of the universe, of which we have any conception, is exterior from the nature or essence of God; nor is it in the nature of things possible for us to receive, or for God to communicate any inspiration or revelation to us, but by the instrumentality of intermediate causes, as has been before observed. Therefore all our notions of the immediate interposition of divine illuminations, inspiration or infusion of ideas or revelations, into our minds, is mere enthusiasm and deception; for that neither the divine mind, nor those of any finite intelligences can make any representation to, or impression on our external senses without the assistance of some adequate

intermediate

intermediate cause. The same is the case between man and man, or with mankind in general, we can no otherwise hold a correspondence but by the aptitude, and through the medium of our senses. Since this is the only possible way in nature by which we can receive any notices, perceptions, or intelligence from God or man, or from those light beings called ministering spirits, angels or any imperceptible intelligences whatever; therefore provided they hold any intercourse with, or communicate any intelligence concerning religion, science or politics to us, they must do it by making use of proper intermediate causes, the same as we do in our mutual correspondence, or by some similar, or at least natural method of communicating their minds to us. For our nature cannot attend to the superior manner of existence and interchangeable correspondence with those superior beings, but they must descend to the inferior capacity of mankind, or keep their distance in the scale of being, and let us *clod-hoppers* alone to our manner of existence, communication of ideas and reasoning, that we may enjoy our book of nature, which undoubtedly is adapted to our various capacities and to our several relations, stations and circumstances in life. Nothing can be more unreasonable, than to suppose, because God is infinitely powerful, that he can

therefore

therefore inspire or infuse perception, reflection or revelation into the mind of man in such a way or manner as is incompatible with the aptitudes and powers of their nature; such a revelation would be as impossible to be revealed by God, as by a mere creature. For though it is a maxim of truth, "That with God all things are possible," yet it should be considered, that contradictions and consequently impossibilities are not comprehended in the difinition of things, but are diametrically the reverse of them, as may be seen in the definition of the word THINGS, *to wit*; "Whatever is." There is no contradiction in nature or truth, which comprehends or contains all things, therefore the maxim is just, " That with God all things are possible," *viz*; all things in nature are possible with God; but contradictions are falsehoods which have no positive existence, but are the negatives to THINGS, or to nature, which comprehends, " Whatever is;" so that contradictions are opposed to nature and truth, and are no THINGS, but the chimeras of weak, unintelligent minds who make false application of things to persons, or ascribe such powers, qualities, dispositions and aptitudes to things, as nature never invested them with; such are our deluded notions of the immediate operations of the holy spirit, or of any mere spirit, on our minds

minds independent of the intervention of some adequate, natural or intermediate cause. To make a triangle four square, or to make a variety of mountains contigiously situated, without vallies, or to give existence to a thing and not to give existence to it at the same time, or to reveal any thing to us incompatible with our capacity of receiving the perception of it, pertains to those negatives to nature and truth, and are not things revealed, nor have they any positive existence as has been before argued; for they are inconsistent with themselves, and the relations and effects which they are supposed to have upon and with each other. It derogates nothing from the power and absolute perfection of God that he cannot make both parts of a contradiction to be true. The figure of a triangle and that of a square is diverse the one from the other in the essentials of their formation, so that the one is not and cannot be of the same shape as the other; for the same figure, which gives the existence of the truth of the triangle, negatives the possibility of its being a square, and the same truth which is predicated on the form and figure of the mountains, necessarily gives being to the figure of the vallies at the same time: The figure of the latter results from, and is necessarily produced by the figure of the former, nor is it possible for Omnipotence itself to give the mountains and the vallies

lies an independent and seperate existence from each other; likewise the same truth, which is predicated on the fact of the existence of any thing, denies the possibility of its not existing at the same time. So also that God should make a revelation to men, or make any discoveries to their minds in a supernatural manner, or incompatible with the aptitudes of their sensitive or mental powers, is as contradictory as either of the before mentioned natural impossibilities; for the same truth which is predicated on the fact of the inability of mankind to receive such revelation, inspiration or illumination, as is incompatible with their nature, absolutely forbids the possibility of their perception of it, and consequently of their understanding any thing less or more about it, it being unnatural and altogether preposterous. But let us reverse the position concerning revelation, and premise that it is accommodated to our capacity of receiving and understanding it, and in this case it would be natural, and therefore possible for us to receive and understand it; for the same truth which is predicated on the sufficiency of our capacity to receive and understand a revelation, affirms at the same time the possibility of our receiving and understanding it. But to suppose that God can make both parts of a contradiction to be true, to reveal and not reveal would be the same as ascribing a falshood to him and to call it by the name of power (tho' it ought to be called by its deformed name of falsehood) is by no means good logic, and only serves to delude weak minds, by dignifying an inconsiderate application of falshood to God, with the ideas, with which, in our language we define the word power. Had the just diffinition of making both parts of a contradiction, to be true, been always called by its right name, *viz:* falshood, and the natural or moral impossibility of it, been rightly understood by mankind (and that instead of honoring and magnifying God, it is nothing less or more than ascribing falshood, contradiction and inconsistency unto him, which is unworthy of God and incompatible with truth,) they had never ascribed it to God, or yielded their reason captive to have believed such absurdities.

THAT God can do any thing and every thing, that is consonant to his moral perfections, and which does not imply a contradiction to the nature of the things themselves, and the essential relation which they bear to each other, none will dispute. But to suppose, that inasmuch as God is all-powerful, he can therefore do every thing, which we in our ignorance of nature or of moral fitness may ascribe to him, without understanding

standing, whether it is either consonant to moral rectitude, or to the nature of the things themselves, and the immutable relations and connections which they bear to each other, or not, is great weakness and folly. That God cannot in the exercise of his providence or moral government, counteract the perfections of his nature, or do any manner of injustice, is manifestly certain; nor is it possible for God to effect a contradiction in the natural world, any more than in the moral: The impossibility of the one results from the moral perfections of God, and the impossibility of the other from the immutable properties, qualities, relations and nature of the things themselves, as in the instances of the mountains, vallies, &c. before alluded to, and in numberless other such like cases.

Some may query in behalf of the doctrine of supernatural or immediate revelations, that though the far greater part of our ideas and succession of thought is natural, and is the result of simple ideas and reflections, naturally flowing from our sensitive and cogitative nature, and that in so obvious a manner that we are not at a loss as to the real cause of their excitement, yet we are often nonplused and surprized with thought and reflection, of which we know not the cause of their excitement, or why such ideas should be produced in our minds, rather than others. But such an inspiration as this would not serve to constitute a revelation sufficient to authorize us to publish it to the world as God's truth, and dictated by his inspiration, when at the same time it consisted (as before observed) of sudden and surprizing reflections, and why they were excited rather than others we knew not, or from whence they came. As to such strange and frightful ideas, which appear to us to be instantaneous, why should they be supposed to be supernatural? For there is not any thing which we can conceive of quicker than thought. It is our superlative comparison to any thing surprizingly sudden to us, that we say, "as quick as thought." But the reason why we are transported with hope or fear, joy or grief, pleasure or pain, is not because those passions, or the ideas that move them, are less natural, but because they are really so, and particularly respect our interest and happiness, either real or imaginary; this is it which surprizes us: but the cause of the excitement of our perceptions, and consequently of our reflections, is in part owing to the multiplicity of the diverse objects of sense, which at different times disclose themselves to the mind and partly to the subject matter of reflection, which

the

the mind alternately pursues in all possible varieties of thinking, contriving and argumentation; so that the chain of reflection more naturally inclines the mind to form such ideas as it does, than others. Besides, there is a great similarity in the objects of sense themselves, and also in the method of reasoning from them, and from the reflections that are produced by simple ideas, which are surprisingly more numerous than those corporeal images are. So that in the course of our perceptions, reflections, speculations and argumentations, our ideas in many instances run one into another; as in the instance of the almost imperceptibleness of the gradations of colours, or the gradual transition from night to day, or from truth to falshood, in remote, perplexed and intricate cases. This great similarity that there is in things, naturally excites similar ideas, or those of a near or more remote resemblance, and those again excite others of a corresponding sort, and so on throughout the course of human perceptions and reflections. These are the great outlines of the natural causes of the excitement, diversity and similarity of our ideas, which to point out with any considerable degree of particularity and accuracy would swell to a volume; which is foreign to my design in this concise system, that treats of a great variety of subjects and therefore demands brevity.

ADMITTING

ADMITTING a revelation to be from God, it must be allowed to be infallible, therefore those to whom it may be supposed to have been first revealed from God, must have had an infallible certainty of their inspiration: so likewise the rest of mankind, to whom it is proposed as a Divine Law, or rule of duty, should have an infallible certainty, that its first promulgators were thus truly inspired by the immediate interposition of the spirit of God, and that the revelation has been preserved through all the changes and revolutions of the world to their time, and that the copies extant present them with its original inspiration and unerring composure, or are perfectly agreeable to it. All this we must have an infallible certainty of, or we fail of an infallible certainty of revelation, and are liable to be imposed upon by impostors, or by ignorant or insidious teachers, whose interest it may be to obtrude their own systems on the world for infallible truth, as in the instance of Mahomet.

BUT let us consult our own constitutions and the world in which we live, and we shall find, that inspiration is, in the very nature of things, impossible to be understood by us; and of consequence not in fact true. What certainty can we have of the agency of the divine mind on ours? Or how can we distinguish the supposed divine illuminations

tions or ideas from those of our own which are natural to us? In order for us to be certain of the interposition of immediate divine inspiration in our minds, we must be able to analyse, distinguish, and distinctly seperate the premised divine reflections, illuminations, or inspiration, from our own natural cogitations, for otherwise we should be liable to mistake our reflections and reasonings for God's inspiration, as is the case with enthusiasts, or fanatics, and thus impose on ourselves, and obtrude our romantic notions on mankind, as God's revelation.

None will (it is presumed) pretend, that the natural reflections of our minds are dictated by the immediate agency of the divine spirit; for if they were thus dictated, they would be of equal authority with any supposed inspired revelation. How then shall we be able to distinguish or understand our natural perceptions, reflections or reasonings, from any premised immediately inspired ones? Should God make known to us, or to any of us, a revelation by a voice, and that in a language which we understand, and admitting that the propositions, doctrines, or subject matter of it, should not exceed our capacity, we could understand it the same as we do in conversation with one another; but this would be an external and natural revelation,

tion, in which God is supposed to make use of language, grammar, logic and sound, *alias*, of intermediate causes, in order to communicate or reveal it, which would differ as much from an immediately inspired revelation, as this book may be supposed to do; for the very diffinition of immediate inspiration precludes all natural or intermediate causes. That God is eternally perfect in knowledge, and therefore knows all things, not by succession or by parts, as we understand things by degrees, has been already evinced; nevertheless all truth, which we arrive at the understanding of, accords with the divine omniscience, but we do not come at the comprehension of things by immediate infusion, or inspiration, but from reasoning; for we cannot see or hear God think or reason any more than man, nor are our senses susceptible of a mere mental communion with him, nor is it in nature possible for the human mind to receive any instantaneous or immediate illuminations or ideas from the divine spirit (as before argued) but we must illuminate and improve our minds by a close application to the study of nature, through the series whereof God has been pleased to reveal himself to man, so that we may truly say, that the knowledge of nature is the revelation of God. In this there can be no delusion, it is natural, and could come from none other but God.

BUT

But should we admit that the divine mind thinks and reflects in our minds, in this case it would not be our mind which thinks and reflects, but the divine mind only; of which we could have no manner of perception or consciousness; for the divine consciousness thereof would not be communicable to us. But if it be our mind only which thinks and reflects, then it excludes the agency of the divine mind, for the divine and human minds are not of the same essence, and consequently the consciousness of the divine mind cannot be the consciousness of ours; though the divine omniscience extends to our consciousness, as such; for God cannot be conscious that our consciousness is his, for it is not true, as we are not of the divine essence. Should we conjecture that the divine mind communes with ours, so as to think or reflect in or with our minds, but in part, and that we also think and reflect in a co-operation with the divinity within us: We argue, that such conjectures are inadmissible, for that it confounds the divine and human essences together; but as they are not of the same essence, so neither can they be conscious of the same consciousness in part, any more than in the whole, as before argued. For we could have no manner of perception, of the conjecture, divine agency, or co-operation of the divine mind, as it could not come within the limits of our own confcioufnefs; and though the divine mind knows all things, and among others the individual confcioufneffes of mankind, yet the divine mind cannot be confcious that our confcioufnefs is his, in part, any more than in the whole, or that there ever was any co-operation, or immediate infufion or communication of ideas or illuminations from the divine to the human mind, inafmuch as it cannot be true. But fhould we admit of a mere mental correfpondence between the divine and human minds, yet, how could we analyfe or diftinguifh the interchangable reflections, which may be fuppofed to pafs between the divine mind and ours, fo as to underftand which were divine and which were human. Unlefs we could do this, we fhould compound them together at a venture, and form a revelation like Nebuchadnezar's idol, "partly iron and partly clay," *alias*, partly divine and partly human. The apoftle Paul informs us, that fometimes he "fpake, and not the Lord," and at other times fpeaks doubtfully about the matter, faying, "and I *think* alfo that I have the fpirit of God," and if he was at a lofs about his infpiration, well may we be diftruftful of it. From the foregoing fpeculations on the fubject of fupernatural infpiration, it appears, that there are infuperable difficulties in a mere mental difcourfe with the divine fpirit; it is what we are unacquainted with, and the law of our nature forbids it. Our method of conversation is vocal, or by writing, or by some sort of external symbols which are the mediate ground of it, and we are liable to errors and mistakes in this natural and external way of correspondence; but when we have the vanity to rely on dreams and visions to inform ourselves of things, or attempt to commune with invisible finite beings, or with the holy spirit, our deceptions, blunders and confusions are increased to fanaticism itself; as the diverse supposed influence of the spirit, on the respective sectaries, even among Christians, may witness, as it manifestly, in their empty conceit of it, conforms to every of their traditions. Which evinces, that the whole bustle of it is mere enthusiasm, for was it dictated by the spirit of truth and uniformity itself, it would influence all alike, however zealots persuade themselves and one another, that they have supernatural communion with the Holy Ghost, from whence they tell us they derive their notions of religion, and in their frenzy are proof against reason and argument, which if we tender them, they tell us, that it is carnal and depraved reasoning, but that their teachings are immediately from God: and then proceed to vent upon us all the curses and punishments, which are written in the book of the law.

THERE has in the different parts and ages of the world, been a multiplicity of immediate and wonderful discoveries, said to have been made to godly men of old by the special illumination or supernatural inspiration of God, every of which have, in doctrine, precept and instruction, been essentially different from each other, which are consequently as repugnant to truth, as the diversity of the influence of the spirit on the multiplicity of sectaries has been represented to be.

THESE facts, together with the premises and inferences as already deduced, are too evident to be denied, and operate conclusively against immediate or supernatural revelation in general; nor will such revelation hold good in theory any more than in practice. Was a revelation to be made known to us, it must be accommodated to our external senses, and also to our reason, so that we could come at the perception and understanding of it, the same as we do to that of things in general. We must perceive by our senses, before we can reflect with the mind. Our sensorium is that essential medium between the divine and human mind, through which God reveals to man the knowledge of nature, and is our only door of correspondence with God or with man.

A premised revelation, adapted to our external senses, would enable our mental powers to reflect upon, examine into, and understand it. Always provided nevertheless, that the subject matter of such revelation, or that of the doctrines, precepts or injunctions therein contained, do not exceed our reason, but are adapted to it as well as to our external senses.

For if a revelation be supposed to surpass our reason, or power of understanding, though the external method of communication it be ever so familiar and natural, yet it would be as supernatural, as though no words or signs, which are the explanations of our ideas, had been made use of in the matter: inasmuch as the ideas themselves are supposed to be above the power of reason, and consequently could not be formed into positions and argumentative deductions or conclusions by it, and after all would remain unintelligible, and therefore not revealed: for that which is beyond the power of reason to understand, is as supernatural to it, as it is to our external senses to correspond with, or form perceptions of imperceptible beings, or of mere spirits. In the one case it would be supernatural to reason, and in the other to sensation; the one may be denominated a mental inability, and the other a bodily inability ty; the one proceeds from the mind, and the other from the body: but in both these cases the impossibility is equal, and in either case precludes the reception of a revelation. But admitting, that a revelation was adapted to our senses, language and reason, still a substantial difficulty would arise, *viz.* to know whether it came with special commission from God or not. For a voice suited to our language and method of speech, or in a grammatical and logical way of speaking, which we could understand, could have no existence, except we admit of intermediate causes between the divine and human minds, *viz.* something fitly organised or rightly constructed and made use of by God to convey to our minds, by the use of speech, the perception, and consequently the knowledge of his revelation; for otherwise, such a grammatical and logical way of speaking would be unnatural, or impossible, which would be the same as supernatural: which has been sufficiently confuted, inasmuch as a proper instrument, rightly fitted to divulge the perception and consequently the understanding of a supposed revelation, would be an essential pre-requisite in order to communicate it to us. To suppose that God, merely from his omnipotence, without the intervention of some adequate intermediate cause,

could

could make use of sound, or grammatical and logical language, or of writing, so as to correspond with us, or to reveal any thing to us, would run into the same sort of absurdity, which we have already confuted; for it is the same as to suppose an effect without a suitable or proportionable cause, or an effect without a cause; whereas effects must have adequate causes or they could not be produced. God is the self-existent and eternal cause of all things, but the eternal cause can no otherwise operate on the eternal succession of causes and effects, but by the mutual operation of those causes on each other, according to the fixed laws of nature. For as we have frequently observed before that of all possible systems, infinite wisdom comprehended the best; and infinite goodness and power must have adopted and perfected it; and being once established into an ordinance of nature, it could not be deviated from by God; for that it would necessarily imply a manifest imperfection in God, either in its eternal establishment, or in its premised subsequent alteration; which will be more particularly considered in the next CHAPTER.

To suppose that almighty power could produce a voice, language, grammar, or logic, so as to communicate a revelation to us, without some

sort

sort of organic or instrumentated machine or intermediate vehicle, or adequate constituted external cause, would imply a contradiction to the order of nature, and consequently to the perfection of God, who established it: therefore, provided God has ever given us any particular revelation, we must suppose, that he has made use of a regular and natural constituted and mediate cause, comprehended in the eternal order of nature, rightly fitted and abilitated to make use of the vocal power of language, which comprises that of characters, orthography, grammar and logic, all which must have been made use of, in communicating a supposed revelation to mankind: which forecloses inspiration.

We will however premise that the christian revelation was of divine authority originally, and communicated or revealed to its first promulgators in an intelligible method of speech, and that the subject-matter thereof was wisely adapted to their capacity of sense and reason; in this case there would have been the same liability of misunderstanding it, as of person's misunderstanding another. When we hear any public discourse, but few of us have a memory to repeat or write it so perfectly that any considerable part would agree with the original. I conclude that

I could not underſtand a revelation thus dictated to me in a vocal manner, ſo as to communicate it to others with any tolerable exactneſs, except it were ſpoken to me in diſtinct ſentences, and I had, as I now have, my pen in hand, and ſo wrote one ſentence firſt, and then have another ſpoken to me, and write that down, and ſo on until I had written the whole; and furthermore, provided I ſhould make any miſtake in writing the ſeveral parts of it, that the dictating voice ſhould notify me of it, and how to rectify it, and ſo on though-out the volume; and provided, I ſhould act the impoſtor in writing any part of it agreeable to my own notions and deſigns, that the heavenly dictating intelligencer, by a voice and proper language, ſhould apprize thoſe of it, upon whom I might otherwiſe impoſe, and whom I might delude with my own inventions, inſtead of God's revelation. Furthermore, this heavenly dictating voice ſhould have been accommodated to all languages, grammars and logical ways of ſpeaking, in which a revelation may have been divulged, as it would be needful to have been continued from the beginning to every receiver, compiler, tranſlator, printer, commentator on, and teacher of ſuch a revelation, in order to have informed mankind in every inſtance, wherein at any time they may have

been

been imposed upon by any spurious adulterations or interpolations, and how it was in the original. These, with the refinements of languages and translations, are a summary of the many ways, wherein we may have been deceived, by giving credit to antiquated written revelation, which would need a series of miracles to promulgate and perpetuate it in the world free from mistakes and frauds of one kind or other, which leads me to the consideration of the doctrine of miracles.

Chapter VII.

SECTION I.

OF MIRACLES.

PREVIOUS to the arguments concerning Miracles, it is requisite that we give a diffinition of them, that the arguments may be clearly opposed to the doctrine of miracles, the reality of which we mean to negative; so that we do not dispute about matters in which we are all agreed, but that we may direct our speculations to the subject matter or essence of the controversy.

We will therefore premise, that miracles are opposed to, and counteract the laws of nature, or that they imply an absolute alteration in either a greater or less degree, in the eternal order, disposition and tendency of it; this, we conclude, is a just diffinition of miraculousness, and is that for which the advocates for miracles contend, in their defining of miracles. For if they were supposed to make no alteration in the natural order of things, they could have no poffitive exiftence, but the laws of nature would produce their effects, which would preclude their reality, and render them altogether fictitious, inafmuch as their very exiftence is premifed to confift in their oppofition to, and alteration of the laws of nature : fo that if this is not effected, miracles can have no poffitive exiftence, any more than nonentity itfelf. Therefore, if in the courfe of the fucceeding arguments, we fhould evince that the laws of nature have not and cannot be perverted, altered or fufpended, it will foreclofe miracles by making all things natural. Having thus defined miracles, and ftated the difpute, we proceed to the arguments.

Should there ever have been a miraculous fufpenfion and alteration of the laws of nature, God muft have been the immediate author of it, as no finite beings may be fuppofed to be able to alter thofe laws or regulations, which were eftablifhed by omnipotent power and infinite perfection, and which nothing fhort of fuch power and perfection can perpetuate. This then is the fingle point at iffue, *viz*; whether God has, or can, confiftent with his nature as God, in any inftance whatever, alter or deviate from the laws, with which he has eternally impreffed the univerfe, or not,

To

To suppose that God should subvert his laws, (which is the same as changing them) would be to suppose him to be mutable; for that it would necessarily imply, either that their eternal establishment was imperfect; or that a premised alteration thereof is so. To alter or change that which is absolutely perfect, would necessarily make it cease to be perfect, inasmuch as perfection could not be altered for the better, but for the worse; and consequently an alteration could not meet with the divine approbation; which terminates the issue of the matter in question against miracles, and authorizes us to deduce the following conclusive inference, *to wit;* that Almighty God, having eternally impressed the universe with a certain system of laws, for the same eternal reason that they were infinitely perfect and best, they could never admit of the least alteration, but are as unchangeable, in their nature, as God their immutable author. To form the foregoing argument into syllogisms, it would be thus:

GOD IS PERFECT,
The LAWS OF NATURE were established by GOD;
Therefore, The LAWS OF NATURE are PERFECT.

But admitting miracles, the syllogism should be thus:

The LAWS of NATURE were in their eternal establishment PERFCT;
The LAWS of NATURE have *been altered*;
Therefore, The *alteration* of the LAWS of NATURE is IMPERFECT.

Or thus; The LAWS of NATURE have been *altered*.
The *alteration* has been for the BETTER;
Therefore, The ETERNAL ESTABLISHMENT thereof was IMPERFECT.

Thus it appears, from a syllogistical as well as other methods of reasoning, that provided we admit of Miracles, which are synonimous to the alterations of nature, we by so doing derogate from the perfection of God, either in his eternal constitution of nature, or in a supposed subsequent miraculous alteration of it, so that take the argument either way, and it preponderates against miracles.

FURTHERMORE, was it possible, that the eternal order of nature should have been imperfect, there would be an end to all perfection. For God might be as imperfect in any supposed miraculous works, as in those of nature; nor could we ever have any security under his natural or moral government, if so be that they were liable to change; for mutability is but another term for imperfection, or is inseperably connected with it.

Was the order of nature to change, the great improvements which have been made in learning and science, would be nullified, in the same proportion as the laws of nature may be supposed to be changed; and the great discoveries of Sir Isaac Newton and others, in astronomy; and their former wise calculations therein, (as far as miracles may be admitted) would be lost to the world in consequence thereof; so that, on the position of miracles, the study or knowledge of nature, would be confounded, by new and diverse impressions suppressing the eternal harmony of nature with subsequent irregularities: in which case we could have but little to do with learning or knowledge, but might figure about the world under awful apprehensions of God's providence, expecting that world will crush upon world, or that the tail of the next comet will set this world on fire; and be constantly looking out for new and unnatural phenomena, and wild and romantic appearances; as in fact the superstitious part of the world do at present, for want of a right understanding of God and of his providence. Nor would the idea of a premised eternal imperfection be confined to the natural world only, but would equally affect the moral world, and sap the foundation of moral good and evil: Some part of mankind, in consequence thereof, might be elected to eternal favour,

vour, and others doomed to eternal perdition, and many other such like chimerical conjectures might take place, were we not thoroughly guarded by eternal and perfect reason.

GOD, the great architect of nature, has so constructed its machinery, that it never needs to be altered or rectified. In vain we endeavour to search out the hidden mistery of a perpetual motion, in order to copy nature, for after all our researches we must be contented with such machanism as will run down, and need rectification again; but the machine of the universe admits of no rectification, but continues its never ceasing operations, under the unerring guidance of the providence of God. Human architects make and unmake things, and alter them as their invention may dictate, and experience may determine to be most convenient and best. But that mind, which is infinitely perfect, gains nothing by experience, but surveys the immense universality of things, with all their possible relations, fitnesses and unfitnesses, of both a natural or moral kind, with one comprehensive view.

To suppose any succession of knowledge in God would be to conceive of him to be finite, as there can be no addition of knowledge (which is the same as succession of it) to that which is perfect, or infinite; therefore, there could not have been a subsequent reason in the divine mind, as a cause of any alteration in his works, or order of nature, providence or moral government: For his omniscience must have eternally comprehended the whole, and his omnipotent power regulated all things accordingly, nor could there possibly have been any more succession in the display or exertion of the power of God, than in the exertion of his omniscience. Inasmuch as a succession in the knowledge or power of God would be incompatable with his absolute perfection, and divest him of his natural attributes; from hence we infer, that as the divine mind cannot admit of succession or addition of knowledge, and as there can be no succession, or addition, of the display of omnipotent power, there can be no new idea to the former, or new exertion of the latter; and consequently no miraculous exertion in the system of the universe.

SECTION

SECTION II.

A succession of Knowledge, or of the exertion of Power in God, incompatible with his OMNISCIENCE *or* OMNIPOTENCE, *and the* ETERNAL *and* INFINITE DISPLAY *of* DIVINE POWER, *forecloses any subsequent Exertion of it* MIRACULOUSLY.

THAT creation is as eternal and infinite as God, has been argued in chapter second; and that there could be no succession in creation, or the exertion of the power of God, in perfecting the boundless work, and in impressing the universe with harmonious laws, perfectly well adapted to their design, use and end.

First. These arguments may be further illustrated, and the evidence of the being of a God more fully exhibited, from the following considerations, *to wit*. Dependent beings and existences must be dependent on some being or cause that is independent; for dependent beings, or existences, could not exist independently: And, in as much as by retrospectively tracing the order of the succession of causes, we cannot include in our numeration the independent cause, as the several successive causes still depend on their preceeding cause, and that preceeding cause on the cause preceeding it, and so on beyond numerical tical calculations, we are therefore obliged (as rational beings) to admit an independent cause of all things, for that a mere succession of dependent causes cannot constitute an independent cause: and from hence we are obliged to admit a self-existent and sufficient cause of all things, for otherwise it would be dependent and insufficient to have given existence to itself, or to have been the efficient cause of all things.

Having thus established the doctrine of a self-sufficient, self-existent, and consequently all-powerful cause of all things, we ascribe an eternal existence to this cause of all causes and effects, whom we call God. And inasmuch, as from the works of nature it is manifest, that God is possessed of almighty power, we from hence infer his eternal existence: Since his premised existence at (and not before) any given æra, would be a conclusive objection to the omnipotency of his power, that he had not existed before, or eternally. For as God is a being self-sufficient, self-existent, and almighty, (as before argued) his power must apply to his own existence as well as to the existence of things in general, and therefore, if he did not eternally exist, it must be because he had not the almighty power of existence in himself, and if so, he never could have existed at all; so that God must have eternally existed or not have existed at all; and inasmuch as the works of nature evince his positive existence and as he could not be dependent on the power, will, or pleasure of any other being but himself, for his existence, and as an existence in time, would be a contradiction to his almighty power of self-existtency, that he had not eternally existed; therefore, his existence must have been (in truth) eternal.

Although it is to us incomprehensible that any being could be self-existent or eternal (which is synonimous) yet we can comprehend, that any being that is not self-existent and eternal is dependent and finite, and consequently not a God. Hence we infer, that though we cannot comprehend the true God (by reason of our own finiteness) yet we can negatively comprehend that an imperfect being cannot be God. A dependent being is finite, and therefore imperfect, and consequently not a God. A being that has existed at a certain æra (and not before) is a limited one, for beyond his æra he was not, and therefore finite, and consequently not a God. Therefore, that being only who is self-existent, infinitely perfect and eternal, is the true God: and if eternally and infinitely perfect, there must have been an eternal and infinite display, and if an eternal and infinite display, it could be nothing short of an eternal and infinite creation and providence.

For

For the illustration of this doctrine, we will premise the existence of a God near six thousand years old (according to Moses's Æra of creation) and compare the idea of the existence of such an imaginary being, with another imaginary God, who has existed, as the Chinesian Chronologist would have it, more than forty thousand years. Now I query, from a comparative idea of the existence of these premised deities, whether the longest existence of the two does not display the most extensive and greatest power of existence and government, and if so, a longer period of the existence and government of a premised God, would still display more power, and so on throughout human numeration, and finally, an eternal existence, creation and providence of a God, would eternally excell and surpass all other conception of a God, and therefore points out to us the true God: And since God is eternal and absolutely perfect in all possible perfection, and possessed of eternal and infinite power; the power of creation and providence, and of sustaining the same, must have been eternal with God, and consequently, could not have failed of eternally producing their effects, which we perceive to be verified, in the creation, regulation, and support, of such part of the universe as comes within our knowledge.

This

This doctrine of eternal creation and providence, naturally and necessarily results from the doctrine of the eternal self-existency, omnipotent power and perfection of God; and is so forcible to a rational and improved mind, that it could not fail of gaining the assent of the learned in Christendom, were it not for prepossession in favor of Moses's theology, which represents creation to have had a beginning and is silent respecting the eternity and infinity of God; the earliest account he gives us of him was in his six days work, and that on the "seventh day" he "*rested* from all his work which" he "had created and made" from this it appears, that the six days work, which included the creation, of "the heavens and the earth" comprised God's creation, and that he bounded the limit of his empire by its circumference; for there is not any thing more evident, than that previous to creation, or beyond its circumference, there could have been no display of creation or providence; and as to the existence of a God, previous to Moses's æra of the first day's work, he does not inform us. The first notice he gives us of a God was of his laborious working by the day, a theory of creation (as I should think) better calculated for the servile Israelitish *Brick-makers* than for men of learning and science in these modern times.

We

We shall now proceed to the further investigation of the order of nature and disprove miracles. Should we admit, that God has countermanded any of his laws, and given nature a different bias or tendency, by a miraculous exertion or interposition of his power, since its establishment, it would not only evince an imperfection in God, either in his eternal constitution of things, or in his supposed subsequent miraculous alteration of the Laws of Nature, as before argued, but would be contrary to our grand position, that the power of God is not and cannot be exercised by succession or degrees, for such an exertion of power would agree with the exercise of it amongst men, and be altogether inadequate to the omnipotent and immense work of creation.

A successive creation had it been continued from any given time forever, could never have completed the boundless work, but it would forever remain a bounded thing; which is the same as to consist of a circumference, beyond which a progressive exertion of power could not extend the amplitude of creation; and therefore a progressive creation could not be immense: For succession cannot extend to infinitude. But as God was eternal and infinitely omnipresent, his almighty exertion of creation and harmonizing nature, was eternally every where, which eternally

and

and immensely gave being and order to the universe, not by succession of time, or addition of parts. And being thus eternally compleat, it was impossible that the act of creation and regulation of nature, could ever be repeated or acted again. Inasmuch as there was an eternal and infinite plenitude and harmony of things, nothing could be added to, or diminished from this perfect system of things, which we call nature. And though the omnipotent and perfectly wise, just, and gracious exertion of God, in creating and regulating nature, could not be by succession, or acted but once, yet nature, with all its productions or formations, is sustained by the same all-sufficient God, who eternally gave being and harmony to it. Nor is it necessary or possible, that there ever should have been any other immediate exertion of infinite power, than in the creation, regulation and sustaining the universe, agreeable to its eternal order, which has been one eternal and infinite exertion of God. Nor could the exertion of the divine power, in sustaining the universe, exert itself by succession, any more than in creation, or in the regulation of nature. For the sustaining power must be co-extensive with the nature of things, which are immense, and therefore cannot admit of succession in its operation or exertion; inasmuch as a progressive exertion of it could not be infinite,

finite, and consequently could not extend to the preservation or upholding of the infinitude of things. From hence we infer, that the creation and harmony of the universe, with its immense fulness, and the sustaining of it agreeable to its eternal laws, was the eternal, infinite and immediate act of almighty God. But the productions of nature, which are the result of the energy of the eternal laws of its establishment, are not the immediate acts of God, but rather mediate, as they pertain to the vast productions of natural causes, and are caused by the mutual co-operation of the effects of the eternal cause, on each other; not by the immediate agency of God himself, but by the intervention and co-operation of intermediate causes on each other, producing others, and so on agreeable to the series of nature's operations, which we call the mediate agency of God; as they are the result of the operations of nature. But these gradations of causes and their effects, resulting therefrom, are dependent on the eternal laws of nature, and those eternal laws dependent on the immediate agency of God who upholds them.

Thus God created the universe, and imparted order and decorum to it, and sustains it by the infinite and immediate agency of his power; this

comprehends

comprehends all the immediate agency of God: For all the productions of nature are only the action of bodies on bodies, or of things on things, and are the mere result of the eternal laws of nature, which we call natural causes, and are the mediate acts of God. It is the want of a right understanding of the divine agency, which makes us imagine that the series of nature's operations, that fall under our notice, is the immediate exertion of God; which is rather the mediate effect of his power and goodness, that constitutes his providence, and being truly natural, is consequently not miraculous.

WORDS cannot express our ideas exactly as they are in our own minds, especially in abstruse reasonings. It is very difficult or impossible, in describing the infinity of creation, and the harmony and upholding of it, or its eternity, to do it in such a manner, as to give the reader the true idea of the writer; which difficulty may lead the reader inadvertently to conclude, that those exertions of God are so many distinct and seperate actions; as first, the eternal act of creation; and secondly, that to invest it with harmony or order was another, and that to impart to both a sustaining power, would be a third successive act of God; which, in the nature of the things themselves can not be true: For the divine act of sustaining the universe, must have been co-eternal and co-extensive with that of creation, or creation could not have existed until the premised progression of the act of sustaining it may be supposed to have taken place; which would have defeated or rendered the premised succeeding act of sustaining the creation useless and impossible: For creation must have vanished, or ceased to be, had not the act of sustaining it been co-eternal and co-extensive with creation itself.

And furthermore, to suppose a succession in the divine exertion of creation and imparting harmony to the creation, would necessarily imply a beginning in the act of harmony, and if so, there must have been an eternity preceding such beginning to harmonize creation, in which eternity, creation must have existed in chaos, which precludes a providence, until order took place. From all which we infer, that there was not and could not be any succession, in the act of almighty God, in creating, sustaining and regulating the universe, but that it was eternal and co-extensive with the infinitude of things. For God never did or can do, but one simple and uncompounded act, which is as eternal and infinite as God. For that the infinite all-comprehending mind can admit of no additional knowledge or succession of ideas, or the exertion of infinite, all-comprehending power, admit of addition or succession of power. For all manner of succession or increase of power is finite, as the succession of ideas, applied to knowledge makes it to be; and as there can be no succession in the immediate exertion of the act of omnipotent power, there never could be a new exertion of it, and therefore no miracle.

THAT a successive creation must have been a limited or finite one, has been argued at large in the second chapter. Provided there has been a succession in the work of creation, one part of it must have succeeded another progressively, and have been done in certain limited operations, viz. days-works, &c. and comprized as many local parts of creation, which added together, would make but a local whole: so that immensity could not be repleted by a successive creation. The same is true of a premised progressive exertion of the divine power in imparting laws, which is the same as harmony to it. So also in the act of sustaining the universe, it could no more be progressive in its exertion than either of the former; for succession is but the same, whether applied to the creation, regulation, or sustaining of the universe. In every of these cases, the creating, regulating or sustaining power must have been immense, and

immensity

immensity the unlimited display of it; and it is but trifling to suppose, that succession or progression of the exertion of power, can extend to infinitude, for the greatest possible addition, of the greatest numerical parts, or the most rapid motion, or any thing of which we can conceive, cannot comprize that which is numberless, boundless, or infinite.

SECTION III.

That which we understand is NATURAL, *and that which we understand not we cannot understand to be* MIRACULOUS.

THOUGH the immediate act of God cannot be progressive, or operate by succession, nevertheless succession is essential to the actions or operations of natural causes, which come within our comprehension, and is the very source out of which time itself with us originated, which is computed from the movements and periodical revolutions of the orbs of our solar system, those worlds of motion which constitute our seasons, with other revolutions immaterial to our present purpose to mention. Furthermore, we compute time from nativities, deaths, and remarkable epochas as, revolutions

lutions of governments and states, and from the productions and dissolutions of animals and vegetables, *as* the age of a man, of an elephant, or a plant, or from the period of the revolution of the planets or comets.

THUS it is that those causes and effects, which are produced in time, have their respective periods and terminations, and operate by succession of seconds, minutes, hours, days, years, centuries, or other parts of duration. But that which is not subject to revolution, change, alteration, succession or progression, as the immediate act of God is not, cannot be computed by time, for that, which is immediate, and without succession, takes no time in its performance; as was eternally the case respecting the immediate act of God, in creating, regulating and sustaining nature; for it was perfectly instantaneous, or it could never have been effected at all as has been already argued. But those things, that are done or produced mediately; *to wit*, by natural causes, are subject to the order of an eternal series of vicissitudes and changes, for that they are the acts or effects of the operations of created beings, or the effects of the operation of matter on matter, or of sensation on mental and cogitative beings. All forms are indebted to creation for their existence, as mere creation unites

with

with, or composes all possible forms; so that all the productions of nature, animate or inanimate, are no more than the production of forms, and their decay and dissolution is no more, than the dissolution of forms, and neither adds to nor diminishes from creation, but are reduced to their original elements again, which by the energy of the laws of nature are changed into new and diverse forms, and thus perpetuate their alternate and never ceasing rounds: so that the particles of matter which compose my body, may have existed in more millions of different forms than I am able to enumerate, and is still liable to fluctuations equally numerous. And though this elementary, fluxility of matter, which is mere creation, is as eternal as God, and its duration immensurable by the fleeting moments of time, yet the respective particular productions, from the eternal elementary mass of creation, which fall under our notice, have their periodical duration, and before they mix with the immense mass, are capable of being calculated, inasmuch as they are the production of natural causes, and have a beginning and an end. But the eternal mass, having neither beginning nor end, cannot come within our calculation of time, for that it is eternal; nor are we able to enumerate the series of nature's operations or productions, for the same reason that they also are eternal.

We can underſtand the order of time, and comprehend the application of it to finite and limited exiſtences, or periods of duration; but as applied to duration without beginning or end, or to that which is boundleſs or endleſs, or to an eternal ſeries of cauſes and events, our mathematical problems and calculations fail us, and all our conceptions are ſwallowed up and loſt in immenſity.

We are not only confounded in our ſpeculations on that which is eternal and infinite, but alſo in that part of the ſeries of nature's operations, which comes under our notice, and conſequently conſideration; their relations, connections, diſpoſitions and eſſences, are in a great meaſure beyond our comprehenſion, but not altogether unknown to us: for was it ſo, our ſpeculations could not extend to them. Thoſe things in nature which we do underſtand, are not miraculous to us, and thoſe things which we do not underſtand, we cannot with any propriety adjudge to be miraculous. Were we to determine every thing to be miraculous, which we cannot comprehend to be natural, or underſtand the reaſon of, our ignorance of nature would, of neceſſary conſequence, determine moſt things to be miraculous.

That God has conſtituted the nature of things, univerſal, will not be diſputed, and that ſhould he

alter

alter them, it would imply mutability in him, has been fully evinced, which militates against miracles. How then is it possible, that we can have an evidence of a miracle, since those things, whereof we understand the natural reasons, are not miraculous, and the things we understand not, we cannot comprehend to be miraculous? But admiting we ever attain to the knowledge of the premised miraculous alterations of nature, it must be respecting some particular things in nature, which we thoroughly comprehend to be natural, and which, by a countermanding power, may be supposed to be inverted, and that we have a certain knowledge, not only that the laws of nature respecting them are suspended, but that they are superceeded by new ones, opposed to, and different from the former. All this we must fully comprehend, before we can have any evidence of a miracle. But to be so perfectly acquainted with the knowledge of nature, as to know its contrary impressions, and distinguish them from the natural, would be difficult or impossible to the greatest philosophers of the age, and wholly exceed the comprehension of ignorant people, who are most fond of miracles.

SECTION

SECTION IV.

Rare and wonderful Phenomenæ no evidence of MIRACLES, *nor are diabolical Spirits able to effect them, or superstitious Traditions to confirm them, nor can ancient* MIRACLES *prove recent* REVELATIONS.

COMETS, earthquakes, volcanoes and nothern lights (in the night) with many other extraordinary phenomenæ or appearances, intimidate weak minds, and are by them thought to be miraculous; although they undoubtedly have their proper or adequate natural causes, which have been in a great measure discovered. Jack-with-a-lanthorn is a frightful appearance to some people, but not so much as the imaginary spectre. But of all the scarecrows, which have made human nature tremble, the Devil has been chief; his family is said to be very numerous, consisting of "Legions," with which he has kept our world in a terrible uproar. To tell of all the feats and diabolical tricks, which this infernal family is said to have played upon our race, would compose a volume of an enormous size. All the magicians, necromancers, wizards, witches, conjurers, gypsies, sybils, hobgoblins, apparitions and the like, are supposed to be under their diabolical government: old Belzebub

bub rules them all. Men will face deftructive cannon and mortars, engage each other in the clafhing of arms, and meet the horrors of war undaunted, but the devil and his banditti of fiends and emiffaries fright them out of their wits, and have a powerful influence in plunging them into fuperftition, and in continuing them therein.

This fuppofed intercourfe between mankind and thofe infernal beings, is by fome thought to be miraculous or fupernatural; while others laugh at all the ftories of their exiftence, concluding them to be mere juggle and deception, craftily impofed on the credulous, who are always gaping after fomething marvellous, miraculous, or fupernatural, or after that which they do not underftand; and are aukward and unfkilful in their examination into nature, or into the truth or reality of things, which is occafioned partly by natural imbecility, and partly by indolence and inattention to nature and reafon.

That any magical intercourfe or correfpondence of mere fpirits with mankind, is contradictory to nature, and confequently impoffible, has been argued in chapter fixth. And that nothing fhort of the omnipotent power of God, countermanding his eternal order of nature, and impreff-

ing

ing it with new and contrary laws, can constitute a miracle has been argued in this, and is an effect surpassing the power of mere creatures, the diabolical nature not excepted. From hence we infer, that Devils cannot work miracles. Inattention to reason, and ignorance of the nature of things makes many of mankind give credit to Miracles. It seems that by this marvellous way of accounting for things, they think to come off with reputation in their ignorance; for if nature was nothing but a supernatural whirligig, or an inconstant and irregular piece of mechanism, it would reduce all learning and science to a level with the fanaticism, and superstition of the weak and credulous, and put the wise and unwise on a level in point of knowledge, as there would not, on this thesis, be any regular standard in nature, whereby to ascertain the truth and reality of things. What is called slight of hand, is by some people thought to be miraculous. Astrological calculations of nativities, lucky and unlucky days and seasons, are by some regarded, and even moles on the surface of the skin are thought to be portentive of good or bad fortune.

"THE Sweedish Laplanders, the most ignorant mortals in" Europe, "are charged with being conjurors, and are said to have done such feats, by the magic art, as do not at all fall short of miracles; that they will give the sailors such winds as they want in any part of their voyage; that they can inflict and cure diseases at any distance; and insure people of success in their undertakings: and yet they are just such poor, miserable wretches as used to be charged with witchcraft here," viz. in England and in New-England, " and cannot command so much as the necessaries of life; and indeed, none but very credulous and ignorant people give credit to such fables at this day, though the whole world seems to have been bewitched in believing them formerly." " The 24th of March, 1735, an act passed in the parliament of Great-Britain to repeal the statute of 1 *Jac*'s, intitled an act against conjuration, witchcraft, and dealing with evil and wicked spirits, and to repeal an act passed in Scotland intitled Aneatis Witchcraft." It is but forty-six years since the supreme legislature of Great Britain became apprized of the natural impossibility of any magical intercourse between mankind and evil and wicked spirits; in consequence whereof they repealed their statute laws against it, as they were naturally void, unnecessary, and unworthy of their legislative restriction. For that such a crime had no possible existence in nature, and therefore could not be acted by mankind; though previous to the repeal of

those

those laws, more or less of the species of that ilk; and had fallen a sacrifice to them; and the relations of those imaginary criminals were stamped with infamy by such executions, which had the sanction of law, *alias* of the legislature and the judges, and in which many learned attornies have demonstrated the turpitude of such capital offences, and the just sanction of those laws in extirpating such pests of society from the earth; to which the clergy have likewise given their approbation, for that those capital transgressors made too free with their Devils.

Furthermore, the repeal of those laws, as far as the wisdom and authority of the British Parliament may be supposed to go, abrogated that paragraph of the law of Moses, which saith " thou shalt not suffer a witch to live," and not only so, but the doctrine of the impossibility of intercourse, or of dealing with wicked spirits, forecloses the supposed miraculous casting out of Devils; of which we have sundry chronicles in the New-Testament.

But to return to the annals of my own country, it will present us with a scene of superstition in the magical way, which will probably equal any that is to be met with in history, *to wit*; The Salem witchcraft in New England; great numbers of the inhabitants of both sexes were judicially

ally convicted of being Wizards and Witches, and executed accordingly; some of whom were so infatuated with the delusion, that at their execution they confessed themselves guilty of the sorcery, for which they were indicted; nor did the fanataciſm meet with a check until some of the first families where accused with it, who made such an opposition to the prosecutions, as finally put an end to any further execution of the Salemites.

Those capital offenders suffered in consequence of certain laws, which, by way of derision, have since been called the *Blue Laws*, in consequence of the multiplicity of superstition, with which they abounded, most of which are repealed; but those that respect sorcery have had favorite legislators enough to keep them alive and in force to this day.

I recollect an account of prodigies said to have been carrying on by the Romish Clergy in France, upon which his most christian majesty sent one of his officers to them, with the following prohibition, *to wit*; " by the command of the King, God is forbid to work any more miracles in this place;" upon which the marvellous work cealed.

THERE has been so much detection of the artifice, juggle and imposture of the pretenders to miracles, in the world, especially in such parts where learning and science have prevailed, that it should prompt us to be very suspicious of the reality of them; even without entering into any lengthy arguments from the reason and nature of things to evince the utter impossibility of their existence in the creation and providence of God.

WE are told, that the first occasion and introduction of miracles into the world, was to prove the divine authority of revelation, and the mission of its first teachers; be it so; upon this plan of evincing the divinity of revelation, it would be necessary that its teachers should always be vested with the power of working miracles; so that when their authority, or the infallibility of the revelation which they should teach, should at any time be questioned, they might work a miracle; or that in such a case God would do it; which would end the dispute, provided mankind were supposed to be judges of miracles which may be controverted. However, admitting that they are possible, and mankind in the several generations of the world to be adequate judges of them, and also that they were necessary to support the divine mission of the first promulgators of revelation, and the divinity which they taught; from the same parity of reasoning miracles ought to be continued to the succeeding generations of mankind, co-extensive with its divine authority, or that of its teachers. For why should we in this age of the world be under obligation to believe the infallibility of revelation, or the heavenly mission of its teachers, upon less evidence than those of mankind who lived in the generations before us? For that which may be supposed to be a rational evidence, and worthy to gain the belief and assent of mankind at one period of time, must be so at another; so that it appears, from the sequel of the arguments on this subject, that provided miracles were requisite to establish the divine authority of revelation originally, it is equally requisite that they be continued to the latest posterity, to whom the divine legislator may be supposed to continue such revelation as his law to mankind.

FURTHERMORE, should we admit the divine mission and authority of the first promulgators of revelation, and the reality of the miracles they wrought, or that God may be supposed to have wrought, as a confirmation of the revelation they then promulgated; yet we cannot for certain determine but that their successors have since corrupted it, and altered it to answer their own sinister designs, and thereby provoked God to withdraw from them the power of working miracles, or to have ceased to work miracles himself, to the intent that they might not obtrude spurious revelations on mankind. For any miraculous works, which may be premised to have been anciently wrought, to evince the divine authority of the first manuscript copies of revelation can bear no testimony to revelation, as we have it according to the present translation, or to the divine mission of the present clergy. Though admitting miracles to have been wrought in the primitive times of the promulgation of revelation, for its then support, and the support of the religion they then taught, it would have been evidential of the divine mission of its first promulgators; but these are matters of speculation to us, and particularly concerned those ages in which revelation may be supposed to have been taught in its purity, and confirmed by miracles; as they supposed, who were the first converts to it, and who are said to have seen and believed; and when this generation is favoured with a miraculous confirmation of the divine mission of our present clergy, and of the authenticity of our present revelation, as it has been handed down to us though the complicated revolutions of the world, and the vicissitudes of human learning, by miracles wrought in open day

light,

light, not only of the sun, but of learning and science (the latter of which the primitive believers had not the advantage of) it will be early enough for us to subscribe to the divine mission of the one, or divinity, or infallibility of the other.

Nothing is more evident to the understanding part of mankind, than that in those parts of the world where learning and science has prevailed, miracles have ceased; but in such parts of it as are barbarous and ignorant, miracles are still in vogue; which is of itself a strong presumption that in the infancy of letters, learning and science, or in the world's non-age, those who confided in miracles, as a proof of the divine mission of the first promulgators of revelation, were imposed upon by fictitious appearances instead of miracles.

Furthermore, The author of Christianity warns us against the impositions of false teachers, and describes the signs of the true believers, saying " And these signs shall follow them that believe, in my name shall they cast out devils, they shall speak with new tongues, they shall take up serpents, and if they drink any deadly thing it shall not hurt them, they shall lay hands on the sick and they shall recover." These are the express words of the founder of Christianity, and are contained in the very commission, which he gave to his eleven Apostles, who were to promulgate his gospel in the world; so that from their very institution it appears, that when the miraculous signs, therein spoken of, failed, they were to be considered as unbelievers, and consequently no faith or trust to be any longer reposed in them or their successors. For these signs were those which were to perpetuate their mission, and were to be continued as the only evidences of the validity and authenticity of it, and as long as these signs followed, mankind could not be deceived in adhearing to the doctrines which the Apostles and their successors taught; but when the signs failed, their divine authority ended. Now if any of them will drink a dose of deadly poison, which I could prepare, and it does not " hurt them," I will subscribe to their divine authority, and end the dispute; not that I have a disposition to poison any one, nor do I suppose that they would dare to take such a dose as I could prepare for them, which, if so, would evince, that they were unbelievers themselves, though they are extremely apt to censure others for unbelief which according to their scheme is a damnable sin.

SECTION

SECTION V

Miracles could not be instructive to mankind.

SHOULD we admit the intervention of Miracles, yet they could not enlarge our ideas of the power of God. For that to unmake nature universally, and to impress it with new and opposite laws from those of its eternal establishment, could require no greater exertion of power, than that which is Omnipotent, and which must have been exerted in the eternal creation, regulation and support of the universe. But any supposed miraculous alteration of nature, must imply mutability in the wisdom of God; and therefore is inadmissable. Should God miraculously raise a dead person to life again, would the restoring life argue a greater exertion of power in God than in first giving existence to that life? surely it could not. From all which we infer, that miracles cannot inlarge our ideas of the power of God. We proceed next to enquire, what advantages could accrue to mankind by them in the way of teaching and instruction? For this must be the great end proposed by them. That they cannot teach us any thing relative to the omnipotence of God, has been evinced; but that they militate against his wisdom: and furthermore, that they cannot prove the divine authority of written revelation, or the mission of its respective teachers to any country, people or nation, any farther or longer than the miraculous works are actually continued, has been sufficiently argued in the proceeding section. It remains farther to be considered, that they are incapable of instructing us in the subject-matter, doctrine, proposition or inference of any premised written revelation; or of giving us any insight into the precepts or injunctions thereof, or to communicate any sort of intelligence or knowledge respecting its contents. The premised, sudden and miraculous alterations of the common course of nature might astonish us; but such alterations or changes, do not evince that they have any thing to do with us, or we with them in the way of teaching and instruction: for truth and falsehood, right and wrong, justice and injustice, virtue and vice, or moral good and evil are in their distinct natures diametrically opposite to each other, and necessarily and eternally will remain so to be, and that, independent of miracles or revealed religion. It is by reason we investigate the knowledge of moral good and evil, it is that which lays us under a moral obligation, and it is not a miracle or revelation that can alter the moral rectitude of things, or prove that to be truth, which in its nature is not so. Therefore admitting ever so many miracles,

and

and revelations, we should still have to recur to reason and argument, the old and only way of exploring truth and distinguishing it from falshood, or understanding true religion from imposture or error. For though miracles might evince the divine mission of the clergy, and the divinity of the christian revelation, to us, were they in fact wrought in this enlightened age for that purpose, yet they are not calculated to expound or explain it, but would perplex and confound us, in our logical and doctrinal speculations, nature and reason being opposed to them as before argued. Such supposed miraculous changes in nature, would to us be mysterious, and altogether unintelligible, and consequently could not come within our deliberation on the right understanding, or comments on a supposed written revelation; the understanding of which, after all the bustle about miracles, must be investigated by reason: and revelation itself be either approved or disapproved by it. From the foregoing reasonings we infer, that miracles cannot be edifying or instructive to us; and though they are strenuously urged as a proof of the divine legation of the first promulgators of revelation, and their successors; nevertheless, where the premised miracles became extinct, their divine authority and the evidence of the infalibility of revelation, became extinct also.

SECTION

SECTION VI.

Prayer cannot be attended with Miraculous Consequences.

BEFORE we conclude our discourse upon miracles, it will be requisite that we consider those supposed miraculous alterations of nature, or of divine providence, which by some are thought to have taken place in the world, merely in conformity to the prayer of Man. The arguments, which have been already advanced against miracles, are in substance equally applicable, to such as may be supposed to be effectuated by prayers, remonstrances or supplications of finite beings. That God should countermand his order of nature, which is the same thing as to alter his providence, merely in dictatorial conformity to the prayers or praises of his creatures, or that he should alter it merely from motives from himself are not essentially different. In as much as the consequence of a supposed alteration from either of the causes before mentioned would equally and necessarily imply mutability in wisdom, in the one case, as in the other; for in both cases the arguments terminate against any supposed miraculous alterations of nature or providence, merely from the consideration of the immutable perfection of the divine nature. For a departure from, or alteration of the

eternal

eternal order, or government of things would be equally derogatory from the absolute perfection of God, whether those alterations are supposed to take place merely in conformity to the prayers or remonstrances of his creatures, or from reasons, which may be supposed to have originated merely from the divine mind itself. There is no thing, which can be mentioned, that would more manifestly argue mutability in God, than that he should alter his order of nature or providence to comply with the prayers of his mutable creatures; or to do that in conformity thereto, which the eternal regulation and government of nature would not have effectuated or accomplished independent of them. For if the eternal laws of nature were absolutely perfect, which must be admitted, a deviation from, or countermanding of them, must unavoidably imply mutability and imperfection, be it from what cause it will.

Sensibly to depend upon God in and through his order of nature, to retain in our minds a grateful sense of his providential goodness to us, to place in him our important hope of immortality, and to act and demean ourselves under all circumstances of life agreeable to reason, or the moral rectitude of things pointed out unto us thereby, is our indispensible duty: it is enjoined by the laws of nature and ought to be taught and cultivated

cultivated among mankind. But prayer to God is no part of a rational religion, nor did reason ever dictate it, but, was it duly attended to, it would teach us the contrary.

To make known our wants to God by prayer or to communicate any intelligence concerning ourselves or the universe to him, is impossible, since his omniscient mind has a perfect knowledge of all things, and therefore is beholden to none of our correspondence to inform himself of our circumstances, or of what would be wisest and best to do for us in all possible conditions and modes of existence, in our never ending duration of being. These, with the infinitude of things, have been eternally deliberated by the omniscient mind, who can admit of no additional intelligence, whether by prayer or otherwise, which renders it nugatory.

We ought to act up to the dignity of our nature, and demean ourselves, as creatures of our rank and capacity in the order of Being ought to do, and not presume to dictate any thing, less or more, to the governor of the universe; who rules not by our proscriptions, but by eternal and infinite reason. To pray to God, or to make supplication to him, requesting certain favors for ourselves, or for any, or all the species, is inconsistent

with

with the relation which subsists between God and man. Whoever has a just sense of the absolute perfection of God, and of their own imperfection, and natural subjection to his providence, cannot but from thence infer the impropriety of praying or supplicating to God, for this, that, or the other thing; or of remonstrating against his providence, inasmuch, as "*known to God are all our wants;*" and as we know, that we ourselves are inadequate judges of what would be best for us, all things considered. God looks through the immensity of things, and understands the harmony, moral beauty and decorum of the whole, and will by no means change his purposes, or alter the nature of the things themselves for any of our intreaties or threats. To pray, intreat, or make supplication to God, is neither more nor less than dictating to Eternal Reason, and entering into the province and prerogative of the Almighty; if this is not the meaning and import of prayer, it has none at all, that extends to the final events and consequences of things. To pray to God with a sense, that the prayer we are making will not be granted any more for our making it, or that our prayer will make no alteration in the state, order or disposal of things at all, or that the requests, which we make, will be no more likely to be granted, or the things themselves conferred upon us by God, than as though we had not prayed for them, would be stupidity or outright mockery, or "to be seen of men," in order to procure from them some temporary advantages. But on the other hand for us to suppose, that our prayers or praises do in any one instance or more alter the eternal constitution of things, or of the providence of God, is the same as to suppose ourselves so far forth to hold a share in the divine government, for our prayers must be supposed to effect somthing or nothing, if they effect nothing, they are good for nothing; but that they should effect any alteration in the nature of things, or providence of God, is inadmissible: for if they did, we should interfere with the providence of God in a certain degree, by arrogating it to ourselves. For if there are any particulars in providence, which God does not govern by his order of nature, they do not belong to the providence of God, but of man; for if in any instance, God is moved by the prayers, intreaties, or supplications of his creatures, to alter his providence, or to do that in conformity thereto, which otherwise, in the course of his providence, he would not have done; then it would necessarily follow, that as far as such alteration may be supposed to take place, God does not govern by eternal and infinite reason, but on the conterary is governed himself by the prayer of man.

Our

Our great proficients in prayer must need think themselves to be of great importance in the scale of being, otherwise they would not indulge themselves in the notion, that the God of nature would subvert his laws, or bend his providence in conformity to their prayers. But it may be objected, that they pray conditionally, *to wit;* that God would answer their prayers, provided they are agreeable to his providential order, or disposal of things; but to consider prayer in such a sense renders it, not only useless, but impertinent; for the laws of nature would produce their natural effects as well without it, as with it. The sum total of such conditional prayer could amount to no more than this, *to wit;* that God would not regard them at all, but that he would conduct the kingdom of his providence agreeable to the absolute perfections of his nature; and who in the exercise of common sense would imagine that God would do otherwise?

The nature of the immense universality of things having been eternally adjusted, constituted and settled, by the profound thought, perfect wisdom, impartial justice, immense goodness, and omnipotent power of God, it is the greatest arrogance in us to attempt an alteration thereof. If we demean ourselves worthy of a rational happiness, the laws of the moral system, already established, will afford it to us; and as to physical evils, prudent œconomy may make them tolerable, or ward most of them off, for a season, though they will unavoidably bring about the seperation of soul and body, and terminate with animal life, whether we pray for or against it.

To pray for any thing, which we can obtain by the due application of our natural powers, and neglect the means of procuring it, is impertinence and laziness in the abstract; and to pray for that which God in the course of his providence, has put out of our power to obtain, is only murmuring against God, and finding fault with his providence, or acting the inconsiderate part of a child; *for example*, to pray for more wisdom, understanding, grace or faith; for a more robust constitution, handsomer figure, or more of a gigantic size, would be the same as telling God, that we are dissatisfied with our inferiority in the order of being; that neither our souls or bodies suit us; that he has been too sparing of his benificence; that we want more wisdom, and organs better fitted for show, agility and superiority. But we ought to consider, that " *we cannot add one cubit to our stature,*" or alter the construction of our organic frame; and that our mental talents are finite; and that in a vast variety of proportions

and

and disproportions, as our Heavenly Father in his order of nature, and scale of being saw fit; who has nevertheless for the encouragement of intelligent nature ordained, that it shall be capable of improvement, and consequently of inlargment; therefore, "*whosoever lacketh wisdom,*" instead of "*asking it of God,*" let him improve what he has, that he may inlarge the original stock; this is all the possible way of gaining in wisdom and knowledge, a competency of which will regulate our faith. But it is too common for great faith and little knowledge to unite in the same person; such persons are beyond the reach of argument and their faith immovable, though it cannot remove mountains. The only way to procure food, raiment, or the necessaries or conveniencies of life, is by natural means; we do not git them by wishing or praying for, but by actual exertion; and the only way to abtain virtue or morality is to practise and habituate ourselves to it, and not to pray to God for it: he has naturally furnished us with talents or faculties suitable for the exercise and enjoyment of religion, and it is our business to improve them aright, or we must suffer the consequences of it. A sense of obligation and dependence on God is a rational devotion, and attended with adoration and thankfulness. We should conform ourselves to reason, the path of moral rectitude,

tude, and in so doing, we cannot fail of recommending ourselves to God, and to our own consciences. This is all the religion, which reason knows or con ever approve of.

Moses the celebrated prophet and legiflator of the Ifraelites, ingraciated himfelf into their efteem, by the ftratagem of prayer, and pretended intimacy with God; he acquaints us, that he was once admitted to a fight of his BACK-PARTS, and that " *No man can see*" his "*face and live;*" and at other times we are told that he " *talked with God, face to face, as a man talketh with his friend;*" and also that at times God waxed wroth with Ifrael, and how Moses prayed for them; and at other times, that he ordered Aaron to offer fweet incenfe to God, which *appeafed his wrath*, and prevented his deftroying Ifrael in his *hot difpleafure*. Thefe are the footfteps, by which we may trace facerdotal dominion to its fource, and explore its progrefs in the world. " *And the Lord said unto Moses, how long will this people provoke me? I will smite them with the pestilence, and disinherit them, and I will make of thee a great nation, and mightier than they,*" but Moses advertifes God of the injury, which fo rafh a proceedure would do to his character among the nations; and also reminds him of his promife to

Ifrael

Israel, saying; "*Now if thou shall kill all this people as one man, then the nations, which have heard the fame of thee will speak, saying, because the Lord was not able to bring this people into the land, which he sware unto them, therefore he hath slain them in the wilderness.*" That Moses should thus advise the omniscient God, of dishonorable consequences which would attend a breach of promise, which he tells us, that God was unadvisedly about to make with the tribes of Israel, had not his remonstrance prevented it, is very extraordinary and repugnant to reason; yet to an eye of faith it would exalt the man Moses, " and make him very great;" for if we may credit his history of the matter, he not only averted God's judgment against Israel, and prevented them from being cut off as a nation, but by the same prayer procured for them a pardon of their sin. "*Pardon I beseech thee, the iniquity of this people,*" and in the next verse follows the answer, "*And the Lord said, I have pardoned according to thy word.*" It seems that God had the power, but Moses had the dictation of it, and saved Israel from the wrath and pestilential fury of a Jealous God; and that he procured them a pardon of their sin, "*for the Lord thy God is a jealous God.*" Jealousy can have no existence in that mind, which possesses perfect knowledge, and consequently cannot without the

greatest

greatest impropriety be ascribed to God, who knows all things, and needed none of the admonitions, advice or intelligence of Moses, or any of his dictatorial prayers, "*And the Lord hearkened unto me at that time also;*" intimating, that it was a common thing for him to do the like. When teachers can once make the people believe that God answers their prayers, and that their eternal interest is dependent on them, they soon raise themselves to oppulency, rule and high sounding titles: as that of *His Holiness*; *the Reverend Father in God*; *The Holy Poker*; *Bishop of Souls*; and a variety of other such like appelations, derogatory to the honor or just prerogative of God; as is Joshua's history concerning the Lord's hearkening unto him at the battle of the Amorites, wherein he informs us, that he ordered the sun to stand still, saying; "*Sun stand thou still upon Gibeon, and thou Moon in the valley of Ajalon, so the Sun stood still and the Moon stayed until the people had avenged themselves upon their enemies; so the Sun stood still in the midst of Heaven, and hasted not to go down about a whole day;*" and then adds, by way of supremacy to himself above all others, and in direct contradiction to the before recited passages of Moses concerning the Lord's hearkening unto him, or to any other man but himself, saying; "*And there was no Day like that before it, or after*

after it, that the Lord hearkened unto the voice of a man," There is not any thing more evident than that if the representation given by Joshua, as matter of fact, is true, those exhibited by Moses, concerning the Lord's hearkening unto him are not: though the representations of fact by Moses and by Joshua are allowed to be both canonical, yet it is impossible that both can be true. However, astronomy being but little understood in the age in which Joshua lived; and the earth being in his days thought to be at rest, and the sun to revolve round it, makes it in no way strange, that he caught himself by ordering the sun to stand still, which having since been discovered to have been the original fixed position of that luminous body, eclipses the miraculous interposition of Joshua. Furthermore, if we but reflect that on that very day Israel vanquished the Amorites with a great slaughter, "*and chaced them along the way that goeth to Bethoron, and smote them to Azekah, and unto Makkedah,*" in so great a hurry of War, clashing of Arms, exasperation and elevation of mind, in consequence of such a triumphant victory, they could make but a partial observation on the length of the day; and being greatly elated with such an extraordinary day's work, Joshua took the advantage of, it and told them that it was an uncommon day for duration;

that he had interposed in the system, and prescribed to the sun to stand still about a whole day; and that they had two day's time to accomplish those great feats. The belief of such a miraculous event to have taken place in the solar system, in consequence of the influence which Joshua insinuated that he had with God, would most effectually establish his authority among the people; for if God would hearken to his voice well might man. This is the cause why the bulk of mankind in all ages and countries of the world, have been so much infatuated by their ghostly teachers, whom they have ever imagined to have had a special influence with God Almighty.

Chapter

Chapter VIII.

SECTION I.

The vagueness and unintelligibleness of the Prophecies, render them incapable of proving Revelation.

PROPHECY is by some thought to be miraculous, and by others to be supernatural, and there are others, who indulge themselves in an opinion, that they amount to no more than mere political conjectures. Some nations have feigned an intercourse with good spirits by the art of Divination; and others with evil ones by the art of magic; and most nations have pretended to an intercourse with the world of spirits both ways.

THE Romans trusted much to their sibyline oracles and soothsayers; the Babylonians to their magicians,

magicians, and astrologers; the Egyptians and Persians to their magicians; and the Jews to their seers or prophets: and all nations and individuals, discover an anxiety for an intercourse with the world of spirits; which lays a foundation for artful and designing men, to impose upon them. But if the foregoing arguments in chapter sixth, respecting the natural impossibility of an intercourse of any unbodied or imperceptible mental beings with mankind, are true, then the foretelling of future events can amount to nothing more than political illusion. For prophecy as well as all other sort of prognostication must be supernaturally inspired, or it could be no more than judging of future events from mere probability or guess-work, as the astronomers ingeniously confess in their calculations, by saying; "Judgment of the weather, &c." So also respecting Astrology, provided there is any such thing as futurity to be learned from it, it would be altogether a natural discovery; for neither Astronomy or Astrology claim any thing of a miraculous or supernatural kind, but their calculations are meant to be predicated on the order and course of nature, with which our senses are conversant, and with which inspiration or the mere co-operation of spirits is not pretended to act a part. So also concerning prophecy, if it be considered to be merely natural, (we will not at present

sent dispute whether it is true or false) upon this position it stands on the footing of probability or mere conjecture and uncertainty. But as to the doctrine of any supernatural agency of the divine mind on ours, which is commonly called inspiration, it has been sufficiently confuted in the sixth Chapter; which arguments need not be repeated, nor does it concern my system to settle the question, whether prophecy should be denominated miraculous or supernatural, inasmuch as both these doctrines have been confuted; though it is my opinion, that were we to trace the notion of supernatural to its source, it would finally terminate in that which is denominated miraculous; for that which is above or beyond nature, if it has any positive existence, it must be miraculous.

The writings of the prophets are most generally so loose, vague and indeterminate in their meaning, or in the grammar of their present translation, that the prophecies will as well answer to events in one period of time, as in another; and are equally applicable to a variety of events, which have and are still taking place in the world, and are liable to so many different interpretations, that they are incapable of being understood or explained, except upon arbitrary principles, and therefore cannot be admitted as a proof of revelation;

tion; *as for instance, " it shall come to pass in the last days, saith God."* Who can understand the accomplishment of the prophecies, that are expressed after this sort? for every day in its turn has been, and will in its succession be the last day; and if we advert to the express words of the prophecy; *to wit, " the last days,"* there will be an uncertain plurality *" of last days,"* which must be understood to be short of a month, or a year; or it should have been expressed thus, and it shall come to pass in the last months or years, instead of days: and if it had mentioned last years, it would be a just construction to suppose, that it included a less number of years than a century; but as the prophecy mentions *" last days,"* we are at a loss, which among the plurality of them to assign for the fulfiling of the prophecy.

FURTHERMORE, we cannot learn from the prophecy, in what month, year, or any other part of duration those last days belong; so that we can never tell when such vague prophecies are to take place, they therefore remain the arbitrary prerogative of fanatics to prescribe their events in any age or period of time, when their distempered fancies may think most eligible. There are other prophecies still more abstruse; *to wit, " And one said unto the man clothed in linnen, which was upon the*

the waters of the river, how long shall it be to the end of these wonders? and I heard the man cloathed in linnen, which was upon the waters of the river, when he held up his right hand and his left hand unto Heaven, and sware by him that liveth forever, that it should be for a time, times and an half." The question in the prophecy is asked " *how long shall it be to the end of these wonders?*" and the answer is given with the solemnity of an oath, " *it shall be for a time, times and a half.*" A *time* is an indefinite part of duration, and so are *times*, and the third description of time is as indefinite as either of the former descriptions of it ; *to wit,* " *and an half ;*" that is to say, *half a time.* There is no certain term given in any or either of the three descriptions of the end of the wonders alluded to, whereby any or all of them together are capable of computation, as there is no certain period marked out to begin or end a calculation. To compute an indefinite *time* in the single number or quantity of duration is impossible, and to compute an uncertain plurality of such indefinite *times* is equally perplexing and impracticable ; and lastly to define *half a time* by any possible succession of its parts, is a contradiction, for *half a time* includes no time at all ; inasmuch as the smallest conception or possible moment or criterion of duration, is *a time,* or otherwise, by the addition of ever so many of those parts together they would not prolong a period; so that there is not, and cannot be such a part of time, as *half a time*, for be it supposed to be ever so momentous, yet if it includes any part of duration, it is *a time*, and not *half a time*. Had the prophet said half a year, half a day, or half a minute, he would have spoken intelligibly; but *half a time* has no existence at all, and consequently no period could ever possibly arrive in the succession or order of time, when there could be an end to the wonders alluded to: and in this sense only, the prophecy is intelligible; *to wit, that it will never come to pass.*

The Revelation of St. John the divine, involves the subject of time if possible in still greater inconsistencies, viz. "*And to the woman was given two wings of a great eagle, that she might fly into the wilderness, into her place: Where she is nourished for a time, and times and half a time.*" "*And the angel which I saw stand upon the sea and upon the earth lifted up his hands to heaven, and sware by him that liveth for ever and ever, who created heaven and the things that therein are, and the earth and the things that therein are, and the sea and the things which are therein, that there should be time no longer.*" Had this tremendous oath been verified there could have been no farther disputations on the calculation

tion of "*time and times and half a time,*" (or about any thing else) for that its succession would have reached its last and final period at that important crisis when time should have been " no longer." The solar system must have ceased its motions, from which we compute the succession of time, and the race of man would have been extinct; for as long as they may be supposed to exist, time must of necessary consequence have existed also; and since the course of nature, including the generations of mankind, has been continued from the time of the positive denunciation of the angel to this day, we may safely conclude, that his interference in the system of nature, was perfectly romantic.

The Apostle Peter, at the first Christian pentecost, objecting to the accusation of their being drunk with new wine, explains the prophecy of the prophet Joel, who prophesied of the events which were to take place in the last days, as coming to pass at that early period; his words are handed down to us as follows; "*But this is that which is spoken by the prophet Joel, and it shall come to pass in the last days, saith God, that I will pour out of my spirit upon all flesh, and your sons and your daughters shall prophesy, and your young men shall see visions, and your old men shall dream dreams.*"

THE history of the out-pouring of the spirit at the pentecost, admitting it to have been a fact, would have been very inadequate to the prophetical prediction, *viz. I will pour out my spirit upon all flesh*; the most favorable construction is that the prophet meant human flesh, *i. e.* all human flesh; but instead of a universal effusion of the spirit, it appears to have been restricted to a select number, who were collected together at Jerusalem, and the concourse of spectators thought them to be delirious. It may however be supposed, that St. Peter was a better judge of the accomplishment of the prophecy than I am: well then, admitting his application of the prophesy of the last days to take place at the first pentecost; it being now more than seventeen hundred years ago, they consequently could not have been the last days.

STILL a query arises, whether every of the prophecies, which were predicted to be fulfilled in the last days, must not have been accomplished at that time; or whether any of the prophecies thus expressed are still to be compleated, by any events which may in future take place; or by any which have taken place since those last days called Pentecost; or whether any prophecy whatever can be fulfilled more than once; and if so, how many times; or how it is possible for us, out of the vast variety

variety of events (in which there is so great a similarity) which one in particular to ascribe to its right prediction among the numerous prophecies.

When we consider the analogy that there is in the series of nature's operations, and those which respect the rise and fall of nations, empires and governments; and also those vicissitudes and changes which respect mankind in less societies, or as individuals; together with the vagueness and uncertainty with which the prophecies are embarrassed: and the difficulties, uncertainties and utter impossibility of understanding what particular event (in the vast series, that already has, or hereafter may take place in the world) to affix to its original and proper prediction, the knowledge of which is essential to the understanding of the prophecies; we shall discover the whole notion of prophecy to be a mere fable. For to understand the prophesies, and point out their events, would require as much inspiration, as may be supposed to have been necessary in their original prediction. Upon the whole, it appears to be at least such a precarious, round-about, and uncertain way of proving revelation, that it is altogether inadmissible.

FURTHERMORE

Furthermore, it would be no ways certain that the prophecies were immediately from God, or from ministering spirits commissioned by him, even admitting it possible for mankind to hold a correspondence with the world of spirits. We are often deceived by wicked hypocritical and designing men, and why not more likely to be imposed upon by invisible wicked beings, whom we might take to be good ones? we are certainly less acquainted with the wiles of diabolical and imperceptible spirits, than with the dissimulations of mankind, and consequently, could not so well guard against them; and if we admit an intercourse with those who are good, we at the same time do it with the bad, as both good and bad spirits have one common nature, the same as virtuous and vicious men: so that if the door of communication is open to the one, it is open to the other, and to distinguish the true chracters of those mental and invisible beings apart, would be impossible, except we make natural reason our director. But such inspirations as these would be no more than natural reasonings, which would spoil them in the opinion of true inspirationists. But if the subject-matter of a supposed inspired revelation is above or beyond our natural capacity, we could have no clue or rule, whereby to understand it, or whether it was from a good or bad spirit; besides, we

should

should be at a loss to distinguish the agency of the divine spirit from that of mere creatures; in these uncertainties we should be confounded, and not know what to rely on concerning any ghostly intelligence from the world of spirits: which reasons, are as applicable to the prophets and first promulgators of revelation, as to us who live in this age of the world.

FURTHERMORE, provided some of the prophecies should point out some particular events, which have since taken place, there might have been previous grounds of probability, that such or such events would in the ordinary course of things come to pass; *for instance*, it is no ways extraordinary, that the prophet Jeremiah should be able to predict that Nebuchadnezzar king of Babylon should take Jerusalem, when we consider the power of the Babylonish empire at that time, and the feebleness of the Jews. "*The word, which came to Jeremiah from the Lord, when Nebuchadnezzar king of Babylon and all his army, and all the kingdoms of the earth of his dominion, and all the people fought against Jerusalem, and against all the cities thereof, saying, thus saith the Lord the God of Israel, go and speak unto Zedekiah king of Judah, and tell him, thus saith the Lord, behold, I will give this city Jerusalem into the hand of the king of Babylon.*" No politicians

politicians could at the time of the prediction be much at a loss respecting the fate of Jerusalem. Nor would it be at all evidential to any candid and ingenious enquirer, that God had any manner of agency in fabricating the prophecies, though some of them should seem to decypher future events; as they might, to human appearance, turn out right, merely from accident or contingency. It is very improbable, or rather incompatable with human nature, that the prophecy of Micah will ever come to pass, who predicts that " *they,*" speaking of mankind, " *shall beat their swords into plough-shares, and their spears into pruning-hooks; nation shall not lift up sword against nation, neither shall they learn war any more.*" Some of the prophecies are so apparently contradictory, that they contain their own confutation; *as for instance*, the prophecy of Michaiah contained in the book of Chronicles, which probably is as absurd as any thing that is to be met with in story, " *and when he was come unto the king, the king said unto him, Micaiah, shall we go to Ramoth Gilead to battle, or shall I forbear? and he said go ye up and prosper, and they shall be delivered into your hand, and the king said unto him, how many times shall I adjure thee, that thou tell me nothing, but that which is true in the name of the Lord? then he said I did see all Israel scattered upon the mountains, as sheep that*

have

have no shepherd, and the Lord said, these have no master, let them return therefore, every man to his house in peace: and the king said unto Jehoshaphat, did not I tell thee, that he would prophecy no good conserning me but evil." *"again he said, therefore hear the word of the Lord, I saw the Lord sitting upon his throne, and all the host of Heaven standing on his right hand and on his left, and the Lord said who shall entice Ahab, King of Israel, that he may go up and fall at Ramoth Gilead, and one spake saying after this manner, and another saying after that manner, then there came out a spirit and stood before the Lord, and said I will entice him, and the Lord said unto him wherewith? And he said I will go forth and be a lying spirit in the mouth of all his prophets, and the Lord said thou shalt entice him and thou shalt also prevail, go out and do even so, now therefore behold the Lord hath put a lying spirit in the mouth of these thy prophets, and the Lord hath spoken evil against thee.* It is observable that the prophet at first predicted the prosperity of Ahab, saying, *"go ye up and prosper, and they shall be delivered into your hand,"* but after a little adjurement by the King, he alters his prediction and prophesies diametrically the reverse. What is more certain than that the event of the expedition against Ramoth Gilead must have comported with the one or the other of his prophecies? Certain it was, that Ahab should take it or not

take

take it, he must either prosper or not prosper, as there could be no third way or mean between these two; and it appears that the prophet was determined to be in the right of it by his prophesying both ways. It farther appears from his prophesy, that there was a great consultation in Heaven to entice Ahab King of Israel to his destruction, and that a certain lying spirit came and stood before the Lord, and proposed to him to go out and be a lying spirit in the mouth of the King's prophets. But what is the most incredible is, that God should countenance it, and give him positive orders to falsify the truth to the other prophets. It appears that Micaiah in his first prophesy, viz. *Go up to Ramoth Gilead and prosper, and they shall be delivered into your hand*, acted in concert with the lying spirit which stood before the Lord, but afterwards acted the treacherous part by prophesying the truth, which, if we may credit his account, was in direct opposition to the scheme of Heaven.

SECTION II.

The Contentions which subsisted between the Prophets respecting their Veracity, and their Inconsistencies with one another, and with the nature of Things, and their Omission in teaching the Doctrine of Immortality, precludes the Divinity of their Prophecies.

WHOEVER examines the writings of the prophets will discover a spirit of strife and contention among them; they would charge each other with fallacy and deception: disputations of this kind are plentifully interspersed through the writings of the prophets: we will transcribe a few of those passages out of many: "*Thus saith the Lord to the foolish prophets that follow their own spirit, and have found nothing, they have seen vanity and lying divination, saying the Lord saith, and the Lord hath not sent them, and they have made others to hope that they would confirm the word.*" And in another place, "*I have not sent these prophets yet they ran; I have not spoken unto them yet they prophesy.*" Again, "*I have heard what the prophets said that prophesy lies in my name, saying, I have dreamed, I have dreamed, yet they are the prophets of the deceit of their own hearts.*" And again, "*Yea they are greedy dogs, which can never have enough, and they are shepherds that cannot understand; they all look to their own way, every one for his gain from his quarter."*

It being the case that there was such a strife among the prophets to recommend themselves to the people, and every art and dissimulation having been practised by them to gain power and superiority, all which artifice was to be judged of by the great vulgar, or in some instances by the political views of the Jewish Sanhedrim, how could those who were cotemporaries with the several prophets, distinguish the premised true prophets from the false? Much less, how can we, who live more than seventeen hundred years since the last of them, be able to distinguish them apart? And yet, without the knowledge of this distinction, we cannot with propriety give credit to any of them, even admitting there were some true prophets among them. Nor is it possible for us to know but that their very institution was merely a reach of policy of the Israelitish and Judaic governments, the more easily, implicitly and effectually to keep their people in subordination, by inculcating a belief that they were ruled with special directions from heaven, which in fact originated from the Sanhedrim. Many other nations have made use of much the same kind of policy.

In the 22d chapter of Genesis, we have a history of a very extraordinary command from God to Abraham, and of a very unnatural attempt of his to obey it. *"And it came to pass after these things that God did tempt Abraham, and he said unto him Abraham, and he said behold here I am, and he said take now thy only son Isaac, whom thou lovest, and get thee to the land of Moriah, and offer him there for a burnt offering upon one of the mountains which I will tell thee of;" "And they came to the place which God had told him of, and Abraham built an altar there, and laid the wood in order, and bound Isaac his son, and laid him on the altar upon the wood; and Abraham stretched forth his hand and took the knife to slay his son."* Shocking attempt! Murder is allowed by mankind in general, to be the most capital crime that is possible to be acted among men; it would therefore be incompatible with the divine nature to have enjoined it by a positive command to Abraham to have killed his son; a murder of all others the most unnatural and cruel, and attended with the most aggravating circumstances, not merely from a prescribed breach of the ties of parental affection, but from the consideration that the child was to be (if we may credit the command) offered to God as a religious sacrifice. What could have been a more complicated wickedness than the obedience of this command would have been?

been? and what can be more absurd than to suppose that it came from God? It is argued, in vindication of the injunction to Abraham to kill his son, that it was merely for a trial of his obedience, and that God never designed to have him do it; to prevent which an angel from heaven called to him and gave him counter orders, not to slay his son; but to suppose that God needed such an experiment, or any other, in order to know whether Abraham would be obedient to his commands, is utterly incompatible with his omniscience, who, without public exhibitions understands all things; so that had the injunction been in itself, fit and reasonable, and also from God, the compliance or non-compliance of Abraham thereto, could not have communicated any new idea to the divine mind. Every part of the conduct of mankind is a trial of their obedience and is known to God, as well as the particular conduct of Abraham; besides in the canonical writings, we read that "*God cannot be tempted with evil, neither tempteth he any man.*" How then can it be "*that God did tempt Abraham*"? a sort of employment which, in scripture, is commonly ascribed to the Devil. It is a very common thing to hear Abraham extolled for attempting to comply with the supposed command of sacrificing his son; but it appears to me, that it had been wiser and more becoming the character

of

of a virtuous man, for Abraham to have replied in answer to the injunction as follows, *to wit*, that it could not possibly have come from God, who was the fountain of goodness and perfection, and unchangeable in his nature; who had endowed him with reason and understanding, whereby he knew his duty to God, his son, and to himself, better than to kill his only son, and offer him as a religious sacrifice to God: for God would never have implanted in his mind such a strong affection towards him, nor such a conscious sense of duty to provide for, protect and succour him in all dangers, and to promote his happiness and well-being, provided he had designed, that he should have laid violent hands on his life. And inasmuch as the command was, in itself, morally speaking, unfit, and altogether unworthy of God, he presumed that it never originated from him, but from some inhuman, cruel and destructive being, who delighted in wo, and pungent grief; for God could not have been the author of so base an injunction, nor could he be pleased with so inhuman and sinful a sacrifice.

Moses in his last chapter of Duteronomy crowns his history with the particular account of his own death and burial. " *So Moses the servant of the Lord died there, in the land of Moab, according to the word of the Lord, and he buried him in a valley, in the land of Moab, over against Bethpeor, but no man knew of his sepulchre unto this day; and Moses was an hundred and twenty years old when he died, his eyes were not dim, nor his natural force abated, and the children of Israel wept for Moses in the plains of Moab thirty days.*" This is the only historian in the circle of my reading, who has ever given the public a particular account of his own death, and how old he was at that decisive period, where he died, who buried him, and where he was buried, and withal of the number of days his friends and acquaintances mourned and wept for him. I must confess I do not expect to be able to advise the public of the term of my life, nor the circumstances of my death and burial, nor of the days of the weeping or laughing of my survivors.

PART of the laws of Moses were arbitrary impositions upon the tribes of Israel, and have no foundation in the reason and fitness of things, particularly that in which he inculcates punishing the children for the iniquities of the father; "*visiting the iniquities of the fathers upon the children, and upon the children's children unto the third and fourth generation.*" There is no reason to be given, why the iniquity of the father might not as well have involved the fifth, sixth and seventh generations, and

so

so on to the latest posterity in guilt and punishment, as the four first generations; for if it was possible, that the iniquity of the father could be justly visited upon any of his posterity, who were not accomplices with him in the iniquity, or were not some way or other aiding or accessary in it, then the iniquity might as justly be visited upon any one of the succeeding generations as upon another, or upon the generation of any indifferent person: for arbitrary imputations of iniquity are equally absurd in all supposable cases; so that if we once admit the possibility of visiting iniquity, upon any others than the perpetrators, be they who they will, we overturn our natural and scientifical notions of a personal retribution of justice among mankind. It is, in plain English, punishing the innocent for the sin of the guilty. But virtue or vice cannot be thus visited or imputed from the fathers to the un-offending children, or to children's children; or which is the same thing from the guilty to the innocent; for moral good or evil is mental and personal, which cannot be transferred, changed or altered from one person to another, but is inherently connected with its respective personal actors, and constitutes a quality or habit, and is the merit or demirit of the respective agents or proficients in moral good or evil, and is by nature unalionable, " *The righteousness*

teousness of the righteous shall be upon him, and the wickedness of the wicked shall be upon him." But as we shall have occasion to argue this matter at large in the twelfth chapter of this treatise, where we shall treat of the imputed sin of Adam to his posterity, and of imputative righteousness, we will discuss the subject of imputation no farther in this place. However, the unjust practice of punishing the children for the iniquity of the father having been an ordinance of Moses, was more or less continued by the Israelites, as in the case of Achan and his children. *"And Joshua and all Israel with him took Achan the son of Zerah, and the silver and the garment, and the wedge of gold, and his sons, and his daughters, and his oxen, and his asses, and his sheep, and his tent, and all that he had, and brought them to the valley of Achor, and all Israel stoned him with stones, and burned them with fire, after that they had stoned them with stones, and they raised over him a great heap of stones unto this day; so the Lord turned from the fierceness of his anger."* 'Fierce anger' is incompatable with the divine perfection, nor is the cruel extirpation of the innocent family, and live stock of Achan, to be accounted for on principles of reason. This flagrant injustice of punishing the children for the iniquity of the father had introduced a proverb in Israel, *viz*, *"The fathers have eaten sour grapes and the childrens teeth*

teeth are set on edge." But the prophet Ezekiel in the 18th chapter of his prophecies, has confuted Moses's statutes of visiting the iniquities of the father upon the children, and repealed them with the authority of *thus saith the Lord,* which was the manner of expression by which they were promulgated. But the prophet Ezekiel did not repeal those statutes of Moses merely by the authority of *thus saith the Lord,* but over and above gives the reason for it, otherwise he could not have repealed them; for Moses enacted them as he relates, from as high authority as Ezekiel could pretend to in nullifying them; so that had he not produced reason and argument, it would have been " *thus saith the Lord,*" against " *Thus saith the Lord.*" But Ezekiel reasons conclusively, viz. " *The word of the Lord came unto me again, saying, what mean ye that ye use this proverb concerning the land of Israel, saying, the fathers have eaten sour grapes and the childrens teeth are set on edge; as I live saith the Lord God, ye shall not have occasion any more to use this proverb in Israel. Behold all souls are mine, as the soul of the father so also the soul of the son is mine; the soul that sineth it shall die, the son shall not bear the iniquity of the father, neither shall the father bear the iniquity of the son, the righteousness of the righteous shall be upon him, and the wickedness of the wicked shall be upon him, therefore I will judge you O house of Israel, every one according to their ways faith the Lord God.* It is observable that the prophet ingeniously says, "*Ye shall not have occasion any more to use this proverb in Israel,*" implicitly acknowledging that the law of Moses had given occasion to that proverb, nor was it possible to remove that proverb or grievance to which the Israelites were liable on account of visiting the iniquity of the fathers upon the children, but by the repeal of the statute of Moses in that case made and provided; which was effectually done by Ezekiel: in consequence whereof the administration of justice became disencumbered of the embarrasments under which it had laboured for many centuries. Thus it appears, that those laws, denominated the laws of God, are not infallible, but have their exceptions and may be dispensed with.

UNDER the dispensation of the law a breach of the Sabbath was a capital offence. "*And while the children of Israel were in the wilderness, they found a man that gathered sticks on the Sabbath day, and the Lord said unto Moses the man shall surely be put to death, and all the congregation shall stone him with stones without the camp; and all the congregation brought him without the camp and stoned him with stones, and he died, as the Lord commanded Moses.*" The very institution of the Sabbath was in itself

itself arbitrary, otherwise it could not have been changed from the last to the first day of the week. For those ordinances which are predicated on the reason and fitness of things can never change: as that which is once morally fit, always remains so, and is immutable, nor could the same crime, in justice, deserve death in Moses's time (as in the instance of the Israelite's gathering sticks) and but a pecuniary fine in ours; as in the instance of the breach of Sabbath in these times.

Time itself is as incapable of being holy or unholy as the figure of a triangle may be supposed to be; for time is not an agent; it is no more than a succession of duration divided into distinct parts, or seperate periods, in the succession whereof agents act and are amenable for its improvement; it is as great an impropriety to call time holy, as it would be to call space so; for that neither of them contain the properties of reflection and consciousness or the knowledge of moral good or evil; these are the properties that constitute an agent, which agent, in some degree may be said to be holy or unholy, as its actions conform to or deviate from moral rectitude. But time is as inadequate by nature for the purpose of holiness, or the contrary, as rain, sunshine, or any other inanimate

animate or unintelligent beings may be supposed to be, which will be further evinced from the consideration, that moral obligation is equally binding on all rational beings, on all days and parts of time alike, therefore one day can have no preeminence above another, as to its purity for religious purposes. Furthermore, the order of nature respecting day and night, or the succession of time, is such, as renders it impossible that any identical part of time, which constitutes one day, can do it to all the inhabitants of the globe at the same time, or in the same period. Day is perpetually dawning, and night commencing to some or other of the inhabitants of the terraqueous Ball without intermission. At the distance of fifteen degrees of Longitude to the eastward of us, the day begins an hour sooner than it does with us here in Vermont, and with us an hour sooner than it does fifteen degrees to the westward, and thus it continues its succession round the Globe, and night as regularly revolving after it, succeeding each other in their alternate rounds; so that when it is midday with us, it is mid-night with our species, denominated the *Periæci*, who live under the same parallel of Latitude with us, but under a directly opposite Meridian; so likewise, when it is midday with them, it is mid-night with us. Thus it appears, that the same identical part of time, which composes our days, compose their nights, and while we are keeping Sunday, they are in their midnight dreams; nor is it possible in nature, that the same identical part of time, which makes the first day of the week with us, should make the first day of the week with the inhabitants on the opposite side of the Globe. The apostle James speaks candidly on this subject, saying, "*Some esteem one day above another, others esteem every day alike let every one be fully persuaded in his own mind,*" and keep the laws of the land. It was unfortunate for the Israelite who was accused of gathering sticks on the Israelitish Sabbath, that he was convicted of it; for though by the law of his people he must have died, yet the act for which he suffered was no breach of the law of nature. Supposing that very delinquent should come to this world again, and gather sticks on Saturday in this country, he might, as an hireling receive his wages for it, without being exposed to a similar prosecution of that of Moses; and provided he should gather sticks on our Sunday, his wages would atone for his crime, instead of his life, since modern legislators have abated the rigor of the law for which he died.

THE

The barbarous zeal of the prophet Samuel in hewing Agag pieces, after he was made a prisoner of war by Saul king of Israel, could not proceed from a good spirit, nor would such a cruelty be permitted towards a prisoner in any civilized nation at this day. "*And Samuel hewed Agag to pieces before the Lord in Gilgal.*" The unmanly deed seems to be mentioned with a phiz of religion. viz. That it was done before the Lord; but that cannot alter the nature of the act itself, for every act of mankind, whether good or evil, is done before the Lord, as much as Samuel's hewing Agag to pieces. The orders which Samuel gave unto Saul (as he says by the word of the Lord) to cut off the posterity of the Amalekites, and to destroy them utterly, together with the cause of God's displeasure with them, are unworthy of God, as may be seen at large in the 15th Chapter of the first Book of Samuel. "*Spare them not, but slay both man and woman, infant and suckling, ox and sheep, camel and ass.*" The ostensible reason for all this was, because the ancestors of the Amalekites, as long before the days of Samuel as when the children of Israel came out of Egypt, which was near five hundred years, had ambushed and fought against Israel, in their passage from thence to the land which they afterwards inhabited: Although it appears from the history of Moses

and

and Joshua, that Israel was going to dispossess them of their country, which is thought to be a sufficient cause of war in these days. It is true they insinuate that the Lord had given those lands to the children of Israel, yet it appears that they had to fight for it and get it by the hardest notwithstanding; as is the case with nations in these days, and ever has been since the knowlege of history.

But be the old quarrel between Israel and Amalek as it will, it cannot on any principle be supposed, the successors of those Amalekites, in the days of Samuel, could be guilty of any premised transgressions of their predecessors. The sanguinary laws of Moses did not admit of visiting the iniquities of the fathers upon the children in the line of succession, farther than to the fourth generation, but the Amalekites against whom Samuel had denounced the wrath of God, by the hand of Saul, were at a much greater remove from those their progenitors, who were charged with the crime for which they were cut off as a nation. Nor is it compatible with reason to suppose, that God ever directed either Moses or Joshua to extirpate the Canaanitish nations. "*And we took all his cities at that time, and utterly destroyed the men and the women, and the little ones of every city, we left none to remain,*" There is not any more propriety in ascribing

cribing these cruelties to God, than those that were perpetrated by the Spaniards against the Mexican and Peruvian indians or natives of America. Every one who dares to exercise his reason, free from bias, will readily discern, that the inhumanities exercised towards the Canaanites and Amorites, Mexicans and Peruvians, were detestibly wicked, and could not be approbated by God, or by rational and good men. Undoubtedly avarice and domination were the causes of those unbounded cruelties, in which religion had as little to do as in the crusades to the holy land (so called.)

THE writings of the prophets abound with prodigies, and strange and unnatural events. The walls of Jericho are represented to have fallen to the ground in consequence of a blast of ram's horns; Balaam's ass to speak to his master, and the prophet Elijah is said to have been carried off bodily into heaven by a chariot, in a whirlwind. Strange stories! But other scriptures tell us "*Flesh and blood cannot inherit the kingdom of God.*" The history of the affront, which the little children of Bethel gave the prophet Elisha, his cursing them, and their destruction by the bears, has the appearance of a fable: That Elisha should be so exasperated at the children for calling him *bald head*, and telling him to *go up*, was rather a sample of ill-breeding: Most

gentlemen

gentlemen would have laughed at the joke, instead of cursing them, or being instrumental in their destruction, by merciless, wild and voracious beasts. Though the children were saucy, yet a man of any considerable candor would have made an allowance for their non-age, " *for childhood and youth are vanity.*" "*And he went up from thence unto Bethel, and as he was going up by the way, there came forth little children out of the city and mocked him, and said unto him go up thou bald head, go up thou bald head, and he turned back and looked on them and he cursed them in the name of the Lord, and there came forth two she-bears out of the wood, and tare forty and two children of them.*" It seems by the children's address to Elisha, that he was an old bald headed man, and that they had heard, that his mate Elijah had gone up a little before; and as it was an uncommon thing for men to kite away into the air, and leave the world after that sort, it is likely that it excited a curiosity in the children to see Elisha go off with himself in the same manner, which occasioned their particular mode of speech to him saying *go up bald head.* The writings of Solomon, king of Israel must needs have been foisted into the canonnical volume by some means or other, for no one passage therein gives the least intimation of inspiration, or that he had any immediate dictation from God in his compositions, but on the contrary he informs us that he acquired his knowledge by applying himself to wisdom "*to seek and to search out concerning all things, that are done under the Sun, this sore travail,*" says he, "*has God given to the sons of men to be exercised therewith.*" And since Solomon never pretended to inspiration, others cannot justly claim his writing to have been any thing more than natural reasonings, for who can with propriety stamp his writings with divine authority, when he pretended no such thing, but to the contrary? His Song of Songs appears to be rather of the amorous kind, and is supposed to have been written at the time he was making love to the daughter of Pharaoh king of Egypt, who is said to have been a princess of exquisite beauty and exceeding coy, and so captivated his affections that it made him light headed, and sing about the "*joints of her thighs*" and "*her belly.*"

The divine legation of Moses and the prophets is rendered questionable from the consideration that they never taught the doctrine of immortality; their rewards and punishments are altogether temporary, terminating at death; they have not so much as exhibited any speculation of surviving the grave: to this is ascribed the unbelief of the Sadducees of the resurrection of the dead, or of an angel or spirit, as they strenuously adhered to the law of Moses: For they could not imagine, but that their great prophet and law-giver would have apprized them of a state of immortality had it been true; and in this the Sadducees seem to argue with force on their position of the divine legation of Moses. For admitting the reality of man's immortality, it appears incredible to suppose, that God should have specially commissioned Moses, as his prophet and instructor to the tribes of Israel, and not withal to have instructed them in the important doctrine of a future existence; the belief and apprehension of which is so essential to the encouragement of morality, and without which our speculations on religious topics would be narrow and contracted, as they would be confined only to the stage of human life; which would depress every exalted and dignified idea of the being, creation, perfection and providence of God; the more so as this is not a world wherein justice universally, and in all cases, takes place, and therefore, without an apprehension and persuasion of another to come, wherein justice, truth and morality will reign triumphant, we could have but a low, unjust, and improper conception of the moral government of God, and our motives to the practice of virtue would be exceeding weak and deficient. In fine, the doctrine of immortality is of such importance to mankind, and to the cause of religion in the

world

world, as to induce us to conclude, that had Moses and the prophets been specially commissioned by God, to instruct mankind in religious matters, they would not have confined their theology to this temporary life only, but would have extended it to an eternal series of existence.

SECTION III.

Dreams or Visions uncertain and chimerical Channel for the conveyance of Revelation; with remarks on the Communication of the Holy Ghost to the Disciples, by the Prayers and laying on of the Apostles Hands, with Observations on the Divine Dictations of the first Promulgators of the Gospel, and an Account of the Elect Lady, and her new Sectary of Shakers.

IT appears from the writings of the prophets and apostles, that part of their revelations were communicated to them by dreams and visions, which have no other existence but in the imagination, and are defined to be " the images which appear to the mind during sleep, figuratively, a chimera, a groundless fancy or conceit, without reason." Our experience agrees with this diffinition, and evinces that there is no trust to be reposed in them. They are fictitious images of the mind,

not

not under the controul of the understanding, and therefore not regarded at this day except by the credulous and superstitious, who still retain a veneration for them. But that a revelation from God to man, to be continued to the latest posterity as a divine and perfect rule of duty or law, should be communicated through such a fictitious and chimerical channel, carries with it the evident marks of deception itself, or of unintelligibleness, as appears from the vision of St. Paul. *"It is not expedient for me doubtless to glory, I will come to visions and revelations of the Lord: I knew a man in Christ above fourteen years ago, whether in the body I cannot tell, or whether out of the body, I cannot tell, God knoweth, such an one caught up to the third heavens. And I knew such a man, whether in the body or out of the body I cannot tell, God knoweth, how that he was caught up unto Paradise and heard unspeakable words which is not lawful for a man to utter."* That God knoweth the whole affair, will not be disputed, but that we should understand it is impossible, for the Apostle's account of his vision is unintelligible; it appears that he was rather in a delirium or stupor, so that he knew not whether he was in or out of the body: He says he heard "*unspeakable words,*" but this communicates no intelligence of the subject-matter of them to us; and that they "*were not lawful for a man to utter,*"

but

but what they were, or wherein their unlawfulness to be uttered by man consisted, he does not inform us. His revelation from his own story was unspeakable and unlawful, and so he told us nothing what it was, nor does it compose any part of revelation, which is *to make known*. He is explicit as to his being caught up to the third heaven, but how he could understand that is incredible, when at the same time he knew not whether he was in the body or out of the body; and if he was in such a delirium that he did not know so domestic a matter as that, it is not to be supposed that he could be a competent judge whether he was at the first, second, third, or fourth heaven, or whether he was advanced above the surface of the earth, or not.

That the Apostles in their ministry were dictated by the Holy Ghost, in the settlement of disputable doctrines, is highly questionable. "*Forasmuch as we have heard that certain, which went out from us have troubled you with words, subverting your souls, saying, ye must be circumcised and keep the law, to whom we gave no such commandment, for it seemed good to the Holy Ghost, and to us, to lay upon you no other burthen than these necessary things.* Acts 15. And after having given a history of the disputations concerning circumcision, and of keeping the law

law of Moses, and of the result of the council, the same chapter informs us, that a contention happened so sharp between Paul and Barnabas, "*that they parted asunder the one from the other.*" Had the Holy Ghost been the dictator of the first teachers of Christianity, as individuals, there could have been no disputable doctrines or controversies, respecting the religion which they were promulgating in the world, or in the manner of doing it, to be referred to a general "*council of the apostles and elders held at Jerusalem;*" for had they been directed by the Holy Ghost, there could have been no controversies among them to have referred to the council. And inasmuch as the Holy Ghost neglected them as individuals, why is it not as likely that it neglected to dictate the council held at Jerusalem or elsewhere? It seems that the Holy Ghost no otherwise directed them in their plan of religion, than by the general council of the apostles and elders, the same as all other communities are governed. "*Paul having passed through the upper coasts came to Ephesus, and finding certain disciples he said unto them have ye received the Holy Ghost since ye believed? and they said unto him we have not so much as heard whether there be any Holy Ghost; and when Paul had laid his hands upon them, the Holy Ghost came on them, and they spake with tongues and prophesied. Now when the Apostles which were at Jerusalem heard that Samaria had received the word of God, they sent unto them Peter and John, who, when they were come down prayed for them, that they might receive the Holy Ghost, for as yet he was fallen on none of them, only they were baptised in the name of the Lord Jesus; then laid they their hands on them and they received the Holy Ghost; and when Simon saw that through the laying on of the Apostles hands, the Holy Ghost was given, he offered them money."* That the Holy Ghost or the Divine Spirit which is in essence the same, should have been given to the disciples, at the option and laying on of the Apostles hands, is inadmissible. What power could there have been in the Apostles, or in their prayers, or what energy in the ceremony of the laying on of their hands on the disciples, to have effected such a marvellous operation? All these things complexly considered, could not have availed any thing in a matter which immediately respected the act of God, *to wit*, the communicative operation of his spirit on his disciples, which, according to the constitution of human nature, is contradictory and impossible; for that the divine spirit or any meer spirit, cannot operate on or co-operate with our spirits without the intervention of a material being, so as to communicate any perceptions to us, as argued at large in chapter sixth.

BUT

But admitting those arguments to be inconclusive, and that the immediate communication or gift of the holy spirit to our spirits, independent of the interposition of intermediate causes, is in nature possible, yet to suppose that the prayers, ceremonies, or exertions of mere creatures, in the instance of the gift of the spirit to the disciples, should have altered the providence of God, or induced him to have done that which otherwise he would not have done, in that or any other instance, would be the same as to suppose, that so far the providence of God was eclipsed, defeated or nullified by the interposition or agency of the Apostles: and as this subject has been fully argued in the sixth section of the seventh chapter, the reader is thereto referred for a more copious disquisition of it.

The spirit of God is that which constitutes the divine essence, and makes him to be what he is; but that he should be dictated, or his spirit be communicated by any acts or ceremonies of the Apostles, is by no means admissible: For such exertions of the Apostles, so far as they may be supposed to communicate the holy spirit to their disciples, would have made God passive in the premised act of the gift of the spirit: for it must have been either the immediate act of God or of the

Apostles; and if it was the immediate act of the one, it could not have been the immediate act of the other.

To suppose that the act of the gift of the spirit was the mere act of God, and at the same time the mere act of the Apostles, are propositions diametrically opposed to each other, and cannot both be true. But it may be supposed that the gift of the spirit was partly the act of God and partly the act of the apostles; admitting this to have been the case the consequence would follow, that the act of the gift of the spirit was partly divine and partly human, and therefore the benificence and glory of the grant of the gift of the spirit unto the disciples, would belong partly to God and partly to the Apostles, and in an exact proportion to that which God and they may be supposed to have respectively contributed, towards the marvelous act of the gift of the spirit. But that God should act in partnership with man, or share his providence and glory with him, is too absurd to demand argumentative confutation, especially in an act which immediately respects the display or exertion of the divine spirit on the spirits of men.

There is a material distinction which ought to be made between the immediate and mediate act of God: the latter respects the series of nature's operations, and the former the creation, support and regulation of it.

What I mean by the mediate act of God, is the same as the eternal series of the exertions of the various parts of nature on each other, which, properly speaking, act intermediately, or between the eternal cause and the succeeding or final event of things; so that the mediate act of God, is defined to be nothing more or less, than the mere operations of nature, which act by succession, and are the complicated exertions of created beings: But the eternal cause cannot act by succession, but is one eternal, infinite and uncompounded exertion of God, giving being, order and support to the universe, and cannot admit of beginning, succession or limitation; so that there could have been no new or succeeding act of God, which is the same as an immediate exertion of the Holy Ghost on the disciples: For if the laying on of the Apostle's hands upon the disciples, or their prayers, or ceremonies, caused the immediate act of the gift of the Spirit of God, it would have subverted the order of nature, and made the Apostles the efficient cause of the act of the gift of the spirit; and the premised immediate act of God therein, would have been transposed into the order of dependent causes,

causes, and instead of being the mover would have been the moved.

FURTHERMORE, to suppose the act of the gift of the spirit to the disciples, to have originated from, and to have been the immediate act of God, it must have been miraculous; as it would imply a divine exertion, which was not comprized in the eternal establishment of things, but took place at a certain subsequent æra of the world, according to the order of time, and not in the order of the series of natural causes, but from the immediate act of God himself. That there cannot be any succession in the immediate act of God, has been particularly urged in the preceding chapter, and is applicable in the case of the premised act of the gift of the spirit: For if we admit of an immediate act of God in the days of the Apostles, it would succeed the eternal act of God in creating, ordering and sustaining the universe, which, if perfectly done, could not admit of a succeeding immediate act or acts of God.

To suppose God in his order of nature to have mediately produced a race of creatures which we call man, and that they stand in need of the immediate exertion of the energy of the divine spirit upon theirs, would be the same as to suppose, that

until

until that miraculous operation of the divine spirit, God had not perfected his workmanship of the nature and salvation of man. Furthermore, provided the gift of the Holy Ghost was requisite to any part of mankind, it would be so to the whole, and on the proviso that it has ever been conferred on any, God could not act consistent with himself, or the wants of his creatures, without a universal effusion of it to mankind: but the doctrine of a partial effusion seems to be the pride of the elect. It appears, that the disciples, of whom we have been frequently speaking, were unacquainted with the spiritual matters then beginning to be in vogue with some people, as may be learned from their answer to the apostle's interrogating them respecting their receiving the Holy Ghost; *" And they said unto him, we have not so much as heard, whether there be any Holy Ghost."* It was a new doctrine, and that of a supernatural kind; and it is natural to suppose, that the disciples were overawed at the expectation of receiving the heavenly infusion; which, together with the sanctimonious parade and ceremonies of the apostles, could not have failed to have heightened their surprize. Their minds thus agitated with hope, fear and religious curiosity, which compounded together might produce the feelings of enthusiastical conceit, and the apostles at the same time insinuating, that it was

the

the Holy Ghost, the disciples most probably might have imagined it to have been a fact.

Such delusions have taken place in every age of the world since history has attained to any considerable degree of intelligence; nor is there at present a nation on earth, but what is more or less infatuated with delusory notions of the immediate influence of good or evil spirits on their minds. A recent instance of it appears in the Elect Lady (as she has seen fit to stile herself) and her followers, called Shakers; this pretended holy woman began her religious scheme at Connestaguna, in the Northwestardly part of the state of New-York, about the year 1769, and has added a new sectary to the religious catalogue. After having instilled her tenets among the Connestagunites, and the adjacent inhabitants, she rambled into several parts of the country, promulgating her religion, and has gained a considerable number of scattering proselytes, not only in the state of New-York, but some in the New-England states. She has so wrought on the minds of her female devotees, respecting the fading nature, vanity and tempting alurements of their ornaments (which by the by are not plenty among her followers) and the deceitfulness of riches, that she has procured from them a considerable number of strings of gold beads and jewels,

and

and amassed a small treasure; and like most sectaries engrosses the kingdom of heaven to herself and her followers, to the seclusion of all others. She gives out that her mission is immediately from heaven, that she travails in pain for her elect, and pretends to talk in seventy two unknown languages, in which she converses with those who have departed this life, and says, that there has not been a true church on earth since the apostles days until she had erected hers. That both the living and the dead must be saved in, by, and through her, and that they must confess their sins unto her and procure her pardon, or they cannot be saved. That every of the human race, who have died since the apostle's time, until her church was set up, has been damned, and that they are continually making intercession to her for salvation, which is the occasion of her talking to them in those unknown tongues; and that she gathers her elect from earth and hell. She wholly refuses to give a reason for what she does or says; but says that it is the duty of mankind to believe in her, and receive her instructions, for that they are infallible.

For a time she prohibited her disciples from propagating their species, but soon after gave them ample licence, restricting them, indiscriminately, to the

the pale of her sanctified church, for that she needed more souls to compleat the number of her elect. Among other things, she instructs those who are young and spritely among her pupils, to practise the most wild, freakish, wanton and romantic gestures, as that of indecently, striping themselves, twirling round, extorting their features, shaking and twitching their bodies and limbs into a variety of odd and unusal ways, and many other extravagancies of external behavior, in the practice of which they are said to be very alert even to the astonishment of spectators, having by use acquired an uncommon agility in such twirling, freakish and romantic practices: The old lady having such an ascendency over them as to make them believe that those extravagant actions were occasioned by the immediate power of God, it serves among them as a proof of the divinity of her doctrines.

A MORE particular account of this new sectary has been lately published in a pamphlet by a Mr. Rathburn, who, as he relates, was, for a time, one of her deluded disciples, but after a while apostarised from the faith, and has since announced to the world the particulars of their doctrines and conduct.

PROBABLY

PROBABLY there never was any people or country, since the æra of historical knowledge, who were more confident than they that they are acted upon by the immediate agency of the divine spirit; and as they are facts now existing in a considerable tract of country, and are notoriously known in this part of America, I take the liberty to mention them, as a knowledge of these facts, together with the concurrent testimony of the history of such deceptions in all ages and nations, might induce my countrymen to examine strictly into the claim and reality of ghostly intelligence in general.

Chapter

Chapter IX.

SECTION I.

Of the Nature of FAITH and wherein it consists.

FAITH in Jesus Christ and in his Gospel throughout the New-Testament, is represented to be an essential condition of the eternal salvation of mankind. "Knowing that a man is not justified by the works of the law, but by the faith of Jesus Christ; even we have believed in Jesus Christ, that we might be justified by the faith of Christ, and not by the works of the law, for by the works of the law shall no flesh be justified." Again, "If thou shalt confess the Lord Jesus Christ, and believe in thine heart that God hath raised him from the dead, thou mayest be saved." And again, "He that believeth and is baptised shall be saved,

saved, but he that believeth not shall be damned." Faith is the last result of the understanding, or the same which we call the conclusion, it is the consequence of a greater or less deduction of reasoning from certain premises previously laid down; it is the same as believing or judging of any matter of fact, or assenting to or dissenting from the truth of any doctrine, system or position; so that to form a judgment, or come to a determination in one's own mind, or to believe, or to have faith, is in reality the same thing, and is synonymously applied both in writing and speaking; for example, *" Abraham believed in God."* Again, *" for he,"* speaking of Abraham, *" judged him faithful who had promised,"* and again, *" his faith was counted unto him for righteousness."* It is not only in scripture that we meet with examples of the three words, to wit, belief, judgment and faith, to stand for the marks of our ideas for the same thing, but also all intelligible writers and speakers, apply these phrases synonimously, and it would be good grammar and sense for us to say that we have faith in a universal providence, or that we believe in a universal providence, or that we judge that there is a universal providence. These three different phrases, in communicating our ideas of providence, do every of them exhibit the same idea, to all persons of common understanding, who are acquainted

with

with the English Language. In fine every one's experience may convince them, that they cannot assent to, or dissent from the truth of any matter of fact, doctrine or preposition whatever, contrary to their judgment; for the act of the mind in assenting to, or dissenting from any position, or in having faith or belief in favor of, or against any doctrine, system or proposition, could not amount to any thing more or less, than the act of the judgment, or last dictate of the understanding, whether the understanding be supposed to be rightly informed or not; so that our faith in all cases is as liable to err, as our reason is to misjudge of the truth; and our minds act faith in disbelieving any doctrine or system of religion to be true, as much as in believing it to be so. From hence it appears, that the mind cannot act faith in opposition to its judgment, but that it is the resolution of the understanding itself committed to memory or writing, and can never be considered distinct from it. And inasmuch as faith necessarily results from reasoning, forcing itself upon our minds by the evidence of truth, or the mistaken apprehension of it, without any act of choice of ours, there cannot be any thing, which pertains to, or partakes of the nature of moral good or evil in it. For us to believe such doctrines or systems of religion, as appear to be credibly recommended to our reason,

can

can no more partake of the nature of goodness or morality, than our natural eyes may be supposed to partake of it in their perception of colours; for the faith of the mind, and the sight of the eye are both of them necessary consequences, the one results from the reasonings of the mind, and the other from the perception of the eye. To suppose a rational mind without the exercise of faith, would be as absurd as to suppose a proper and compleat eye without sight, or the perception of the common objects of that sense. The short of the matter is this, that without reason we could not have faith, and without the eye or eyes we could not see, but once admitting that we are rational, faith follows of course, naturally resulting from the dictates of reason.

Furthermore, It is observable, that in all cases wherein reason makes an erroneous conclusion, faith is likewise erroneous, and that in the same proportion as the conclusion may be supposed to be faulty and irregular: for it is the established order of human nature, that faith should always conform to the decrees of the judgment, whether it be right or wrong, or partly both. From hence it follows, that errors in faith, and consequently in practice, are more or less unavoidable. We are therefore obliged to substitute sincerity in the place of knowledge, in all cases wherein knowledge is not attainable, for we cannot look into the eternal order of unerring reason and perfect rectitude, so as in all cases to regulate our minds and consciences from thence. We must therefore adopt the principle of sincerity, since it is always supposed to aim at perfection, and to come as near it as the infirmities of our nature will admit, (for otherwise it could not be sincerity) which is the highest pretension to goodness, that we can lawfully aspire to. There are therefore good or bad designs and intentions, which crown all our actions, and denominate them to be either good or bad, virtuous or vicious. Those who are vicious and abandoned to wickedness, may, and often do, possess more knowledge, and consequently a more extensive faith than those who are ignorant and virtuous: their sin does not consist in the want of understanding or faith, but in their omission of cultivating in their own minds the love and practice of virtue, or in not bringing their designs, intentions, dispositions and habits to a conformity thereto. A good conscience, predicated on knowledge as far as that is attainable, and on sincerity for the rest of our conduct, always was and will be essential to a rational happiness, which results from a consciousness of moral rectitude, and thus it is that mankind, by seeking after the truth, and conforming

ing (as far as human frailty will permit) to moral rectitude, may attain to the enjoyment of a good conscience, although in doctrinal or speculative points of religion, or in creeds, they may be supposed to be ever so erroneous.

SECTION II.

Of the Traditions of our Forefathers.

IT may be objected, that the far greater part of mankind believe according to the tradition of their forefathers, without examining into the grounds of it, and that argumentative deductions from the reason and nature of things, have, with the bulk of them, but little or no influence on their faith. Admitting this to have been too much the case, and that many of them have been blameable for the omission of cultivating or improving their reason, and for not forming a better judgment concerning their respective traditions, or a juster and more exalted faith; yet this does not at all invalidate the foregoing arguments respecting the nature of faith: for though it be admitted that most of the human race do not, or will not reason, with any considerable degree of propriety, on the traditions of their forefathers, but receive them implicitly

plicitly, they neverthelefs eftablifh this one propofition in their minds, right or wrong, *that their respective traditions are right*, for none could believe in them were they poffeffed of the knowledge that they were wrong. And as we have a natural bias in favor of our progenitors, to whofe memory a tribute of regard is juftly due, and whofe care in handing down from father to fon fuch notions of religion and manners, as they fuppofed would be for the well being and happinefs of their pofterity in this and the coming world, naturally endears tradition to us, and prompts us to receive and venerate it. Add to this, that the priefts of every denomination are " *inftant in feafon and out of feafon*," in inculcating and inftilling the fame tenets, which, with the foregoing confiderations, induces mankind in general to give at leaft a tacit confent to their refpective traditions, and without a thorough inveftigation thereof, believe them to be right and very commonly infallible, although their examinations are not attended with argumentative reafonings, from the nature of things; and in the fame proportion as they may be fuppofed to fall fhort of conclufive arguing on their refpective traditions they cannot fail to be deceived in the rationality of their faith.

But

BUT after all it may be that some of the human race may have been traditionally or accidentally right, in many or most respects. Admitting it to be so, yet they cannot have any rational enjoyment of it, or understand wherein the truth of the premised right tradition consists, or deduce any more satisfaction from it, than others whose traditions may be supposed to be wrong; for it is the knowledge of the discovery of truth alone, which is gratifying to that mind who contemplates its superlative beauty.

THAT tradition has had a powerful influence on the human mind is universally admitted, even by those who are governed by it in the articles or discipline of their faith; for though they are blind with respect to their own superstition, yet they can perceive and despise it in others. Protestants very readily discern and expose the weak side of Popery, and papists are as ready and acute in discovering the errors of heretics. With equal facility do Christians and Mahometans spy out each others inconsistencies, and both have an admirable sagacity to descry the superstition of the heathen nations. Nor are the Jews wholly silent in this matter; "*O God the heathen are come into thine inheritance, thy holy temple have they defiled.*" What abomination must this have been in the opinion of a nation who had monopolized all religion to themselves! Monstrous vile Heathen, that they should presume to approach the *sanctum sanctorum!* The Christians call the Mahometans by the odious name of infidels, but the Musselmen, in their opinion, cannot call the Christians by a worse name than that which they have given themselves, they therefore call them *Christians.*

WHAT has been already observed upon tradition, is sufficient to admonish us of its errors and superstitions, and the prejudices to which a bigoted attachment thereto exposes us, to which is abundantly sufficient to excite us to a careful examination of our respective traditions, and not to rest satisfied until we have regulated our faith by reason.

SECTION III.

Our Faith is governed by our Reasonings, whether they are supposed to be conclusive or inconclusive, and not merely by our own Choice.

IT is written that " *Faith is the gift of God.*" Be it so, but is faith any more the gift of God than reflection, memory or reason are his gifts? Was it not for memory, we could not retain in our minds, the judgment which we have passed upon things,

things, and was it not for reasoning, in either a regular or irregular manner, or partly both, there could be no such thing as judging or believing; so that God could not bestow the gift of faith seperate from the gift of reason, faith being the mere consequence of reasoning, either right or wrong, or in a greater or less degree, as has been previously argued.

STILL there is a knotty text of scripture to surmount, viz. "*He that believeth shall be saved, but he that believeth not shall be damned.*" This text is considered as crouding "*damned*" hard upon unbelievers in Christianity; but when it is critically examined, it will be found not to militate at all against them, but is merely a Jesuitical fetch to overawe some and make others wonder. We will premise, that an unbeliever is destitute of faith, which is the cause of his being thus denominated. The Christian believes the Gospel to be true and of divine authority, the Deist believes that it is not true and not of divine authority; so that the Christian and Deist are both of them believers, and according to the express words of the text "*shall be saved,*" and a Deist may as well retort upon a Christian and call him an infidel, because he differs in faith from him, as the Christian may upon the Deist; for there is the same impropriety in applying

the

the cant of infidelity to either, as both are believers; and it is impossible for us to believe contrary to our judgments or the dictates of our understanding, whether it be rightly informed or not. Why then may there not in both denominations be honest men, who are seeking after the truth, and who may have an equal right to expect the favour and salvation of God.

But if the foregoing exposition of the text should be dissatisfactory to Christians, and they should still be of opinion that themselves only have an exclusive right to the title of believers, and that those who disbelieve Christianity (believe whatever else they will) must inevitably be damned, and that merely in consequence of such their unbelief; I shall dispute the justice of it, and appeal to the decision of the righteous judge of the universe: In the mean time I offer it as my candid opinion, that a proffer of religion to mankind, which tenders salvation to them, merely upon condition of believing it, *alias* its teachers, and which dooms all those who disbelieve it to damnation, has too much the appearance of human craft, and ought to be suspected as to its divinity, and rejected; being utterly incompatible with the nature of faith, as has been before argued, and also with the moral perfections of God.

It is frequently objected by believers in the Christian system, against the Deists, that provided Christianity should eventually turn out to be true, then they have God's word for it, that "*he that believeth not shall be damned,*" whereas, on the contrary, both Christians and Deists, upon the principles of the law of nature, will be admitted to future proficiency in knowledge, faith and action, and to such a salvation as the Law of Nature may admit of; from hence the Christians infer, that at least it is most prudent to be a Christian. But it ought to be considered, that we cannot believe or disbelieve contrary to the result of the evidence for and against Christianity, as it appears to us upon deliberation. All that we have to do, as rational and accountable creatures, is to govern our assent to or dissent from it by reason and candid argument; and are by no means left at loose from the evidence originating from the reason of things, to play politics, and believe or not believe, just as we please, independent of the evidence concerning Christianity; so that there is no possibility in nature for the exercise of such a prudent or political faith: our minds must be determined in all matters by our reasonings, whether they are conclusive or otherwise; for mere traditional faith has its inconclusive arguments for its support, viz. father believed and so did the parson of the parish,

and

and they were very good men and are both gone to Heaven, *ergo*, I will believe too, that I may go to Heaven also.

But after all that has been said on this subject, provided that " *he that believeth not,*" in Christianity " *shall be damned;*" what will become of the Deists? Why to be honest about the matter, I suppose, that on this position they will be damned sure enough: Which may be a gratification to some believers, when all other arguments fail them.

Chapter

Chapter X.

SECTION I.

A Trinity of Persons cannot exist in the Divine Essence, whether the Persons be supposed to be finite or infinite: With Remarks on St. Athanasius's Creed.

OF all the errors which have taken place in religion, none have been so fatal to it as those that immediately respect the divine nature. Wrong notions of a God, or of his Providence, sap its very foundation in theory and practice, as is evident from the superstition discoverable among the major part of mankind; who, instead of worshipping the true God, have been by some means or other

infatuated

infatuated to pay divine homage to *mere creatures*, or to idols made with hands, or to such as have no existence but in their own fertile imaginations.

God being incomprehensible to us, we cannot understand all that perfection in which the Divine Essence consists; we can nevertherless (negatively) comprehend many things, in which (positively) the divine essence does not and cannot consist.

That it does not consist of three persons, or of any other number of persons, is as easily demonstrated, as that *the whole* is *bigger* than a *part*, or any other proposition in mathematics.

We will premise, that the three persons in the supposed Trinity are either finite or infinite; for there cannot in the scale of being be a third sort of beings between these two; for ever so many and exalted degrees in finiteness is still finite, and that being who is infinite admits of no degrees or enlargement; and as all beings whatever must be limited or unlimited, perfect or imperfect, they must therefore be denominated to be finite or infinite: we will therefore premise the three persons in the Trinity to be merely finite, considered personally and individually from each other, and the question would arise, whether the supposed trinity of finites though united in one essence, could be more than finite still. Inasmuch as three imperfect and circumscribed beings united together, could not constitute a being perfect or infinite, any more than absolute perfection could consist of three imperfections; which would be the same as to suppose that infinity could be made up or compounded of finiteness; or that absolute, uncreated and infinite perfection, could consist of three personal and imperfect natures. But on the other hand, to consider every of the three persons in the supposed Trinity, as being absolutely infinite, it would be a downright contradiction to one infinite and all comprehending essence. Admitting that God the father is infinite, it would necessarily preclude the supposed God the Son, and God the Holy Ghost from the god-head, or essence of God; one infinite essence comprehending every power, excellency and perfection, which can possibly exist in the divine nature. Was it possible that three absolute infinites, which is the same as three Gods, could be contained in one and the self-same essence, why not as well any other number of infinites? But as certain as infinity cannot admit of addition, so certain a plurality of infinites cannot exist in the same essence; for real infinity is strict and absolute infinity, and only that, and cannot be compounded of infinites or of parts, but forecloses all addition: A personal or circumscribed God, implies as great and manifest a contradiction as the mind of man can conceive of; it is the same as a limitted omnipresence, a weak Almighty, or a finite God.

FROM the foregoing arguments on the trinity, we infer, that the divine essence cannot consist of a trinity of persons, whether they are supposed to be either finite or infinite.

THE Creedmongers have exhibited the doctrine of the Trinity in an alarming point of light, viz. *"Whoever would be saved, before all things it is necessary that he hold the catholic faith, which faith, except every one doth keep whole and undefiled, without doubt he shall perish everlastingly."* We next proceed to the doctrine, *"The father is eternal, the son is eternal, and the holy ghost is eternal, and yet there are not three eternals but one eternal."* The plain English is, that the three persons in the trinity are three eternals, individually considered, and yet they are not three eternals but one eternal.

To say that there are three eternals in the trinity, and yet that there are not three eternals therein, is a contradiction in terms, as much as to say, that there are three persons in the trinity and yet there are not three persons in the trinity.

The first proposition in the creed affirms, that "*the Father is eternal,*" the second affirms that "*the Son is eternal,*" the third affirms that "*the Holy Ghost is eternal,*" the fourth affirms that "*there are not three eternals,*" and the fifth that there is "*but one eternal.*"

The reader will observe, that the three first propositions are denied by the fourth, which denies that there are three eternals, though the three first prepositions affirmed, that there were three eternals by name; *viz.* The Father, Son and Holy Ghost. The fifth proposition is unconnected with either of the former, and is undoubtedly true; *viz.* "*but there is one eternal.*" "*The Father is God, The Son is God, and the Holy Ghost is God, and yet there are not three Gods but one God.*" Here again we have three God's by name, affirmed to have an existence by the three first propositions, by the fourth they are negatived, and the fifth affirms the truth again, viz. that there is "*but one God.*"

ADMITTING the three first propositions to be true, *to wit,* that there are three Gods, the three could not be one and the same God, any more than Diana, Dagon and Moloch, may be supposed to be the same; and if three Gods, their essences and providences would interfere, and make universal confusion and disorder.

"*The Father is Almighty, the Son is Almighty, and the Holy Ghost is Almighty, and yet there are not three Almighties but one Almighty.*" Here we have three Almighties and at the same time but one Almighty. So that the point at issue is brought to this simple question, *viz.* whether three units can be one, or one unit three, or not? Which is submitted to the curious to determine. Our creed further informs us, that the three persons in the Trinity are co-eternal together and co-equal, but in its sequel we are told that one was begotten of the other; and when we advert to the history of that transaction, we find it to be not quite eighteenhundred years ago, and took place in the reign of Herod, the King of Judea, which faith, except "*we keep whole and undefiled,*" we have a threat, that "*without doubt we shall perish everlastingly.*"

SECTION II.

Essence being the Cause of Identity, is inconsistent with Personality in the Divine Nature.

ONE God can have but one essence, which must have been eternal and infinite, and for that reason precludes all others from a participation of his nature, glory, and universal and absolute perfection.

WHEN we speak of any being who by nature is capable of being rightfully denominated an individual, we conceive of it to exist in but one essence; so that essence as applied to God, denominates the divine nature; and as applied to man, it denotes an individual: for although the human race is with propriety denominated the race of man, and though every male of the species, is with equal propriety called man, for that they partake of one common sort of nature and likeness, yet the respective individuals are not one and the same. The person of A is not the person of B, nor are they conscious of each others consciousness, and therefore the joy or grief of A, is not and cannot be the joy or grief of B; this is what we know to be a fact from our own experience. The reason of this personal distinction is founded in nature, for though we partake of one common nature and likeness, yet we do not partake of one and the same essence. Essence is therefore, in the order of nature, the primary cause of identity or sameness and cannot be divided.

THE essence of any beings is that by which they are distinguished from each other, and which constitutes and gives being to identity itself. A more downright contradiction cannot be expressed in words than to affirm, that three persons do each

and

and every of them pertain to one and the same essence; for was it so, the consciousness of the one would be the consciousness of the other without distinction; nor would it be possible for them to have a seperate knowledge, interest, or consciousness; but their premised plurality of persons and being, would be swallowed up and lost in one essence and individuality. So that their actions, interest, honor, happiness or misery, would be all one and the same, as much as their essence may be supposed to be: or, in fine, it would constitute a compleat identity.

Now, inasmuch as we know, from our own experience, that three persons cannot exist in one essence, how unreasonable is it to ascribe a trinity of persons to the divine nature; which, if admitted to be true, overturns all our notions of identity; for if three persons are one and the same, they can no more be three, than three units may be one, or one may be three, which is mathematically impossible.

It is as contradictory that three persons should exist in one essence, as that three essences should exist in one person, when at the same time essence is the identical nature of a person and makes him to be essentially what he is; or is the very consciousness or quintessence of him, comprehending

all

all that by reason of which he is not something else, which is a just idea of identity, and therefore cannot consist of an aggregate assemblage of distinct natures, and consequently cannot consist of more persons or essences than one: For no person can have a positive existence without an essence, this being the same as to exist without an existence, essence being essential to existence itself.

But should we, for argument sake, admit, that there are three persons, and consequently three essences in the Godhead, then it would follow, that they could not be privy to, or conscious of each others consciousness: for if they were, it would reduce the three supposed essences, and consequently the trinity of persons, into one essence only, for consciousness proceeds from identity of essence, without distinction of persons, and includes the divine nature in one entire and infinite essence, which cannot admit of parts or units, but is infinitely removed from personality. But on the contrary, provided the three premised persons in the Trinity, are not privy to or conscious of each others consciousness, it would reduce the omniscience of the supposed Trinity to a finite comprehension, so that if the three persons in the premised Trinity, are not privy to, or conscious of each other's consciousness, it would necessarily imply imperfection in knowledge, and consequently in government,

vernment, and each of the perfections of a God; and therefore precludes the trinity from the essence of God.

The three supposed persons in the Trinity must be conscious of each other's consciousness, or not conscious of it; if they are supposed to be conscious thereof it would amount to but one entire consciousness, and would be comprehended in one and the same essence, as before argued, and foreclose the trinity of persons from the divine essence. But if there be in the trinity a personal and distinct consciousness, of which each other are not conscious, they would constitute but three finite minds; a trinity of which would fall infinitely short of a God.

From hence we infer, that the doctrine of the Trinity is destitute of foundation, and tends manifestly to superstition and idolatry.

SECTION III.

The imperfection of Knowledge in the Person of Jesus Christ, incompatible with his Divinity, with Observations on the Hypostatical Union of the Divine and Human Natures.

THAT Jesus Christ was not God is evident from his own words, where, speaking of the day of judgment, he says, "*Of that day and hour knoweth no man, no not the angels which are in Heaven, neither the Son, but the Father.*" This is giving up all pretension to divinity, and acknowledging in the most explicit manner, that he did not know all things, but compares his understanding to that of man and of angels; "*of that day and hour knoweth no man, no not the angels which are in heaven, neither the son.*" Thus he ranks himself with finite beings, and with them acknowledges, that he did not know the day and hour of judgment, and at the same time ascribes a superiority of knowledge to the father, for that he knew the day and hour of judgment.

That he was a mere creature is further evident from his prayer to the father, saying, "*Father if it be possible, let this cup pass from me, nevertheless not my will but thine be done.*" These expressions speak forth the most humble submission to his father's will, authority and government, and however becoming so submissive a disposition to the divine government would be, in a creature, it is utterly inconsistent and unworthy of a God, or of the person of Jesus Christ, admitting him to have been a divine person, or of the essence of God.

What notions can we entertain that the divine essence should be divided, and one part assume an authority over the other; or that the other should yield obedience; this is a contradiction, inasmuch as essence cannot be divided, but is the same, without distinction, either in its nature, authority or government.

To suppose one part of the divine nature to exercise authority over another, is the same as to suppose, that part of the essence of God was weak and imperfect, and not capable of holding a share in the divine government, which would reduce it to the state and condition of a creature, and divest it of its divinity. Nor would the consequences of such a supposed imperfection in the essence of God end here, but would necessarily involve the divine nature, in weakness, misery and imperfection; and extinguish every idea of the existence of a God: This is the necessary consequence of deifying Christ. But if Jesus Christ was not of the essence of God, he must have been a mere creature; as there cannot be any being but who is either finite or infinite, as has been before argued.

But we are told of a hypostatical union of the divine and human nature. But wherein does it consist? Does it unite the two natures so as to include

clude the human nature in the essence of God? If it does not it does not deify the person of Christ; for the essence of God is that which makes him to be what he is; but if the hypostatical union includes human nature in the divine, then there would be an addition of the human nature to the essence of God, in which case the divine nature would be no longer perfectly simple, but compounded, and would be diverse from what it may be supposed to have been the eternity preceding such premised union; in which connection the divine nature must have changed from its eternal identity. He could not be the same God he was previous to his union with humanity; for if the union of natures is supposed to have made no alteration in the divine essence, it is a contradiction to call it a union; for the hypostatical union must be supposed to be something or nothing, if it be nothing, then there is no such union, but if it is any thing real, it necessarily produces mutability in the divine nature. Now, if the divine nature was eternally perfect and compleat, it could not receive the addition of the nature of man, but if it was not perfect in the eternity preceding the premised hypostatical union, it could not have been perfected by the addition of another imperfection.

THE

The doctrine of the *incarnation* itself, and the *virgin mother*, does not merit a serious confutation and therefore is passed in silence, except the mere mention of it.

Chapter

Chapter XI.

SECTION I.

OBSERVATIONS *on the State of* MAN, *in* MOSES's PARADISE, *on the* TREE OF KNOWLEDGE OF GOOD AND EVIL, *and on the* TREE OF LIFE: *with Speculations on the* DIVINE PROHIBITION *to* MAN, *not to eat of the fruit of the former of those Trees, interspersed with Remarks on the* MORTALITY *of* INNOCENT MAN.

THE mortality of animal life, and the dissolution of that of the vegetable, has been particularly considered in chapter 3, section 4, treating on physical evils. We now proceed to make an application of those arguments, in the case of our reputed first parents, whose mortality is represented

presented by Moses to have taken place in consequence of their eating of the forbidden fruit.

Moses, in his description of the garden of Eden acquaints us with two chimerical kinds of fruit trees, which, among others, he tells us were planted by God in the place appointed for the residence of the new made couple; the one he calls by the name of "*the Tree of Knowledge of Good and Evil*," and the other by the name of "*the Tree of Life*." And previous to his account of the apostacy, he informs us, that God expressly commanded the man and woman, saying, "*be fruitful and multiply and replenish the earth and subdue it, and have dominion over the fish of the sea, and over the fowl of the air, and over every living thing that moveth upon the earth; and God said, behold I have given you every herb bearing seed, which is upon the face of all the earth, and every tree, in which is the fruit of a tree yielding seed, to you it shall be for meat.* Again, "*and the Lord commanded the man saying, of every tree of the garden thou mayest freely eat, but of the Tree of Knowledge of good and evil thou shalt not eat of it, for in the day that thou eatest thereof thou shalt surely die.*" "*And the Lord said, it is not good for man to be alone, I will make him an help meet for him; and the Lord God caused a deep sleep to fall upon Adam, and he slept, and he took out one of his ribs, and closed up up the flesh instead thereof, and the rib which the Lord God had taken from man made he a woman."*

Thus it appears from Moses's representation of the state of man's innocency, that he was commanded by God to labour, and to replenish the earth; and that to him was given the dominion over the creatures; and that at two several times he was licenced by God himself to eat of every of the fruit of the trees, and of the herbage, except of the tree of knowledge of good and evil; and because it was not good that the man should be alone, but that he might multiply and replenish the earth, our amorous mother Eve, it seems, was formed, who I dare say well compensated father Adam for the loss of his rib.

This short description of man's state and condition in innocency, agrees with the state and circumstances of human nature at present. Innocent man was required to labour and subdue the earth, out of which he was to be subsisted; had a license to eat of the fruit of the trees, or herbage of the garden, which pre-supposeth, that his nature needed refreshment the same as ours does; for otherwise it would have been impertinent to have granted him a priviledge incompatable with his nature, as it would have been no priviledge at all, but an outright mockery, except we admit, that

innocent

innocent human nature was liable to decay, needed nutrition by food, and had the quality of digestion and perspiration; or in fine, had the same sort of nature as we have; for otherwise, he could eat but one belly-full, which without digestion would remain the same, and is too romantic to have been the original end and design of eating. And though there is nothing mentioned by Moses concerning his drinking, yet it is altogether probable, that he had wit enough to drink when he was thirsty. That he consisted of animal nature is manifest, not only from his being subjected to subdue the earth, out of which he was to be subsisted, and from his eating and drinking, or his susceptibility of nutrition by food, but also from his propensity to propagate his kind; for which purpose a help-mate was made for him.

Nothing could more fully evince, that Moses's innocent progenitors of mankind, in that State, were of a similar nature to our's, than their susceptibility of propogating the species; and as they required nutrition, their nature must have had the quality or aptitude of digestion and perspiration, and every property that at present we ascribe to an animal nature; from hence we infer, that death, or mortality, must have been the necessary consequence. What would have prevented them from having been crushed to death by a fall from a precipice

precipice, or from suffering death by any other casualty, to which human nature is at present liable? will any suppose that the bodies of those premised innocent progenitors of the human race were invulnerable; were they not flesh and blood? surely they were, for otherwise they could not have been male and female; as it was written, *"male and female created be them:"* and inasmuch as animal life has, from its original, consisted of the same sort of nature, and been propogated and supported in the same manner, and obnoxious to the same fate, it would undoubtedly, in the premised day of Adam, have required the same order in the external system of nature, which it does at present, to answer the purposes of animal life.

WAS it possible that the laws of Nature, which merely respect gravatation, could be and were suspended, so as not to be influential on matter, our world would be immediately disjointed and out of order, and confusion would succeed its present regularity; in the convulsions whereof animal life could not subsist. So that not only the laws which immediately respect animal nature in particular, but the laws which respect our solar system, must have been the same in man's innocency, as in his whimsically supposed state of apostacy; and consequently, his mortality the same. From hence we infer,

infer, that the curses, which Moses informs us of in chapter 3: as being by God pronounced upon man, saying; "*dust thou art, and unto dust thou shalt return*," could not have been any punishment, inflicted as a penalty for eating the forbidden fruit; for turn to dust he must have done, whether he ate of it or not; for that death and dissolution was the inevitable and irreversible condition of the law of nature, which wholly precludes the curse, of which Moses informs us, from having any effect on mankind.

The story of the "*tree of life,*" is unnatural. And their being but one of the kind, it may be called an only tree, the world not having produced another of the sort; the fruit of which, according to Moses, had such an efficacious quality, that had Adam and Eve but eaten thereof, they would have lived forever. "*And now lest he put forth his hand and take also of the tree of life, and eat, and live for ever.*" To prevent which, they are said to be driven out of the garden, that the eating thereof might not have reversed the sentence of God, which he had previously pronounced against them, denouncing their mortality. "*So he drove out the man, and he placed at the east of the garden of Eden, Cherubims, and a flaming sword, which turneth every way to keep the way of the tree of life;*" a bite of this fruit

fruit it seems would have reinstated mankind, and spoiled priestcraft. Yet it is observable, that there are no travellers or historians, who have given any accounts of such a tree, or of the Cherubims or flaming sword, which renders its existence disputable, and the reality of it doubtful and improbable; the more so, as that part of the country, in which it is said to have been planted, has for a long succession of ages been populously inhabited.

Yet it may be objected, that the tree may have rotted down and consumed by time. But such conjectures derogate from the character of the quality of the tree. It seems, that so marvelous a tree, the fruit of which would have preserved animal life eternally, would have laughed at time, and bid defiance to decay and dissolution, and eternally have remained in its prestine state under the protection of the flaming sword, as a perpetual evidence of the divine legation of Moses, and the reality of man's apostacy for ever. But alas! it is no where to be found, it is perished from off the face of the earth, and such a marvellous fruit is no more, and consequently no remedy against mortality remains.

Another part of the Chronicles of Moses, which demands our serious attention and wise improvement, we may find recorded in the 2d Chapter

ter of Genesis at the ninth verse, the latter clause of the verse. "*The tree of Knowledge also of good and evil.*" This tree, if we may credit the history, appears to be as stupenduous in its nature, and in the quality of its fruit, as that of the tree of life, though of a different kind. Some are of opinion, that the eating of this fruit gave our reputed first parents to understand the distinction between moral good and evil, and others, that it could do no more than communicate to them an experiment of natural good and evil.

THAT the premised innocent couple acquired the principle of reflection or reason by eating of the fruit of the tree of knowledge of good and evil, is preposterous; for it is the same as supposing, that previous to their eating of that fruit, they were not rational creatures, and if so, not accountable for their eating of it, but incapable of agency in the matter of any supposed command. Nor could their eating of that fruit, on the position that they did not know moral good and evil, have amounted to the transgression of any law, for "*where there is no law there is no transgression.*" Nevertheless, the eating of that or of any other fruit, might have given them the experimental knowledge of natural good or evil, for that fruit which is agreeable and rightly adapted to our nature,

ture, imparts health, strength and vigor to it, and affords us an experiment of natural good. So on the other hand, that fruit which is disagreeable and noxious to our nature, impairs our strength, and health, and to us would be an experiment of natural evil. So that natural good or evil might have been the consequence of our premised first parents eating of that fruit, as it may have affected themselves. But should we premise, that there was in the forbidden fruit such a baneful quality, that it poisoned the original source of human nature, and implanted the seeds of mortality, yet it would have restricted it to the generation of Adam and Eve to the exclusion of the brutal, and every other part of the universal creation, who are equally obnoxious to mortality with mankind. We must therefore take a retrospective speculation into animal nature in general, and search into it from its foundation, and that previous to, and independent of the eating of the forbidden fruit; and by thus exploring the original cause of mortality, we at the same time include that of man, and consequently render Moses's account of it altogether fictitious. For should we admit, that the eating of the forbidden fruit would have rendered the nature of man mortal, had it not been so previous to the eating of it, nevertheless it could not produce mortality in a nature, which was

mortal

mortal before, for this would be the same as to suppose two original causes of mortality; which is inadmissible, as there cannot be two first causes to any event whatever.

THAT mortality was the condition of animal life universally, has been particularly argued in the 4th Section of the 3d Chapter, treating on physical evils, to which the reader is referred.

NOTWITHSTANDING the great bustle, which has been in the world concerning the "*tree of knowledge of good and evil*," and the woeful consequences of it's fruit to mankind, it is no ways probable, that so baneful a tree was ever permitted by divine providence to have existed; which should not only prove to be the death of all mankind, but that of the only begotten son of God, and eventually terminate in the damnation of the greatest part of the human species.

ACCORDING to this tradition it might well have "*repented the Lord, that he had made man on the earth;*" or at least that he had made such a tree, or that he had permitted the devil to have ensnared the two first great babies of mankind, the story of which will not bear a rational examination. For if the fruit is supposed to have been good for food, gratifying to their appetites, and pleasing to their eyes,

eyes, there can be no reason assigned for the prohibition of the eating thereof.

We will premise that the eating of this fruit must have been attended in its consequences with a physical or moral evil, or no evil at all, inasmuch as there is no third sort of evil in the universe; and as there could not have been an original intrinsic evil of either a physical or moral nature; in the use and enjoyment of that food, which Moses represented to be "*good*," and "*pleasant*," it would have been unworthy of God to have prohibited the enjoyment of it.

That God should foreclose any of his creatures from doing or enjoying, that which is in itself fit and rational, by a positive command, would be the same as to suppose that the injunction was unreasonable, and therefore such a positive prohibition is groundless. For the innocent couple could not, with any propriety, have been laid under any manner of restriction from God, respecting the gratification of their natural and consequently innocent appetites; or the refreshing and strengthening their nature in the use and nutriment of any or every of the good and desirable fruit of the garden. Had they eaten to excess, there might have been a blamable accusation against them, but in this case the punishment of a vomit

vomit would probably have atoned for the offence; as their knowledge of the proportion of food must have been learned from experience.

In this view of the case, original sin (so called) does not appear with that turpitude and hell-deserving vindictive punishment, which it is commonly from the pulpit represented to deserve. Be this as it will, provided that there was not, in the eternal reason and fitness of things, any impropriety, or evil, either of a physical or moral nature, in the use and nutrition of the fruit of the "*Tree of knowledge of good and evil,*" no after premised prohibition from God could make the use and nutrition of it to be so.

For the eternal reason and fitness of things is immutably the same, and cannot be changed, nor could there ever arise in the divine mind a reason, why they should change; inasmuch as omniscience itself had eternally comprehended all the possible relations, agreements and fitness of things, both moral and natural; so that in the order of time there could never be an addition to, diminution of, or deviation from eternal rectitude, which must have eternally had the divine sanction and support. From hence we infer, that God could never have given any positive laws to the first

first progenitors of mankind, or to any of his creatures, laying them under any other injunction or prohibition, but such as result from the reason and fitness of things; which precludes the prohibition of Moses before alluded to, leaving Adam and Eve and all other creatures on the footing of the law of nature.

SECTION II.

Pointing out the natural impossibility of all and every of the diverse Species of Biped Animals, commonly termed Man, to have lineally descended from Adam and Eve, or from the same original Progenitors; with Remarks on the uncertainty, whether the WHITE, BLACK *or* TAWNY *Nations are hereditary to* ORIGINAL SIN, *or who of them it is that needs the* ATONEMENT : *With Remarks on the Devil's beguileing Adam and Eve.*

IT is altogether improbable and manifestly contradictory to suppose, that the various and diverse nations and tribes of the earth, who walk upon two legs, and are included under the term *man*, have or possibly could have descended by ordinary generation, from the same parents, be they supposed to be who they will.

Those adventurers, who have sailed or travelled to the several parts of the globe, inform us, in their respective histories, that they find the habitable part of it more or less populated by one kind or other of rational animals, and that considered as tribes or nations, there is evidently a gradation of intellectual capacity among them, some more exalted and others lower in the scale of being; and that they are specifically diverse from each other with respect to their several animal natures, though in most respects they appear to have one sort of nature with us, viz. more like us than like the brute creation; as they walk erect, speak with man's voice, and make use of language of one sort or other, though many of them are more or less inarticulate in their manner of speaking: and in many other particulars bear a general likeness to us. They are nevertheless considered as distinct tribes or nations, are of different sizes, and as to complexion, they vary from the two extremes of white and black, in a variety of tawny mediums.

The learned nations can trace their genealogies, (though somewhat incorrect) for a considerable time, but are certain to be sooner or later lost in the retrospect thereon, and those that are of an inferior kind, or destitute of learning or science have no other knowledge of their genealogies, than they

retain

retain by their respective traditions, which are very inconsiderable. They are likewise diverse from each other in their features and in the shape of their bodies and limbs, and some are distinguished from others by their rank smell and the difference in their hair, eyes and visage, but to point out the distinctions minutely would exceed my design.

The Ethiopeans though of a shining black complexion, have regular and beautiful features, and long black hair (one of those female beauties captivated the affections of Moses) they differ very materially from the negro blacks, so that it appears impossible that they should have descended in a lineal succession from the same ancestors. They are uniformly in their respective generations essentially diverse from each other, so that an issue from a male and female of the two nations would be a mongrel, partaking partly of the kind of both nations. So also concerning the difference which subsists between us and the negroes; their black skin is but one of the particulars in which they are different from us; their many and very essential differences fully evince, that the white nations and they could not according to the law of their respective generations, have had one and the same lineal original, but that they have had their diverse kind of original progenitors.

It

It is true that the several nations and tribes of the earth, comprehended under the general term man, notwithstanding their diversity to each other in bodily shape and mental powers, bear a nearer resemblance to one another than the brute kind, for which reason they are known by one common appellation: though it is manifest that they could never have lineally descended from the same first parents, whether their names were Adam and Eve or what not.

But inasmuch as our genealogies are wholly insufficient for the purpose of explaining our respective originals or any or either of them, or to give us or any of us, considered as individuals or nations, who fall under the denomination of the term man, any manner of insight or knowledge from whom we are lineally descended, or who were our respective original ancestors, or what their names were: We must therefore reason on this subject from the facts and causes now existing, which abundantly evince, that we are of different kinds, and consequently are not of the same lineage.

But how many specifically distinct original progenitors there have been, from whom the progenies of rational animals have lineally descended, is to us unknown. Moses has given us a history of one Adam and his helpmate Eve, whom he affirms to have been the first parents of mankind; but whether they were of a white, black or tawny complexion he does not inform us; so that it remains precarious and undetermined, admitting his chronicle to be true, whether we who are of the white nations or those of the black or tawney were their descendants, for that the whole could not (as will be further argued.) And consequently it remains also uncertain whether our mortality took place in consequence of the eating the forbidding fruit. For admitting that to have been the cause of mortality to Adam and his posterity, yet it would have been restricted to his lineal descendants, and therefore could not have been the cause of mortality to those diverse and specifically distinct nations or tribes of the earth, which have had their lineage from other original progenitors, any more than to the beasts of the field.

As it remains uncertain and altogether precarious whether we are the posterity of Adam or not (admitting that there was such a man, and that he apostatized and brought mortality on himself and upon his descendents) it is equally uncertain whether it is the white, black, or tawny nations, who are guilty of original sin, so called, on the position
that

that Adam was the fœderal head and representative of his posterity, and capable of sinning for them. And lastly, the same uncertainty still remains, admitting the foregoing positions, whether it is the white, black, or tawny nations, who need an atonement for their apostacy, or whether it may not be the Etheopians, negroes or some other distinct lineage of people called mankind. In all these matters we are in the dark, (admitting the reality of the apostacy) and unable to apply the apostacy with its consequences, or the redemption with its consequences either to ourselves or to others: inasmuch as all nations and tribes of people, called man, could not possibly have been the offspring of Adam; and consequently suspence and uncertainty in these matters must unavoidably perplex and confound the believer in the christian scheme, unless they are resolved to believe, that the white nations and that of the negroes, Etheopians, Hottentots, and all other nations and tribes of the earth, who walk on two legs, sprang from the lineage of a supposed father Adam: though at the same time common sense stares every one in the face, and testifies to the contrary.

The acquaintance, which we have had with the negroe nation in particular, fully evinces the absurdity of supposing them to be of the same blood and

and kindred with ourselves. But that there are some original intrinsic and hereditary diversity or essential difference between us and them, which cannot be ascribed to time, climate, or to mere contingence.

For that we and they are in nature inherently and uniformly diverse from each other in our respective constitutions and generations, and have been so time immemorial. So that the negroes are of a different species of rational beings from us, and consequently must have had their distinct lineal original; was it not so, there could be no such thing as a mongrel or mulatto, who is occasioned by a copulation between the males and the females of the respective diverse species, the issue partaking of both natures.

Had all the nations and tribes of the world, who are denominated rational, been lineally descended from the same progenitors, mongrelism could never have taken place among them, as in this case they would have been all of the same kind: from hence we infer, that they have had their respective original progenitors. The Dutch colony at the Cape of Good Hope, have enacted laws to punish with death such of their Dutch subjects as may be convicted of copulating with the Hottentots;

Hottentots; for that their nature is adjudged to be of an inferior species to theirs, so that mixing their nature with them would essentially degenerate and debase their own.

Although it is manifestly absurd to trace the geneology of every of the species of two-legged intelligent animals from one and the same progenitors. Admitting every of them to have lineally descended from a premised father Adam; yet the scripture story of the apostacy is in itself incredidle.

To suppose that the craft of Hell, by the interposition of its infernals, should have been permitted by divine providence to have been exerted against a premised new made couple, is inadmissible. It appears from Moses, that they were destitute of learning or instruction; having been formed at full size, in the space of one day, and consequently void of experience; from hence we may with propriety infer, that they would have been but poorly able to cope with the wiles of the Devil; who in this progressive age of the world is allowed to be more than a match for any one man (especially if in connection with a woman.) One man bears no more proportion to him than Jonas did to the whale, which swallowed him.

THE Clergy have been combined against the devil for more than seventeen hundred years last past, and it is their constant cry that he has been all this time gaining ground of them, seducing more souls to hell, than they have savingly converted to Heaven; so as that we are told, the former is much more popular than the latter.

THIS infernal monster, who has so disturbed our world, is said to have made war in heaven, he is called by the name of the dragon, and is described to be of a red colour, whose tail drew a third part of the stars of heaven, and cast them to the ground; "*And there was war in Heaven, Michael and his Angels fought against the Dragon, and the Dragon fought and his Angels.*"

WHEN we consider, what a diabolical, powerful malicious, spiteful, designing, cunning and ensnaring rascal the Devil, Satan, the Dragon or the old Serpent is represented to be, we cannot reconcile it to divine providence to have permitted so pernicious and artful a being to have transformed himself into the likeness of a serpent, thereby capacitating himself to work his premeditated villainy with a woman who just before had been taken out of Adam's broad-side, whose experience had been none or trifling, and by deluding her pave the way to enfnare Adam alfo, together with their numerous offspring. This is too much craft to have been permitted to be exercifed towards fuch an innocent ignorant and new made twain, as there is no proportion between the knowledge, malice and fkill of the tempter on the one part, and the innocency and imbecillity of the vanquifhed on the other. From whence we infer, that divine goodnefs never permitted thofe tranfactions of Satan. But admitting the facts, Adam and Eve had an undo̲   ̲ plead non-age, and lay the blame on   ho, according to Mofes, was the efficient caufe of the apoftacy.

SECTION III.

Of the Origin *of the* Devil *or of* Moral Evil, *and of the* Devil's *talking with* Eve; *with a Remark that the Doctrine of* APOSTACY *is the* FOUNDATION *of* CHRISTIANITY.

INASMUCH as the devil is reprefented to have had fo great and undue an influence in bringing about the apoftacy of Adam, and ftill to continue his temptations to mankind, it may be worth our while to examine into the nature and manner of his being and the mode of his exhibiting his temptations.   AND

And first we will premise, that the devil is neither self-existent, eternal, nor infinite; and

Secondly, that God never made him a devil; and now there remains but one possible way more to account for his existence as a devil, which is, to suppose him to have been made a good and probationary finite being, and that by a misimprovement of his talents, or by making a bad or immoral use of his liberty, which is the same as departing from moral rectitude, he acquired the opposite habit of sin and wickedness; which constitutes a vicious or wicked being, whom we may as well call by the name of devil, satan, or the old serpent, as by any other name; and thus accounting for a devil (which is the same as giving a diffinition of the origin of moral evil) does at the same time prescribe a way whereby any and every of mankind, or any other finite mental beings, may become vicious or sinful, the same as the devil has been previously supposed to do, in order to have made himself a devil, and that altogether independent of any supposed devil or of any of his temptations. For if this supposed creature whom we call the devil, was originally a salvable probationary being, and by a bad use of liberty became a sinner, why may not any other probationary creatures, by a bad use of their liberty, become sinners also, and that as free from any influence or seducement of any supposed

devil,

devil, as the premised devil himself may be supposed to have been from the influence or seduction of any previous devil or tempter.

On these principles the scheme of some first tempter or devil is chimerical and without foundation, and we may as well account for our own temptations or sins as for his; for the question, run it up to the origin of moral evil, terminates the same in a supposed devil as in man or any other agent of trial whatever. For all possible moral evil that ever did or can take place in the infinitude of the creation of God, is neither more nor less than the deviation of moral agents from moral rectitude; and such deviations take place in consequence of a wrong and vicious use of liberty: This is the only possible origin of moral evil, and is equally possible to all probationary agents, as there always was, and ever will be the same liability to transgression or sin in all finite probationists, as to any premised devil. And to this the Apostle James agrees: *"But every man is tempted when he is drawn away of his own lust and enticed."*

Undoubtedly there has been a greater variety in the order of intelligent beings, in God's immense creation, than we are able to enumerate, who may every of them more or less have transgressed the rules of eternal unerring order and reason

son, which is the same as moral fitness; and who may have been or will be restored to a participation of morality, and consequently to a rational happiness again, as has been argued in Chapter 3, treating on the subject of infinite and eternal punishment; which is needless to be here repeated, for it is easier to the reader, if he should be so minded to satisfy himself on this subject, to turn to that Chapter and read it, than it is for me to write it over again.

But if it be admitted, that the creature called the Devil (who must be supposed to be under the divine government, as much as any other creature) could become inflexible, and perpetually rebellious and wicked; incapable of a restoration, and consequently subjected to eternal punishment (which to me appears to be inconsistent with the wisdom and goodness of the divine government, and the nature, end and design of a probationary agent) yet it would by no means follow from hence, that so stubbornly wicked and incorrigible a creature, would have been permitted, by the providence of God, to tempt, ensnare or seduce mankind, by plying his temptations to their weak side. One thing we are certain of, viz. that the Devil does not visit our world in a bodily or organized shape, and there is not in nature a second way, in which it it is possible for him to make known himself to us, or that he could have done it to our progenitors, nor could he ever have communicated to them or to us, any temptations or ideas whatever, any otherwise than by making a proper application to our external senses, so that we could understand him, or receive the ideas of his temptations in a natural way. For supernatural intercourse with the world of spirits or invisible beings has been shown to be contradictory and impossible in the arguments contained in the sixth Chapter, to which the reader is referred. Those arguments will hold equally good as applied to either good or evil spirits, and are demonstrative of the utter impossibility of mankind's holding any manner of intercourse or intelligence with them.

But should we premise, that, according to the history of Moses, it was in the power of the Devil to assume a bodily shape, and that he did in very deed transform himself into the figure, likeness and organization of a snake, yet by and with that organ he could not have spoken or uttered the following articulate words, which Moses charged him with; *to wit,* " *And the serpent said unto the woman, ye shall not surely die, for God doth know, that in the day ye eat, thereof, that your eyes shall be opened, and ye shall be as gods knowing good and evil.*"

A3

As the serpent is by nature incapable of speech, it must have put the Devil into the same predicament, admitting that he transformed himself into the same figure or likeness, and consequently for want of the proper and adequate organs of speech, he must necessarily have been incapable of any other language than that of rattling his tail, and therefore could never have spoken those recited words unto Eve, or communicated any of his temptations unto her by language, while in that similitude. However, admitting that the first parents of mankind were beguiled by the wiles of the Devil to transgress the divine law, yet of all transgressions it would have been the most trivial (considered under all the particular circumstances of it) that the mind of man can conceive of.

Who in the exercise of reason can believe, that Adam and Eve by eating of such a spontaneous fruit could have incurred the eternal displeasure of God, as individuals? Or that the divine vindictive justice should extend to their un-offending offspring then unborn? And sentence the human progeny to the latest posterity to everlasting destruction? As chimerical as Moses's representation of the apostacy of man manifestly appears to be, yet it is the very basis, on which christianity is founded, and is anounced in the New-Testament to be the very cause why Jesus Christ came into this world, "*that he might destroy the works of the Devil*," and redeem fallen man, *alias*, the elect, from the condemnation of the apostacy; which leads me to the consideration of the doctrine of imputation.

Chapter

Chapter XII.

Of Imputation.

SECTION I.

Imputation cannot change, alienate or transfer the personal Demerit of Sin, and personal Merit of Virtue to others, who were not active therein, although this Doctrine supposes an alienation thereof.

THE doctrine of imputation according to the christian scheme, consists of two parts; first, of imputation of the apostacy of Adam and Eve to their posterity, commonly called original sin; and secondly, of the imputation of the merits or righteousness of Christ, who in scripture is called the second Adam, to mankind, or to the elect. This is a concise definition of the doctrine, and which will undoubtedly be admitted to be a just one by every denomination of men, who are acquainted with christianity whether they adhere to it or not. I therefore proceed to illustrate and explain the doctrine by transcribing a short, but very pertinent conversation, which in the early years of my Manhood I had with a Calvinistical divine, but previously remark, that I was educated in what is commonly called the Armenian principles, and among other tenets. to reject the doctrine of original sin, this was the point at issue between the clergyman and me. In my turn I opposed the docrine of original sin with philosophical reasonings, and as I thought had confuted the doctrine. The Reverend gentleman heard me through patiently, and with candor replied, " your metaphysical reasonings are not to the purpose; inasmuch as you are a christian, and hope and expect to be saved by the imputed righteousness of Christ to you; for you may as well be imputedly sinful as imputedly righteous. Nay said he, if you hold to the doctrine of satisfaction and atonement by Christ, by so doing you pre-suppose the doctrine of apostacy or original sin to be in fact true; for said he, if mankind were not in a ruined and condemned state by nature, there could have been no need of

a

a redeemer, but each individual of them would have been accountable to his creator and judge upon the basis of his own moral agency. Further observing, that upon philosophical principles it was difficult to account for the doctrine of original sin, or of original righteousness, yet as they were plain fundamental doctrines of the christian faith, we ought to assent to the truth of them, and that from the divine authority of revelation. Notwithstanding, said he, if you will give me a philosophical explanation of original imputed righteousness, which you profess to believe, and expect salvation by, then I will return you a philosophical explanation of the doctrine of original sin; for it is plain, said he, that your objections lie with equal weight against original imputed righteousness, as against original imputed sin." Upon which I had the candor to acknowledge to the worthy ecclesiastic, that upon the christian plan, I perceived that the argument had fairly terminated against me. For at that time I dared not distrust the infallibility of revelation, much more to dispute it. However, this conversation was uppermost in my mind for several months after, and after many painful searches and researches after the truth respecting the doctrine of imputation, resolved at all events to abide the dicision of rational argument in the premises, and on a full examination of both parts of the doctrine, rejected the whole; for on a fair scrutiny, I found, that I must concede to it entirely or not at all, or else believe inconsistently as the clergyman had argued.

Having opened and explained the doctrine we proceed argumentatively to consider it. Imputation of sin or righteousness includes an alteration or tranferring of the personal merits or demerits of sin or righteousness, from those who may be supposed to have been active in the one or the other, to others, who are premised not to have been active therein, otherwise it would not answer the Bible notion of imputation. For if sin or righteousness, vice or virtue, are imputable only to their respective personal proficients or actors, in this case original sin must have been imputed to Adam and Eve, to the exclusion of their posterity, and the righteousness of Christ as exclusively imputed to himself, precluding all others therefrom; so that both the sin of the first Adam and the righteousness of the second, would, on this stating of imputation, have been matters which respect merely the agency, or the demerits or merits of the two respective Adams themselves, and in which we could have had no blame, reward or concern, any more than in the building of Babel.

This

This then is the question that determines the sequel of the dispute for or against the doctrine of imputation; viz. Whether the personal merit or demerit of mankind, that is to say their virtue or vice, righteousness or wickedness can be alienated, imputed to, or transferred from one person to another, or not? If any should object against this stating of the question now in dispute, it would be the same in reality as disputing against the doctrine of imputation itself, for imputation must transfer or change the personal merit or demerit of the sin or righteousness of mankind or not do it; if it does not do it, the whole notion of original sin or of righteousness, as being imputed from the first and second Adams to mankind, is without foundation, consequently, if there is any reality in the doctrine of imputation, it must needs transfer or change the guilt of original sin, or of the apostacy of Adam and Eve, to their posterity, or otherwise they could need no atonement or imputative righteousness, as a remedy therefrom, but every individual of "mankind would have stood accountable to their creator and judge on the basis of their own moral agency," which is undoubtedly the true state of the case, respecting all rational and accountable beings; so that if the transferring of the individual merits or demerits of one person to another, is not contained in the act or doctrine of imputation

putation, it contains nothing at all, but is a sound without a meaning, and after all the talk which has been in the world about it, we must finally adopt the old proverb, *viz.* every tub stands upon its own bottom.

SECTION II.

The Punishment of Sin, or the Reward of Virtue, as it respects the Mind, can have no positive Existence abstractly considered from the Demerits of the one or Merit of the other; with an Explanation of the Scripture Doctrine of IMPUTATION.

THOSE who believe in the doctrine of imputation, will consequently undoubtedly suppose, that the sinful act of the apostacy of Adam was imputed to his posterity, as soon as the order of generation permitted them a positive existence; for 'til that time they could not have been denominated either guilty or innocent, any more than mere non entity. So that if we admit the suffering and atonement of Christ and the imputed sin of Adam to his lineal descendants, those generations which have been born since Christ's crucifixion, cannot be made partakers of the atonement; for it is since that we have been made imputedly sinners, if at all

and

and therefore could not be included in the atonement which was more than seventeen hundred years ago.

We will however consider this doctrine, as it respected the generations of mankind, previous to the sufferings of Christ. If Jesus Christ suffered for the imputed sin of Adam to the generations of mankind, previous to the era of the atonement, it follows of consequence, that the demerit of original sin was changed and transferred from those respective generations of Adam (or from the elect) and imputed to be the sin of Christ, and for which he suffered; so that the imputation of sin consists of imputation and re-imputation; *viz.* the imputation of Adam's sin to his posterity, and the re-imputation of it to the person of Jesus Christ.

Those who subscribe to this doctrine believe, that God "*laid on him the iniquity of us all,*" at least of the elect; and that "*by his stripes they were healed;*" and that "*Christ was bruised for their iniquities, and wounded for their transgressions.*" They will suppose that the suffering of Christ in the garden, upon the cross, and in his death, in the agonies of which he is said to have borne the vindictive wrath of God, was for original re-imputed sin.

None

None who adhere to Christianity will suppose, that Christ suffered merely on his own account, or that he was any otherwise a sinner than imputedly so. Therefore all the sufferings of Christ must be admitted to have been wholly to redeem more or less of mankind from the supposed ruin and condemnation of the apostacy. This I take to be the Scripture notion respecting the imputation and re-imputation of sin.

But it may be objected, that it was merely the punishment of original sin which was re-imputed to Christ, and not the guilt or criminality of it; but this would be only punishing the innocent in the person of Christ, and the guilty would be guilty still, and still ought to be punished for the sin for which Christ is supposed to have once suffered the penalty: so that there would, on this position, be a double punishment inflicted for the sin of the apostacy, the one on Christ, and the other on those he is said to have redeemed; and consequently, the suffering of Christ would be of no avail; for the original cause of punishment must have consisted in the criminal nature; guilt or demerit of sin, and there would forever remain the same reason why mankind or any of them should be punished for it, as long as they remain sinners, as there was previous to the premised suffering of Christ for it; and

and thus, by supposing the imputation of punishment, abstractedly from the sin, and guilt, which demerited it, could be of no avail to mankind, or to any of them, but would leave them in the same condition in which such an atonement found them: so on the other hand a supposed imputation of the consolation and mental happiness of Christ's righteousness, without imputing the real merit or principle of it, would be contradictory and impossible; for the want of the real merit or principle of virtue or righteousness, is the cause of misery or punishment, in a moral sense; so that the identical merit or principle of the righteousness of Christ must needs have been imputed to believers, otherwise they could not receive any consolation or intellectual happiness therefrom: for that a principle of virtue or righteousness is pre-requisitely necessary to a moral happiness.

To suppose the existence of such an happiness, without its pre-requisite, would be the same, as to suppose an effect without a cause, which is too absurd to pretend to. From this we infer, that the identical act or demerit of original sin, or the sin of Adam, according to the christian plan, must have been transferred, made over, or imputed to his posterity, and from them, or the elect, reimputed to be the identical act and demerit of Jesus Christ,

Christ, and that he suffered and atoned for it, and lastly, that the merit or identical act of the righteousness of Christ, should be made over, transferred or imputed to mankind, or to the elect, in order to redeem them from the condemnation of the apostacy, commonly called original Sin, to the end that they should be restored to the favor and Salvation of God.

SECTION III.

The IMPUTATION of MORAL GOOD or EVIL is incompatible with our own consciousness of the one or of the other of those agencies, and therefore cannot affect our mental Happiness or Misery.

THAT moral good or evil, with their respective concomitant mental happiness or miseries, are the personal and inherent merit or demerit of the respective individual agents, who make proficiency in either the one or the other of those opposite agencies, is one of the self evident axioms, which can be made but little if any plainer, or more evident by argumentation than by the mere stating therof, and if true over turn the doctrine of imputation.

IT is repugnant to the first perceptions of common-sense to suppose, that the body of A and the body of B which are the bodies of two individuals, are nevertheless one and the same body: or that the mind, which actuates the body of A, is the same, which is united to and actuates the body of B; common sense will further agree that A and B have a distinct exclusive personality in their respective bodies and minds, and that the one is not the other, and consequently that the doings, actions, or agency of the mind and body of A, are not the identical doings, actions or agency of the mind and body of B: from hence we infer, that A's virtuous or vicious agency, or his proficiencies in either virtue or vice, is his own personal merit or demerit, to the exclusion of all others. And further that A, and A only, in truth, justice and equity, should be either commended or discommended, rewarded or punished, according as his agency may be supposed to be either virtuous or vicious, or to deserve praise or blame, happiness or misery; and that the same is true of every individual of mankind.

THE argument applies as justly to the agency of a premised Adam and Eve, as to their supposed posterity, so that, there could be no more propriety, justice or possibility of imputing the act, doing or agency of original sin, or the penal consequences of it to the then unborn offspring of Adam, than there would be in imputing the agency of the man in the moon to them. The same impropriety, injustice and impossibility would attend the supposed imputation of original righteousness, commonly called the righteousness of Christ, to any or all of mankind; for if that righteousness is Christ's, it is a downright contradiction to suppose that it is the righteousness of mankind or of the elect; the same as to suppose that the righteousness of A is the righteousness of B, which has just before been evinced to be impossible. But why should A be commended or discommended, punished or rewarded for his virtuous or vicious agency, any more than B, or any other person whatever? because A's conduct whether it be virtuous or vicious, good or evil, is, in the truth, justice and equity of things, his own individual and inherent property; for that A's principle, disposition, quality and temper of mind, be they what they will, is in truth his identical merit or demerit, exclusively, which we may properly call his property. For mankind, considered as individuals, may as well be said to have a property in their personal actions or habits, virtues or vices, as in lands and chattels, though the latter may be alienated or transferred, but the former not, because that A and he only is conscious of the state and condition of his own mind, his good or bad dispositions, habits and intentions, joy or grief, happiness or misery of body or mind. The same may be said of every individual of mankind, that we are not and cannot be conscious of each others consciousness, and consequently cannot be intelligently happy or miserable for what another does, suffers or enjoys. Those, who are co-temporaries, may be remotely happy or miserable by way of sympathy, or in consequence of the management of the public interests of the community or society, to which they belong; but not by way of merit or desert. We cannot be miserable for the sin of Adam, or happy in the righteousness of Christ, in which transactions we were no ways accessory or assisting as accomplices, or otherwise concerned; and are not at all conscious of those antient matters; all we know about it is from the history of Moses, the Evangelist's and Apostles: nor is it possible for us to feel ourselves guilty of any remorse of conscience, concerning a premised eating a pleasant apple, which may have been the spontaneous production of nature in paradise. Nor on the other hand are we at all conscious of any merit or virtue, in consequence of any supposed suffering or mediation for the premised crime of eating that apple.

WHAT have those old and obsolete matters to do with our virtues or vices, or with our consciousness of righteousness or wickedness, happiness or misery, reward or blame? For it is manifestly absurd to suppose, that moral good or evil can possibly be imputed from one person to another, except it was in nature possible that one person could be conscious of another's consciousness.

But inasmuch as the laws of nature, which are the laws of God, forbid it, we may therefore infer the impossibility of the reality of the scripture doctrine of imputation. We will premise, that a great and tremendous sin was imputed to me, or to the reader, or to us both, and at the same time we had no consciousness or knowledge of it, or of its punishment; would any one suppose, that we should not be as composedly and mentally happy, as though it had not been imputed to us? In my opinion it would be a matter of perfect indifference to us, whether sin or righteousness, goodness or badness was imputed to us, or what degrees of either of them, if so be we had no sensation, perception or consciousness of it.

To suppose it in nature possible, that moral good and evil with the rewards and punishment naturally concommitant with them, respectively could be imputed or transferred from one individual

dual to another, is so great an absurdity, that it wants a name; for it is saying neither more or less, than that there is no intrinsic or essential distinction between the personal merit or demerit of mankind; so that admitting the doctrine of imputation; the wicked might as likely share the joys and salvation of the righteous, as the righteous themselves; and the righteous be subjected to the miserable condition of the wicked, which is altogether preposterous. If the advocates for imputation should object, that it would be incompatible with the justice of God, thus universally to impute the sin of the wicked to the righteous, or the righteousness of the righteous to the wicked, with the rewards and punishments, naturally and respectively connected with them, it would be the same as objecting against the whole scripture doctrine of imputation. For if it is possible, that imputation should take place in one instance, why not in another, and so on until it becomes universal; so that the advocates for imputation must admit the possibility of its taking place universally, or not at all, lest, by advancing reason and argument, they overturn the fundamental doctrine of christianity; for the reason, justice and fitness of things, is the same, whether applied to one instance of imputation or more, or to a universal preposterous application thereof, which is too glaringly absurd to demand a serious

argument

argument for its confutation, was it not, that great numbers of mankind, learned as well as unlearned, have embraced it as the ground of their religion and faith.

SECTION IV.

The MORAL RECTITUDE *of Things forecloses the Act of* IMPUTATION.

IMPUTATION confounds virtue and vice, and saps the very foundation of moral government, both divine and human. Abstract the idea of personal merit and demerit, from the individuals of mankind, justice would be totally blind, and truth would be nullified; or at least excluded from any share in the administration of government. Admitting that moral good and evil has taken place in the system of rational agents, yet, on the position of imputation, it would be impossible, that a retribution of justice should be made to them by God or by man, except it be according to their respective personal merits and demerits; which would fix us upon the basis of our own moral agency and accountability, and preclude the imputation of righteousness or sin.

TRUTH respects the reality of things, as they are in their various complicated and distinct natures, and necessarily conforms to all facts and realities. It exists in, by and with every thing that does exist, and that which does not and cannot exist, is fictitious and void of truth, as is the doctrine of imputation. It is a truth that some of the individuals of mankind are virtuous, and that others are vicious, and it is a truth, that the former merit peace of conscience and praise, and the latter horror of conscience and blame: for God has so constituted the nature of things, that moral goodness, naturally and necessarily tends to happiness in a moral sense, and moral evil as necessarily tends to the contrary; and as truth respects every thing, as being what it is, it respects nature, as God has constituted it, with its tendencies, dispositions, aptitudes and laws; and as the tendency of virtue is to mental happiness, and vice the contrary, they fall under the cognizance of truth, as all other facts necessarily do; which tendencies will for ever preclude imputation, by making us morally happy or miserable according to our works.

TRUTH respects the eternal rules of unalterable rectitude and fitness, which comprehends all virtue, goodness and true happiness; and as sin and wickedness is no other but a deviation from the rules of eternal unerring order and reason, so truth respects it as an unreasonable, unfit, unrighteous and unhappy deviation from moral rectitude, naturally tending to misery. This order of nature, comprehended under the term of truth, must have been of all others the wisest and best; in fine it must have been absolutely perfect; for this order and harmony of things, could not have resulted from any thing short of infinite wisdom, goodness and power, by which it is also upheld; and all just ideas of equity, or of natural or moral fitness must be learned from nature, and predicated on it; and nature predicated on the immutable perfection of a God; and to suppose that imputation, in any one instance, has taken place, is the same as to suppose, that the eternal order, truth, justice, equity and fitness of things has been changed, and if so, the God of nature must needs have been a changeable being, and liable to alter his justice or order of nature, which is the same thing: for without the alteration of nature, and the tendency of it, there could be no such thing as imputation, but every of the individuals of mankind would be ultimately happy or miserable, according as their respective proficiencies may be supposed to be either good or evil, agreeable to the order and tendency of nature, before alluded to. For all rational and accountable agents must stand or fall upon the principles of the laws of nature, except imputation alters the nature and tendency of

things;

things; of which the immutability of a God cannot admit.

FROM what has been already argued on this subject, we infer, that as certain as the individuals of mankind, are the proprietors of their own virtues or vices, so certain, the doctrine of imputation cannot be true. Furthermore, the supposed act or agency of imputing or transferring the personal merit or demerit of moral good or evil, *alias*, the sin of the first Adam, or the righteousness of the second Adam, to others of mankind, cannot be the act or exertion of either the first or second Adam, from whom original sin and righteousness is said to have been imputed: Nor can it be the act or doing of those individuals, to whom the supposed merit or demerit of original sin or righteousness is premised to be imputed; so that both Adam and each individual of mankind are wholly excluded from acting any part in the premised act of imputation; and are supposed to be altogether passive in the matter, and consequently it necessarily follows, that if there ever was such an act as that of imputation, it must have been the immediate and sovereign act of God, to the preclusion of the praise or blame of man. But to suppose, that God can impute the virtue or vice of the person of A, to be the virtue or vice of the person of B, is the same as to suppose, that God can impute or change

truth

truth into falsehood, or falsehood into truth, or that he can reverse the nature of moral rectitude itself, which is inadmissible. But admitting, that imputation was in the power and at the option of man, it is altogether probable that they would have been very sparing in imputing merit and happiness, but might nevertheless have been vastly liberal in imputing demerit and misery, from one to another, which is too farcical.

SECTION V.

A state of Condemnation equally affected the Character of CHRIST, *as far as he may be supposed to have partaken of the nature of* MAN, *as well as the rest of* MANKIND; *with Remarks on the Atonement and Satisfaction for* ORIGINAL SIN.

THE doctrine of imputation is in every point of view incompatible with the moral perfections of God. We will premise, that the race of Adam in their respective generations was guilty of the apostacy, and obnoxious to the vindictive justice and punishment of God, and accordingly doomed to either an eternal or a temporary punishment therefor, which is the Bible representation of the matter. What possibility could there have been of reversing the divine decree? It must be supposed

posed to have been just, or it could not have had the divine sanction, and if so, a reversal of it would be unjust. But it would be still a greater injustice to lay the blame and vindictive punishment of a guilty race of condemned sinners upon an innocent and inoffensive being, for in this case the guilty would be exempted from their just punishment, and the innocent unjustly suffer for it, which holds up to view two manifest injustices; the first consists in not doing justice to the guilty, and the second in actually punishing the innocent, which instead of atoning for sin, would add sin to sin, or injustice to injustice; and after all, if it was ever just, that the race of Adam should have been punished for the imputed sin of their premised original Ancestor, be that punishment what it will, it is so still, notwithstanding the atonement, for the eternal justice and reason of things can never be altered. Thus justice always defeats the possibility of satisfaction for sin by way of a Mediator.

PROVIDED any advocates for imputation should explain it differently from what I have done, in order to clear it from the inconsistencies previously pointed out, by premising, that as all mankind, including both soul and body, descended from Adam by natural generation, are therefore to be considered but as so many individual parts of the

same

same Adam, and consequently became guilty of original sin, not by imputation of it from Adam to them, but by being actually Adam, are to be considered as actually guilty. And as "*Christ took not on him the nature of Angels, but the seed of Abraham,*" or nature of man, and thereby became one of the members of the extensive nature of Adam, and actually guilty of original sin, in which nature he suffered for it, not by imputation, but in consequence of his being actually a part of Adam himself: Such an exposition of imputation, explains it all away, and holds up to view no other sin, but what is actual, or no other punishment but what resulted from it, as just. But admiting that Christ was of the sinful nature of Adam, and that he suffered for his own actual transgression, yet this could not extend the satisfaction of his suffering for sin any farther than to himself. To suppose his sufferings to be applied to any other parts of this great and extensive Adam, who is premised to have lived and died in every generation of mankind to this day, would re-fix us in the doctrine of imputation. For there could be no justice in laying all the blame and punishment of original sin, or the sin of Adam on that part of Adam only who existed in the person of Christ; when on this position of an Adam, many millions of other persons (thereof) in their respective generations and

periods

periods of existence must be supposed to be as sinfully guilty, as the person of Christ, on this thesis, may be premised to be, and consequently, according to justice, must suffer as he has done, for otherwise we come within our former explanation of the scripture doctrine of the imputation, of the sin and righteousness of one to others, which has been previously confuted.

That physical evils may and have been propagated by natural generation, none can dispute, for that the facts themselves are obvious. But that moral evil can be thus propagated, is altogether chimerical, for we are not born criminals, nor on the contrary are we born morally good, so as to be commended for it. To be innocently or harmlessly good, is as much as the state of nature can admit of. To be praise-worthy, requires that we should be cogitatively, designedly and actually virtuous, and that from principle. We are not to be commended or discommended, punished or rewarded in a moral sense, merely for being born, or for belonging to this, that or the other race of creatures; and if we partake of the same kind of nature, as Adam did, yet he and we are not personally or identically the same; nor is his agency and ours the same, any more than the agency of A, can be the agency of B, as before argued;

ed. Simple innocence is a sufficiency of righteousness for a state of childhood, but from a state of maturity, the law of nature demands a habit of virtue, a deficiency whereof is punished with a want or negation of intelligent happiness; and positive mental evil. But to return to our subject; admitting that mankind are sinners by nature, and in a state of condemnation, it would necessarily follow, that Jesus Christ was in the same predicament, for the scriptures inform us, that "*he took not on him the nature of Angels, but the seed of Abraham,*" or nature of man: so far therefore as he was of the nature of man he must have been either innocent or guilty, as the nature of man may be supposed to be. If the nature of man was innocent, there was no need of a redeemer, but if was naturally guilty and under condemnation of everlasting damnation, as some believe, it would follow, that Christ, considered as a sinful creature, and under that condemnation, instead of suffering three days and three nights in hell for the sins or condemnation of mankind, or the elect, must have suffered forever on account of the sin and condemnation of his nature, as a descendent from Adam. And as the divine nature is at an infinite remove from sin or suffering, it was impossible, that Christ could have suffered as a God, therefore his suffering, merely as man, for three days and three

three nights would have been but trifling, had it been equally divided among the proprietors of original sin, *viz.* among the whole progeny of Adam.

THAT Christ as a sponsor, according to the Christian scheme, must have suffered the same quantity or degree of punishment, as the posterity of Adam must have done, had it not been for a premised redeemer's suffering of it, will probably be conceded to by all parties. For if the punishment may be supposed to have been cancelled, as inflicted on the person of the sponsor, why might it not as well have been abated, as it respected mankind at large, for whom it is supposed that Christ had become sponsible? Or if it was possible that the punishment could have been in the least mitigated, why not the whole remitted, without the ceremony of a suffering mediator?

IF the sin of the apostacy was imputed from Adam and Eve to their posterity, they must have been acquited from it themselves, and discharged therefrom either in whole or in part, as the original sin may be supposed to have been, in whole or in part imputed to their offspring; for it is contradictory to suppose that sin could be imputed and not imputed at the same time, which must have

been

been the case provided it was imputed from the first parents of mankind to their posterity, and they were not acquited or discharged therefrom in consequence thereof. Nor could the posterity of Adam and Eve be required to suffer a greater penalty or weight of punishment, admitting that original sin was imputed to them, than Adam and Eve must have done, and was able to have sustained, had they borne the penalty of it themselves, which would have been of no considerable consequence, had it been equally divided and inflicted among their numerous descendants; likely it would have been no more than the prick of a pin to each individual.

But if the penalty is supposed to be merely of the mental kind, there could not be any punishment at all inflicted on the race of Adam, as we cannot be conscious of the guilt or blame of original sin, in the transaction whereof we had no manner of agency or concernment.

SECTION VI.

The Person of JESUS CHRIST, *considered in a variety of different Characters, each of which are incompatible with a Participation of the Divine Nature. That a* REDEMPTION, *wrought out by inflicting the Demerits of* SIN *upon the* INNOCENT, *would be* UNJUST, *and that it could contain no* MERCY *or* GOODNESS *to the universality of Being, considered inclusively.*

IT is impossible that God should suffer or change, or the person of Jesus Christ, as far as he may be supposed to be of the essence of God; for the absolute perfection of the divine nature exempts it from suffering, weakness, or any manner of imperfection. Therefore Jesus Christ, in the nature in which he is premised to have suffered, could not be God.

BUT on the position that Christ was a mere creature, as the *Arians* believe, though ever so exalted, all the obedience or righteousness he could have acquired or attained to, would have been necessary for the discharge of his own duty as an accountable creature. Admitting that he had imputed it to others, he must have been miserable himself for the deficiency thereof, except his righteousness had been acquired by works of supererrogation, or except he is supposed to be capable of a moral happiness without righteousness or goodness, and if he may be supposed to have been capable of such a happiness without those moral qualifications requisite thereto, why might not mankind in general have been capable of it upon the same footing of deficiency, without his imputed righteousness? However it is no way probable admitting it to be possible, that any exalted, wise and understanding being would part with the essentials of his own happiness; *viz.* his morality to others; and for them, and in their stead, actually suffer a great and dreadful weight of misery, and thus at an equal expence of his own happiness and goodness, redeem a race of sinful and guilty creatures; for there could not on this thesis, be any advantage to the system of finite beings, considered collectively, or any mercy or goodness displayed to being in general. What mercy would there be in reprieving or restoring a race of condemned creatures from misery, by inflicting an equal condemnation or punishment on a premised innocent and exalted finite being, which should have been inflicted on the guilty? Humanity obliges us to be kind and benevolent, but never obliges us to suffer for criminals (nor could such a suffering

excuse

excuse them from their just demerits) but justice and self-preservation forbids it; for all finite beings are under greater obligations to themselves than to any other creature or race of creatures whatever; so that there could be no justice or goodness in one being's suffering for another, nor is it at all compatible with reason to suppose, that God was the contriver of such a propitiation.

THE practice of imputing one person's crime to another, in capital offences among men, so that the innocent should suffer for the guilty, has never yet been introduced into any court of judicature in the world, or so much as practised in any civilised country; And the manifest reason in this, as in all other cases of imputation, is the same, viz. it confounds personal merit and de-merit.

THE murderer ought to die for the demerit of his crime, but if the court exclude the idea of personal demerit (guilt being always the inherent property of the guilty and of them only) they might as well sentence one person to death for the murder as another: for justice would be wholly blind was it not predicated on the idea of the fact of a personal demerit, on the identical person who was guilty of the murder: nor is it possible to reward merit abstractly considered from its personal agents. These are facts that universally hold good in human governments. The same reasons cannot fail to hold good in the divine mind as in that of the human, for the rules of justice are essentially the same whether applied to the one or to the other, having their uniformity in the eternal truth and reason of things.

But it is frequently objected, that inasmuch as one person can pay, satisfy and discharge a cash debt for another, redeem him from prison and set him at liberty, therefore Jesus Christ might become sponsible for the sins of mankind, or of the elect, and by suffering their punishment atone for them, and free them from their condemnation. But it should be considered, that comparisons darken or reflect light upon an argument according as they are either pertinent or impertinent thereto; we will therefore examine the comparison, and see if it will with propriety apply to the atonement.

Upon the Christian scheme, Christ the son was God, and equal with God the father, or with God the Holy Ghost, and therefore original sin must be considered to be an offence equally against each of the persons of the premised Trinity, and being of a criminal nature could not be discharged or satisfied by cash or produce, as debts of a civil contract

contract are, but by suffering; and it has already been proved to be inconsistent with the divine or human government, to inflict the punishment of the guilty upon the innocent, though one man may discharge another's debt in cases where lands, chattles or cash are adequate to it; but what capital offender was ever discharged by such commodities?

STILL there remains a difficulty on the part of Christianity, in accounting for one of the persons in the premised trinity's satisfying a debt due to the impartial justice of the unity of the three persons. For God the son to suffer the condemnation of guilt in behalf of man, would not only be unjust in itself, but incompatible with his divinity, and the retribution of the justice of the premised trinity of persons in the godhead (of whom God the son must be admitted to be one) toward mankind; for this would be the same as to suppose God to be judge, criminal and executioner, which is inadmissible.

BUT should we admit for argument's sake, that God suffered for original sin, yet taking into one complex idea the whole mental system of being, universally, both finite and infinite, there could have been no display of grace, mercy, or goodness to being in general, in such a supposed redemption

of

of mankind; inasmuch as the same quantity or degree of evil is supposed to have taken place upon being, universally considered, as would have taken place, had finite individuals, or the race of Adam, suffered according to their respective demerits.

SHOULD we admit that there is a trinity of persons in the divine essence, yet the one could not suffer without the other, for essence cannot be divided in suffering, any more than in enjoyment. The essence of God is that which includes the divine nature, and the same identical nature must necessarily partake of the same glory, honor, power, wisdom, goodness and absolute uncreated and unlimited perfection, and is equally exempted from weakness and suffering. Therefore, as certain as Christ suffered he was not God, but whether he is supposed to be God or man, or both, he could not in justice have suffered for original sin, which must have been the demerit of its perpetrators as before argued.

SUPPOSING Christ to have been both God and man, he must have existed in two distinct essences, *viz.* the essence of God and the essence of man. And if he existed in two distinct and seperate essences, there could be no union between the divine

vine and human natures. But if there is any such thing as an hypostatical union between the divine and human natures, it must unite both natures in one essence, which is impossible: for the divine nature being infinite, could admit of no addition or enlargement, and consequently cannot allow of a union with any nature whatever. Was such an union possible in itself, yet, for a superior nature to unite with an inferior one in the same essence, would be degrading to the former, as it would put both natures on a level by constituting an identity of nature: the consequences whereof would either deify man, or divest God of his divinity, and reduce him to the rank and condition of a creature; inasmuch as the united essence must be denominated either divine or human.

That God should become a man, is impossible, and that man should become a God, is equally impossible and absurd. But if the divine nature retains its absolute perfection, and the nature of man its infirmity, then a premised hypostatical union between them would imply a union of weakness and imperfection to the nature and essence of God; for so certain as human nature is imperfect and united with the divine, so certain perfection must be supposed to unite with imperfection, but it is contradictory and unworthy of the divine nature to form such a hypostatical junction. Furthermore to suppose that two essences are contained in one, is as great a contradiction, as to suppose, that two units are one, and one unit is two; for if two essences have a positive existence, they must exist in two distinct and seperate natures, for that, which constitutes but one nature, is and necessarily must be contained in but one essence, so *vice versa*, that which constitutes two essences, at the same time gives existence to two natures, for a nature cannot exist without an essence, nor an essence without a nature; for essence is identity itself. But that there should be two identities in the same nature or essence, is impossible and contradictory, therefore Jesus Christ could not be both God and man, for this plain reason, that if he was one of them, he could not be the other; for God and man are not and cannot be one and the same, for that there is an infinite disproportion between them; for which reason they cannot be hypostatically united in one nature or essence. The divine mind comprehends all possible knowledge, with one entire and infinite reflection without a succession of thinking. Nor is it compatible with the omnipresence of God to ascribe motion to him, for it would imply absence in him from place, and be a down right contradiction to his being every where present; therefore that mind, which intuitively

understands

understands all things, and is every where present, is exalted above our narrow conceptions or traditions of uniting with the animal or cogitative nature of man, any more than with the universe in general. Our intelligence would contribute nothing to his mind, and the body of man would be but a circumscribed and inconsistent vehicle to enwrap, or inclose that mind, which is eternal and infinite. A man is finite and cannot be in but one place at the same time, his motion from one place to another as regularly and necessarily excludes him from one place, as it introduces him into another; he thinks by succession and by parts, and is liable to errors and mistakes in theory and practice; and ignorance, vanity and infirmity are more or less the lot of humanity. How arrogant is it then in man to pretend a union with the divine nature, who is infinitely above our praises or adoration? But we are told, that the hypostatical union is a mysterious one. Nevertheless it is a union or not a union, if it is a union of the divine and human natures, they must be comprized in one and the self-same essence, or otherwise it is such a mysterious union, that it is not a union, which is no mystery at all, but a barefaced absurdity. For that which we can comprehend to be unreasonable and contradictory, is by no means mysterious. That only is mysterious, which we cannot understand to be reasonable or unreasonable, true or false, right or wrong, which is not the case respecting the hypostatical union; for admitting it to be true, the human mind must reflect, reason and judge of things in and with the divine mind. But as the divine mind does not think or reflect by succession, and the human mind cannot exert its thinking faculty any otherwise than by succession, it could not think or reflect in or with the divine mind at all; for the divine omniscience, comprehending all things, would also comprehend the thoughts and reasonings of the human mind, whether they are supposed to be right or wrong. But the finite mind would be lost and swallowed up in the divine, without adding any thing to it, except it be imperfection. Nor is it possible in itself, that an intelligent finite being, who thinks by succession, should be united in one essence with that mind, which is infinite, and does not think by succession: For infinity of intelligence cannot admit of addition, nor could the infinite and finite mind think together in one and the same mind, as the manner of their perceptions, as well as the extent of them, would be infinitely different, and consequently there could be no union between them. But the human mind, by a progressive and finite mode of reflection, would act and judge of things, not only distinctly from, but opposite to the eternal mind

which

which naturally obstructs or precludes the union. Besides, if the human mind acts seperately and individually from the divine mind, it acts in the same manner as our minds do, and like them would be liable not only to imperfection, but to sin and misery; a union too wretched to be ascribed to the divine nature. But admitting the union between the infinite and finite minds, they would be but one mind, and conscious of the same consciousness, for otherwise they could not be the same, or pertain to the same essence. But that a finite mind could be concious of an infinite or all comprehending consciousness, or compose any part of it, is absurd; as a consciousness is not compounded of parts, as parts cannot comprize infinity. And as to moral and physical evil, the infinite mind is at as great a remove therefrom as from finiteness itself, and consequently could not jointly suffer with the person of a supposed mediator.

But it may be objected that Jesus Christ was not possessed of a human mind, and that the hypostatical union consisted in the uniting of the divinity with the animal part of the nature of man only. But such a union would of consequence subject the divine nature to a state of suffering, and obnoxiously expose it to physical evils. To suppose that it did not, is the same as to suppose, that

that there was no such union, for if it be really a union, it must be attended with the necessary consequences of a union of the divine nature with the animal part of the nature of man, or otherwise it is a contradiction to call it a union. But if the divine nature did not suffer in the person of Christ, and he was by nature void of a human mind, then it follows, that it was the mere animal body of Christ that suffered for original sin, in which, intelligent nature, either divine or human, did not bear a part. But if it be supposed, that the hypostatical union united the divine nature with that of the human, consisting of cogitation and sensation, then the previous arguments stand fairly opposed to the doctrine of the hypostatical union, which is submitted to the reader.

Chapter

Chapter XIII.

SECTION I.

Of the impossibility of translating an Infalliable Revelation from its original copies, and preserving it entire through all the revolutions of the World, and Vicissitudes of human learning to our time.

ADMITTING for argument sake that the scriptures of the old and new Testament were originally of divine supernatural inspiration, and that their first manuscript copies were the infallible institutions of God, yet to trace them from their respective antient dead languages, and different and diverse translations, from the obscure
hieroglyphical

hieroglyphical pictures or characters, in which they were first written, through all the vicissitudes and alterations of human learning, prejudices, superstitions, enthusiasms and diversities of interests and manners, to our time, so as to present us with a perfect edition from its premised infallible original manuscript copies, would be impossible. The various and progressive methods of learning, with the insurmountable difficulties of translating any supposed antiquated written revelation would not admit of it, as the succeeding observations on language and grammar will fully evince.

In those early ages of learning, hieroglyphical pictures were expressive of ideas; as for instance, a snake quirled (a position common to that venomous reptile) was an emblem of eternity, and the picture of a lion, a representation of power, and so every beast, bird, reptile, insect and fish, had in their respective pictures, particular ideas annexed to them, which varied with the arbitrary custom and common content of the several seperate nations, among whom this way of communicating ideas was practiced, in some sense analogous to what is practised at this day by different nations in connecting particular ideas to certain sounds or words written in characters, which according to certain rules of grammar constitute the several

languages

languages. But the hieroglyphical manner of writing by living emblems, and perhaps in some instances by other pictures, was very abstruse, and inadequate to communicate that multiplicity and diversity of ideas, which are requisite for the purpose of history, argumentation or general knowledge in any of the sciences or concerns of life; which mystical way of communicating ideas underwent a variety of alterations and improvements, though not so much as that of characters and grammar has done; for in the hierogliphical way of communicating their ideas, there was no such thing as spelling, or what is now called orthography, which has been perpetually refining and altering, ever since characters, syllables, words or grammar have been brought into use, and which will admit of correction and improvement as long as mankind continue in the world. For which reason the original of all languages is absorbed and lost in the multiplicity of alterations, and refinements, which have in all ages taken place, so that it is out of the power of all the Etymologists and Lexiconists now living, to explain the ideas, which were antiently connected with those hieroglyphical figures or words, and which may have composed the original of any language, written in characters, in those obselete and antiquated ages, when learning and science were in

their

their infancy: Since the beneficial art of printing has arrived to any considerable degree of perfection, the etymology of words, in the scientifical and learned languages, has been considerably well understood; though imperfectly, as the various opinions of the learned concerning it may witness. But since the æra of printing, the knowledge of the ancient learning has been in a great measure, or in most respects, wholly lost; and inasmuch as the modern substitute is much better, it is no loss at all. Some of the old English authors are at this day quite unintelligible, and others in their respective later publications, more or less so. The last century and an half has done more towards the perfecting of grammar, and purifying the languages, than the world had ever done before.

I do not understand Latin, Greek or Hebrew, in which languages, it is said, that the several original manuscripts of the scriptures were written; but I am informed by the learned therein, that, like other languages, they have gone through their respective alterations and refinements, which must have been the case, except they reached their greatest perfection in their first composition; or which the progressive condition of man could not admit. So that the learned in those languages, at

this

this day, know but little or nothing how they were spoken or written when the first manuscript copies of the scriptures were composed; and consequently, are not able to inform us, whether their present translations do, any of them, perfectly agree with their respective original premised infallible manuscript copies, or not. And inasmuch as the several English translations of the Bible do materially differ from each other, it evinces the confused and blundering condition in which it has been handed down to us.

The clergy often inform us from the desk, that the translation of the Bible, which is now in use in this country, is erroneous, after having read such and such a passage of it, in either Latin, Greek or Hebrew, they frequently give us to understand, that instead of the present translation, it should have been rendered thus and thus in English, but never represent to us how it was read and understood in the antiquated and mystical figures or characters of those languages, when the manuscripts of scripture were first written, or how it has been preserved and handed down entire, through every refinement of those languages, to the present condition of Latin, Greek and Hebrew. Probably this is too abstruse a series of retrospective learning for their scholarship, and near or quite as foreign

eign from their knowledge as from that of their hearers.

It is not to be supposed that all the alterations which have taken place in language, have been merely by improving it. In many instances, ignorance, accident and custom has varied it to its disadvantage, but it has nevertheless been subject to correction, and generally speaking has been altered for the better, yet, by one means or other has been so fluctuating and unstable, as that an infallible revelation could not have been genuinely preserved, through all the vicissitudes and revolutions of learning, for more than seventeen hundred years last past to this day.

The diversity of the English language is represented with great accuracy by Mr. Samuel Johnson, the celebrated lexicographer, in the samples of different ages, in his history of the English language, subjoined to the preface of his Dictionary, to which the curious are referred for the observance of the various specimens.

SECTION

SECTION III.

Remarks concerning Mr. Ditton's Conceffions and conclufion refpecting the authority of the Evangelical, and other ancient Authors, and of the Errors, Corruptions and fpurioufnefs, to which they are expofed.

Mr. DITTON (a celebrated writer in vindication of the Chriftian revelation) frankly admits, that the fcripture writings may have been liable to contract faults, and have been fubject to the common calamity, as he calls it, which has more or lefs attended all books, ever fince there have been books in the world. His own words are thefe, "I do not fuppofe every letter, fyllable, or word, is exactly the fame as when the laft hands of their refpective authors were fet to them; the learned know well enough, that there are a multitude of ways, by which books may be abufed, and that perhaps no book in the world, of any moment, has ever efcaped this fate, but had its fhare of corruption in the common calamity at one time or other, either more or lefs.

"They know how writings may be worn out and defaced by time, the great confumer of all things, as well as to what injuries they may be expofed, by the ordinary accidents of life: how easy it is for mistakes to arise by a bare omission in points of distinction, or from the use of symbols and characters, or any sort of contractions and abridgments in writings. "How he, that dictates to another may possibly not judge rightly of the several letters whose beauty is either lost by age, or perhaps was but basely written at first. How he may mistake those letters which are of a resembling shape and figure, one for another; how inaccurately he might pronounce his words, and so lead him that transcribes into an error, or perhaps seeing the same word or words various times repeated, might easily skip from one to the other, and so leave out all in the author that was between them; or perhaps for want of skill or judgment in the matter he is concerned in, may transfer ordinary notes and glosses from the margin into the text or body of the book.

"THE learned know likewise, that those who write, as well as those who dictate may commit many mistakes; they may hear what is dictated to them imperfectly and by halves; they may be more intent upon some notions in their own minds than the business lying before them, and so write not so much what they hear as what they are at that time thinking of; or at least may possibly shape and modify what they hear, too much according to their

own

own way of speaking and thinking; but above all by want of skill in grammar, especially the knowledge of the ancient orthography, by which means, all the changes in the forms of letters would be unknown to them.

"It is not unlikely, that many such errors should be committed, as would require some skill and judgment to discover and correct afterwards. I need not add the carelessness of those who have the inspection of libraries, the rash and presumptuous attempts of critics, and the sly, villainous practices of impostors, in some circumstances, may be the occasion of mischief and disorder this way.

"All these things must be allowed, because they are certainly true in fact, as might be proved, were this a proper place for it. Now upon these and such like considerations, I very easily allow, that the writings of the old christian authors, might, in prosess of time, be exposed in some measure, to the ordinary fate of the world; I mean, that such corruptions may have crept into them, as are very possible and likely to arise from some or other of the aforementioned causes; but what will any man infer from this? We all agree that this derogates nothing from the credit of any writing; we do not reject a book because we

have

have some proofs of its having suffered in matters of less moment; for if we should proceed upon this principle, it is demonstrable in fact, that we should leave ourselves no authors to read or quote, but must abandon them by whole catalogues to the flames, even those whose authority we lay the greatest stress upon, and think it infinitely ridiculous to question.

"I MUST therefore make a stand here with this conclusion, before I proceed any further, *viz.* that we must either not reject the writings of the Evangelists and Apostles as spurious, or fundamentally corrupted, upon the account of such faults as we find to be common with them and the works of other authors, which we receive as genuine; or else we must agree to reject both the one and the other, and so, together with the New Testament, deny the credit of all books, that we cannot demonstrate to have been less abused than the system of the Christian Religion has been; and if so, I believe, I may safely ask the critics, and all those men whose learning lies only in great reading, what is become of all your boasted knowledge? and to what purpose have you spent your time in poring upon a parcel of old authors, which you are perfectly cheated in, and who never talked any of those things, which you so much value and admire.

admire in them? So that laying all these matters together, the many ways that there are, by which writings may come to contract faults, as also what has actually come to pass in the certain abuse or corruption of books, which celebrated men of old so freely owned, and complained of; it would be an indiscreet and ridiculous piece of zeal to say, that every letter syllable or word of those evangelical and apostolical books, had been preserved, in the same good order and purity, with which they were at first composed, through all the succeeding ages and revolutions of the world down to the present time. On the other hand, I am ready to allow, that they may in length of time have suffered some of those common misfortunes, which books have always been exposed to ever since there were books in the world. But what I affirm, is this, *viz.* that those writings which are now in our hands, are the very writings which the Evangelists and Apostles left behind them; and that not only as to the main matter and substance of them, but also as to all circumstances of necessary moment to Christian doctrine and practice; so far are they from being the inventions of other persons imposed on the world in their name and stead."

This writer having ingeniously enumerated a great variety of probable natural causes of the corruptions and abuses of antient writings, part of which are manifestly unavoidable, as well with respect to the productions of the old Christian authors, as of books in general, particularly from the " want of skill in grammar, and especially of the knowledge of the antient orthography, by which means" also " the changes in the forms of letters" are forgotten and unknown, from all which, together with a complication of other possible and probable causes of the abuse of books, he observes, when speaking of the evangelical and apostolical writings, " I do not suppose, that every letter, syllable or word is exactly the same, as when the last hands of their respective authors were set to them. The learned know very well, that there are a multitude of ways, by which books may be abused, and that perhaps no book in the world of any moment has ever escaped this fate, but had its share of corruption in the common calamity ;" further adding, that " it would be an indiscreet and ridiculous piece of zeal, to say, that every letter, syllable or word, of these evangelical and apostolical books, had been preserved in the same good order and purity, with which they were first composed, through all the succeeding ages and revolutions of the world down to the present time. On the other hand I am ready to allow, that they may in length of time have suffered some of those common misfortunes, which books have always been exposed to, ever since there were books in the world. But what I affirm, is this, *viz.* that those writings, which are now in our hands, are the very writings, which the Apostles and Evangelists left behind them, and that not only as to the main matter and substance of them, but also as to all circumstances of necessary moment to Christian doctrine and practice: so far are they from being the invention of other persons imposed upon the world in their name and stead."

That these writings now in our hands are the very writings which the Apostles and Evangelists left behind them, cannot be in fact true in any sense whatever, except it be pre-supposed, that the ideas now exhibited, in the different languages, in their present translations, are perfectly the same, as they may be supposed to have been in their original composition, by the premised dictation of the divine spirit. For none will pretend that at this day we have the original copies, or if we had, that the present generation would be able to understand them in consequence of the perpetual alterations

terations and refinements in language, (from those hieroglyphical and mystical times) and consequently of communicating the ideas of the human mind; which at best was very imperfectly done in the early ages of the world and infancy of learning, when the scripture writings were first composed, and promulgated; as has been discussed in the preceeding section.

It is by letters, syllables and words, that we receive the ideas of the present translations, o those supposed christian authors; and if every letter, syllable and word are not "exactly the same, as when the last hands of their respective authors were set to them," or at least, that the same original ideas without variation must have been handed down through all the vicissitudes of languages ages and revolutions of the world to our time; or in fact "those writings now in our hands," or any others denominated scriptural, are not the very same writings which the original Bible writers left behind them: This then is the question, admiting that the Bible in its original manuscript copies was infallible, whether there could have been an infallible compiling, re-drafting, translating, re-printing and perpetuation of it, so that the present translation could exhibit to us perfectly the same ideas as were contained in its premised original infallible copies, or not?

Mr.

Mr. Ditton, after recapitulating a multiplicity of causes of the corruptions and abuses of ancient books in general, part of which are manifestly unavoidable, some possible, and others in the highest degree probable, says, " but what will any man infer from this? We all agree that this derogates nothing from the credit and authority of any writing; we do not reject a book as spurious, because we have some proofs of its having suffered in matters of less moment; for if we should proceed upon this principle, it is demonstrable we should leave ourselves no authors to read or quote, but must abandon them by whole catalogues to the flames."

On the position of an immediate revelation of God to mankind, the divine authority of it to succeeding generations, depends altogether upon an infallible method of preserving and perpetuating of it entire and uncorrupted. For it is of no importance to us at this age of the world, whether revelation was, in its original, divinely inspired or not, if so be that the present translations, either through imperfection or imposture, have become spurious.

But it may be objected, in favor of revelation, that probably some part of it may have been preserved,

served, agreeable to the original supposed inspiration of it. But, who but God can tell us, which part it is, admitting that any of it still remains genuine. Allowing this position, it stand in eminent need of a re-inspiration, and a few miracles as a proof of the certainty of it.

In human compositions, alterations, corrections, abridgements, and the like, are most generally serviceable and useful to mankind; but whether we approve of ancient or modern authors, or of the refinements of either or both of them, it matters not, provided we attend to the best reasonings in order to perfect our minds. But if, through accident or imposture, or the corruption common to books, any of them may be depreciated and perverted, yet there are no rules of pretended infallibility; we judge of them according to our reason. To such part as recommends itself to our understanding we give credit, and the residue we reject for human performances; whether oral or written they claim no divine authority over us; but we judge that to be the most divine in which there is the most reason; and thus it is that human writings are always subject to be corrected by reason.

But

But there is all odds with respect to a supposed divine revelation to man, for this claims an authority of controuling human reason (and well it might, if it was the infallible revelation of God.) In order that it should be dignified with such authority, it should have been exempted from the common calamity which has attended books in general. Other books are not of that importance to the salvation of mankind, as it is pretended those scriptural writings are, so that reason would prompt us to conclude, that books, which claim such a character (among other peculiarities that of infallible) should have been exempted from that liability of contracting faults, to which other books are exposed in this deceptible world; shining in their original lustre and purity, thereby convincing the world of God's care of them, and consequently of their divine original."

But it may be objected, that those divine writings having been once delivered to the world, must necessarily be subject to the common calamity or corruptions of books in general, inasmuch as they are, like other books, committed to the care and preservation of man.

This objection operates against revelation conclusively, and evinces the cogency of the foregoing

ing arguments, that the refinements of language, the alterations of orthography, of grammar, tranflations, and the like, muft have deprived the Bible of its premifed original infallibility; or in fine is a conceffion, that the manner of preferving and continuing it in the world, is weak, imperfect, and fubject to errors and corruptions of various kinds; and confequently, at this æra of the world, not infallible; which reduces it to the the ftate and condition of other writings. For the fcriptures muft be confidered as being either fallible or infallible, fince there is no third way or mean between thefe two; for that which is not abfolutely infallible and perfect, is fallible and imperfect; and fince the prefent tranflation of the Bible is manifeftly of the latter of thefe characters, it is not authorized to control human reafon; but on the other hand, reafon ought to control the Bible, in thofe particulars in which it may be fuppofed to deviate from reafon.

By comparing the before quoted conceffion of Mr. Ditton with refpect to the corruptions and abufes of books, which fays he, " celebrated men of old have fo freely owned and complained of," with his affirmation, that appoftolical and evangelical " writings, which are now in our hands, are the very writings, which the Apoftles and Evangelifts

gelifts left behind them; and not only as to the main matter and substance of them, but also as to all circumstances of necessary moment to Christian doctrine and practice," it will amount nearly to a contradiction in terms. Upon what principles can any persons assure themselves, that the several books of the old Christian authors might not as likely suffer, by contracting errors or faults in their manner of being handed down to us, in the substance and essentials of them, as in matters trivial, and of less moment? Certainly the want of skill in grammar, or of the knowledge of the antient orthography, would render it, not only precarious and uncertain, but impossible, for modern translators rightly to understand the original ideas, annexed to the several symbols and sorts of characters, which were grown or growing by degrees out of use, and had become, or were becoming obsolete and unintelligible; which perplexities would equally affect every part of revelation, whether essential or trivial. The same may be argued respecting all and every of the natural impediments attending the preserving entire and uncorrupted the writings of an antiquated revelation.

From what has been already observed, we may infer, that the errors, mistakes or abuses of the books of revelation, might as probably happen with respect to the substance or subject matter and essential doctrines thereof, as with respect to such parts as may be supposed to be of little or no consequence "to Christian doctrine and practice," inasmuch as the main system, together with its subordinate parts must have been exposed to all and singular of the beforementioned causes of abuses and corruptions, common to the books of the old Christian authors, except in the instance of cunning and sly impostors, who would more likely strike at the essential doctrines of a supposed revelation, than at the less or more inconsiderable parts thereof. For an impostor could gain no valuable advantage to himself, or propose such a motive, unless he could alter it very essentially by adding to or diminishing from it. Mahomet himself did "not deny the mission of Moses or of Christ, or the divine authority of the scriptures, but charged both Jews and Christians with perverting them, and insinuated that he was sent by God to purge them from their errors, and restore the law of God to its primitive purity." In fine, he managed his pretentions with that art and address, that he entirely new modeled the scriptures, as he pretended was agreeable to the patriarchal purity; and it is altogether probable, that the Popes, and Romish clergy have made near or quite

as

as great alterations in it. At the reformation the Protestant clergy exploded the Apocrypha, condemning the story of Tobit and his Dog; but the rest of the scriptures they accepted as cannonical, just as the Popes and their creatures had coined it to their hands, of which more will be observed in the sequel of this chapter.

But to return to the thread of this discourse; we will premise, that the Christians will allow that there was not, in the original of the Bible writings, any part so trivial as to be of no moment or importance "to Christian doctrine and practice;" for if they do not, they would be hard put to it to justify the wisdom of God in making it in the first place any part of their revelation. They must therefore be obliged to own, that every part was of importance as to doctrine and practice, and that the least, as well as greatest variation, from its original composition (which they suppose to have been dictated by the divine spirit) is in fact, so far forth as the variation may be supposed to have taken place in the present translation, a derogation from, and subversion of God's supposed revelation. Mr. Ditton admits, that it would be "a ridiculous piece of zeal to say that every letter," syllable or word "of those Evangelical and Apostolical books had been preserved in the same

good

good order and purity, with which they were first composed, through all the suceeeding ages and revolutions of the world down to the present time." Nor is it possible for any or all the Christian world, at this day, to understand, how far, or in what particulars, the present translations of the scriptures may have been varied from their several originals, or what they were, or whether the whole is not essentially corrupted and become spurious. Of one thing we may be certain, which is, that it is, in the nature of things (the laws of the world we live in, and the condition of mankind therein duly considered, particularly the vicissitudes of learning and manner of translating and preserving the writings and ideas of antient authors) utterly impossible, that there could have been a genuine and perfect compiling and translation thereof. It would be the greatest arrogance and vanity for any individuals or councils to pretend to sever the errors and impostures, which, at one time or other, may have crept into them, from that which may be supposed still to be genuine, or to distinguish the premised perfect from imperfect; which would require the omniscience of a God, instead of the fallible knowledge acquired by the erudition of man, and is manifestly subversive of the infallibility and divine authority of revelation.

FROM

FROM which we infer, that ancient written revelations were never of divine authority; for it is inconsistent with the wisdom and goodness of God to have made a revelation of his mind and will to mankind, for a rule of duty and practice to them, and to be continued to the latest generations as such, when at the same time it is demonstrable, that God has so constituted the laws and course of the world, and the circumstances of mankind therein, as would, in the nature of things, necessarily make a revelation void, on account of the unavoidable obstacles, which his providence in the constitution of things, has laid in the way, as an impregnable barrier against a perfect translation and perpetuation thereof.

SECTION III.

The variety of Annotations and Expositions of the Scriptures, together with the diversity of Sectaries evinces their fallibility.

EVERY commentary and annotation on the Bible, implicitly declares its fallibility; for if the scriptures remained genuine and entire, they would not stand in need of commentaries and expositions, but would shine in their infallible lustre and purity without them. What an idle phantom

tom is it for mortals to assay to illustrate and explain to mankind, that which God may be supposed to have undertaken to do, by the immediate inspiration of his spirit? Do they understand how to define or explain it better than God may be supposed to have done? This is not supposable; upon what ground then do these multiplicity of comments arise, except it be pre-supposed that the present translations of the Bible have, by some means or other, become fallible and imperfect, and therefore need to be rectified and explained? and if so, it has lost the stamp of divine authority; provided in its original composition it may be supposed to have been possessed of it.

To construe or spiritualize the Bible is the same as to inspire it over again, by the judgment, fancy or enthusiasm of men; and thus the common people, by receiving God's supposed revelation at secondary hands (whether at the thousandth or ten thousandth remove from its first premised inspiration they know not) cannot in fact be taught by the revelation of God. Add to this the diverse and clashing expositions of the Bible, among which are so many flagrant proofs of the fallibility and uncertainty of such teachings, as must convince even bigots, that every one of those expositions are erroneous, *except their own*.

It has been owing to different comments on the scriptures, that christians have been divided into sectaries. Every commentator, who could influence a party to embrace his comment, put himself at the head of a division of Christians; as Luther, Calvin, and Arminius, laid the foundation of the sectaries who bear their names; and the Socinians were called after the scismatical Socinius: The same may be said of each of the sectaries. Thus it is that different commentaries or acceptations of the original meaning of the Scriptures, have divided the Christian world into the divisions and subdivisions of which it consists at present. Nor was there ever a division or subdivision among Jews, Christians or Mahometans, respecting their notions or opinions of religion, but what was occasioned by commentating on the scriptures, or else by later pretended inspired revelations from God in addition thereto. The law of Moses was the first pretended immediate revelation from God, which respects the Bible, and after that in succession the several revelations of the prophets, and last of all (in the Christian system) the revelations of Jesus Christ and his apostles, who challenged a right of abolishing the priesthood of Moses; Christ claiming to be the antitype of which the institution of sacrifices and ceremonial part of the law of Moses was emblematical; but this infringement of the prerogative of the Levitical priests gave such offence, not only to them, but to the Jews as a nation, that they rejected christianity, and have not subscribed to the divine authority of it to this day, holding to the law of Moses and the prophets. However Christianity made a great progress in the world, and has been very much divided into sectaries, by the causes previously assigned.

"Mahomet taking notice of the numerous sects and divisions among Christians, in his journies to Palestine, &c. thought it would not be difficult to introduce a new religion, and make himself high priest and sovereign of the people." This he finally effected, prosecuting his scheme so far; that he new modelled the scriptures, presenting them (as he said) in their original purity, and called his disciples after his own name. He gained great numbers of proselytes and became their sovereign, in civil, military and spiritual matters, instituted the order of the mystical priesthood, and gave the world a new Bible by the name of the Alcoran; which he gives us to understand was communicated to him from God, by the intermediate agency of the angel Gabriel, chapter by chapter. "His disciples at this day inhabit a great part of the richest countries in the world, and are supposed to be more numerous than the Christians," and are

are as much if not more divided into sectaries, from causes similar to those which produced the division of Christians, viz. the different commentatories on and expositions of the Alcoran. The Mufti, or priests, represented the doctrines and precepts of the Alkoran in a variety of lights different from each other, each of them claiming the purity of the original and infallible truths prescribed to the world by Mahomet, their great reformer of christianity. For though the several sectaries of Mahometans differ, respecting the meaning of their Alkoran, yet they all held to the truth and divine authority thereof, the same as the Christian sectaries do concerning their Bible: so that all the different opinions which ever did, or at present do subsist, between Jews, Christians and Mahometans, may be resolved into one consideration, viz. the want of a right understanding of the original of the scriptures. All sat out at first, as they imagined, from the truth of God's word, (except the impostors) concluding, that they had an infalible guide, and have, by one means or other, been guided into as many opposite faiths as human invention has been capable of fabricating; each sect among the whole, exulting in their happy ignorance, believing that they are favored with an infallible revelation for their direction.

It alters not the present argument, whether the scriptures were originally true or not; for though they be supposed to have been either true or false, or a mixture of both, yet they could never have been handed down entire and uncorrupted to the present time, through the various changes and perpetual refinements of learning and language; this is not merely a matter of speculative and argumentative demonstration, the palpable certainty of it stands confessed in every Jewish, Christian and Mahometan sectary.

SECTION IV.

On the compiling of the Manuscripts of the Scriptures into one Volume, and of its several Translations. The Infallibility of the Popes, and of their chartered Right to remit or retain Sins. And of the Impropriety of their being trusted with a Revelation from God.

THE manuscripts of scripture, which are said to have been originally written on scolls of bark, long before the invention of paper or printing, and are said to compose our present Bible, were in a loose and confused condition, scattered about in the world, deposited nobody knows how or where, and at different times were compiled into one volume. The four gospels are by the learned generally

ally admitted to have been wrote many years after Christ, particularly that of St. John: and sundry other gospels in the primitive ages of christianity were received as divine by some of its then sectaries, which have unfortunately not met with orthodox approbation in subsequent æras of the despotism of the church.

The translation of the scriptures by Ptolemy Philadelphus, king of Egypt, was before Christ, and therefore could not include the writings of the new testament in his translation, and " whether by seventy two interpreters, and in the manner as is commonly related, is justly questioned." But where, at what time, and by whom, the scriptures of the old and new testament were first compiled into one volume, is what I do not understand: but was it a longer or shorter period after Christ, it alters not the present argument materially, since the scattered manuscripts were in a loose and confused condition for a long time; and the grand query is, when the compilers of those manuscripts collected them together in order to form them into one volume, how they could have understood the supposed divine writings, or symbolical figures, with the ideas originally connected with them, and distinguish them from those which were merely human, and in comparison of the others are called

ORACLES

led prophane. To understand this distinction would require a new revelation, as much as may be supposed necessary for composing the original manuscripts themselves; but it is not pretended that the compilers or translators of the Bible were inspired by the divine spirit in the doing and compleating their respective business; so that human reason, fancy, or some latent design, must needs have been substituted, in distinguishing the supposed divine and human writings apart, and in giving a perfect transcript of the original manuscripts. Now admitting that the compilers were really honest principled men (which is more than we are certain of) it would follow, that they would be obliged to cull out of the mixed mass of premised divine and human writings, such as to them appeared to be divine, which would make them to be the sole arbitrators of the divinity that they were compilng to be handed down to posterity as the infallible word of God, which is a great stretch of prerogative for mortal and fallible man to undertake, and as great a weakness in others to subcribe to it, as of divine authority.

Mr. Fenning, in his Dictionary diffinition of the word Bible, subjoins the following history of its translations; "The translation of this sacred volume was begun very early in this kingdom,'
[England]

[England] "and some part of it was done by King Alfred. Adelmus translated the Psalms into Saxon in 709, other parts were done by Edfrid or Ecbert in 730, the whole by Bede in 731. Trevisa published the whole in English in 1357. Tindals was brought higher in 1534, revised and altered in 1538, published with a preface of Cranmers in 1549. In 1551, another translation was published, which was revised by several bishops, was printed with their alterations in 1560. In 1607 a new translation was published by authority, which is that in present use." From this account it appears, that from the first translation of the Bible by Trevisa, into English, in 1357, it has been revised, altered, and passed through six different publications, the last of which is said to have been done by authority, which I conclude means that of the King, whose prerogative in giving us a divine revelation, can no more be esteemed valid than that of other men, though he may be possessed of an arbitrary power within the limits of his realm to prevent any further correction and publication of it. As to the changes it underwent previous to Trevisa's translation, in which time it was most exposed to corruptions of every kind, we will not at present particularly consider, but only observe that those translations could not, every one of them, be perfect, since they were diverse from

from each other, in consequence of their respective revisions and corrections; nor is it possible that the Bible, in any of its various editions could be perfect, any more than all and every of those persons who have acted a part in transmitting them down to our time may be supposed to be so: for perfection does not pertain to man, but is the essential prerogative of God.

The Roman Catholic's, to avail the evils of imperfection, fallibility and imposture of man, have set up the Pope to be infallible; this is their security against being misguided in their faith, and by ascribing holiness to him, secure themselves from imposture; a deception, which is incompatible with holiness. So that in matters of faith, they have nothing more to do, but to believe as their church believes. Their authority for absolving or retaining sins is very extraordinary; however, their charter is from Christ (admitting them to be his Vicars, and the successors of St. Peter) and the present English translation of the Bible warrants it. The commission is in these words; "*And I will give unto thee the keys of the kingdom of Heaven, and whoever thou shalt bind on Earth, shall be bound in Heaven; and whatsoever thou shalt loose on Earth, shall be loosed in Heaven. Whosoever sins ye remit, they are remitted unto them and whosoever sins ye retain, they are retained.*" That St.

St. Peter or his successors should have a power of binding and determining the state and condition of mankind in the world to come by remitting or retaining sins, is too great a power to be intrusted in men, as it interferes with the providence and prerogative of God, who on this position would be exempted from judging the world (as it would interfere with the chartered prerogative of the Popes in their remitting or retaining of sins, admitting it to have been genuine) precluding the divine retribution of justice; we may therefore from the authority of reason, conclude it to be spurious. It was a long succession of ages that all Christendom were dupes to the See of Rome, in which time it is too evident to be denied, that the Holy Fathers obtruded a great deal of pious fraud on their devotees; all public worship was read to the people in unknown languages, as it is to this day in Roman Catholic countries. Nor has the Bible, in those countries, to this time, been permitted to be published in any but the learned languages, which affords great opportunity to the Romish church to fix it to answer their lucrative purposes. Nor is it to be supposed that they want the inclination to do it. The before recited grant of the power of the absolution of sin, to St. Peter in particular, was undoubtedly of their contrivance.

In short, reason would prompt us to conclude, that had God, in very deed, made a revelation of his mind and will to mankind, as a rule of duty and practice to them, and to be continued as such to the latest posterity, he would in the course of his providence have ordered matters so that it should have been deposited, translated, and kept, in the hands of men of a more unexceptionable character than those Holy Cheats can pretend to.

Witchcraft and Priestcraft, were introduced into this world together, in its non-age; and has gone on, hand in hand together, until about half a century past, when witchcraft began to be discredited, and is at present almost exploded, both in Europe, and America. This discovery has depreciated Priestcraft, on the scale of at least fifty per cent. per annum, and rendered it highly probable that the improvement of succeeding generations, in the knowledge of nature, and science, will exalt the reason of mankind, above the tricks and imposture of Priests, and bring them back to the religion of nature and truth; ennoble their minds, and be the means of cultivating concord, and mutual love in society, and of extending charity, and good will to all intelligent beings, throughout the universe; exalt the divine character, and lay a perminent foundation for truth and reliance on providence; establish our hopes and prospects of

immortality

immortality, and be conducive to every defirable confequence, in this world, and that which is to come; which will crown the fcene of human felicity in this fublunary ftate of being and probation; which can never be compleated, while we are under the power and tyranny of Priefts, fince as it ever has, it ever will be their intereft, to invalidate the law of nature and reafon, in order to eftablifh fyftems incompatible therewith.

Chapter

Chapter XIV.

SECTION I.

An Historical Testimony of Miracles insufficient to prove irrational Doctrines.

THE method which the advocates for the Christian revelation have most generally taken, to prove its divine authority, is, by making use of the miracles, which are said to have been done by Moses and the Prophets, and by Christ and his Apostles, for that purpose. These miracles, they either take for granted to be facts, or by a circumlocution of argumentative conclusions, deduced from the antiquated history of miracles, and principally from the scripture writings themselves, they pretend to evince the reality of them. This historical narrative of the facts of the miracles, they call by the name of a moral evidence, which, they tell us, lays an indispensible obligation on those of mankind to whom it is proposed, to assent to the truth of the miracles. Having thus, as they premise, evinced the fact of the miracles, they proceed to make use of them as being demonstrative of the divine authority of revelation; the same as though the miracles were incontestibly true; arguing, that it would be inconsistent with the moral perfections of God, to exert his power to work miracles for the confirmation of the divinity of revelation, and mission of promulgators, was it not of the institution of God; for otherwise, say they, "God by working the miracles, would have set his own seal to the delusion;" and thus, they think they have proved the truth and divine authority of the Christian revelation; which inference must be admitted to be just, if so be that in very deed, God had wrought the miracles for that purpose; but admitting the essential doctrines of their revelation, or its main system, to be repugnant to right reasoning, and to the divine character, the inference must follow, that God never wrought the miracles to confirm it; for that, by working them, he would (as in the other premised case) " have set his own seal to the delusion." It is therefore, absolutely incumbent on the advocates of revelation, in the first place, to evince from reason, that their respective revelations are consistent with truth and the moral perfections of God, or they cannot, with any propriety, make use of the evidence of miracles, as a proof their divinity, or of the divine legation of their respective promulgators; which consideration naturally prompts the inquisitive to a reconsideration of the arguments contained in the preceding chapters, concerning revelation, and the Bible doctrines thereof, and to determine whether they are conclusive or not. If those arguments are just, they preclude miracles in general from having any existence in the creation and providence of God; but should those reasonings be thought inconclusive, yet, as we have before observed, that as miracles are urged as a proof of the divine institution of revelation, admitting the fundamental doctrines thereof are repugnant to reason and truth, it must of consequence, invalidate the evidence of the fact of the miracles; for as the Christians justly infer, if God wrought the miracles to confirm revelation, it must be admitted to be of divine authority; so on the other hand, if the principle doctrines of revelation are inconsistent with reason, or the moral rectitude of things, then it follows, that God did not work the miracles to evince the truth of it; for that, it would be the same as exerting his Almighty power miraculously, to prove an unreasonable revelation to be of his special institution, to reasonable beings; which is inadmissible. From hence we infer, that any revelation,

doctrine

doctrine or preposition whatever, which, in the principles or subject of them are false, can never be proved to be truth, or of divine authority, by evidence deduced from the history of miracles; but on the contrary, such revelation or its doctrines disprove the fact of the miracles, which are brought for their support. And as the scriptures contain their own confutation, in the repugnancy of the fundamental doctrines thereof to reason, as has been argued before, it is in the highest degree unjust in argument to deduce evidence from (pretended) miracles, in support of their divinity, at the same time, relying on uncertain, antiquated, interesting and precarious history, for the evidence of the fact of the miracles; an evidence of all others the weakest, and most liable to deception; when on the other hand, the evidence against the divine authority of revelation, arising from its own inconsistencies (of which this generation must judge for itself) is as strong as reason can possibly conceive of, or the truth and fitness of things, as resulting from God, can make it to be; and in a superlative sense overturns the evidence for the fact of the miracles which could not have been wrought to prove contradictions; and, as the stronger evidence should controul the weaker, we reject the history of miracles, for that we can be rationally certain that the miracles, which are said to have been done by Moses and the prophets, and by Christ and his Apostles, in testimony of their revelation, were not in fact true; since the fundamental doctrines which they have promulgated to the world are not reasonable.

It is not my design to examine particularly into the history of Miracles, which would swell a volume, shall therefore observe that an historical representation of facts, which are said to have taken place in remote periods or parts of the world, are neither true nor false merely in consequence of an historical existence. Nor is it in our power to detect any misrepresentation of matters of fact, recorded in ancient history, except they are improbable or impossible to be true; for such events as probably, or possibley may have taken place, and which are handed down to us by history, or by tradition, as having taken place in remote epocha's of the world, whether they are true or false, we cannot at this time determine, inasmuch as that which is probable or possible, might have taken place for any thing we can know about it. But such historical representations of matters of fact as are inconsistent in themselves, or with the reason and fitness of things, we are authorized from reason to detect as fallacious or spurious. For instance, an historical testimony that two and three

three was four could not be true; as those numbers added together, make five: Nor could such a testimony make virtue red, white, or any other colour; or justice to consist of mere solidity, figure, motion or extension, or make a body occupy two distinct parts of space, at one and the same instant of time. Furthermore, an historical testimony that Adam's sin is my sin, or that of any of his supposed descendants, could not be in fact true; or that the merits or righteousness of Christ is that of the elect; or in other words it is impossible that the doctrine of imputation should be true, as argued in the 12th chapter. Nor is it possible that the doctrine of supernatural inspiration, or revelation, or of a mysterious revelation, or a mere spiritual intercourse of invisible and imperceptible beings with mankind, should be in fact true, as argued in the 6th chapter. Nor is it possible that there should ever have been any truth in miracles, as argued in the 7th chapter. Nor is it possible that prophecy could have amounted to any thing more than human art, or illusion, as argued in the 8th chapter. Nor is it possible that faith could be the condition of Salvation, as argued in the 9th chapter. Nor is possible that the doctrine of the trinity should have been in fact true, as argued in the 10th chapter. Nor is it possible that all the human specie descended, by ordinary generation

ation, from the same original progenitors, as argued in the 11th chapter? Nor could a written or printed reveltion have possibly been consistent with a progressive state of knowledge, or applicable to the various circumstances of action and duty which concern mankind, who, after all, must have been necessitated to adopt the religion of nature or reason, as argued in the 2nd section of the 5th chapter; nor has it been possible that there should have been a perfect compiling, or translation of the scriptures, from the antient manuscripts and dead langurges, through all the refinements and vicissitudes of learning, down to our time, as argued in chapter 13th. The doctrine here alluded to, and their appendages, compose the main system of the christian revelation, the rationality of which, may be better judged of in this enlightened age of the world, than in those times of ignorance and superstition, in which it was promulgated. None will pretend, but that the learned nations of the earth at present, are far advanced, in arts, sciences and logical reasonings, above the primative Christians: let us therefore examine, and candidly criticise for ourselves, left the credulity of former ages obtrude their unphilosophical and inconsistent revelations upon us, as sacred and infallible truth. It is high time we were roused from our lethargy and superstition and that we demand of our spiritual teachers, reason and solid

argument

argument, for the ground of our faith and confidence.

Should we admit that miracles were wrought to confirm the divine authority of primitive christianity, and the mission of its first teachers, yet, those miracles could not confirm the divinity of its present translation, or the authority of its present teachers; for that the main system of it, as it is now handed down to us, is, in its principles, repugnant to truth and the moral character of God, as argued in the chapters already alluded to. We infer from hence, that if miracles have been wrought in the early æra of the promulgation of the christian revelation, to confirm its (then) authority, and that of its teachers, it has since that æra, by some means or other, become spuriously altered from its primitive supposed purity; and that those premised miracles cannot evince the truth of the present copies of revelation, or the divine authority of the present clergy; for that the copies now extant, will not bear the scrutiny of reason. But if the present copies of the revelation are perfectly or essentially the same as they were in their primitive composure, we may be morally certain, that God never wrought miracles to perpetuate and confirm such irrational doctrines as are therein contained, at the great expence of the treasures and understandings of mankind.

SECTION

SECTION II.

Morality, derived from Natural Fitness, and not from tradition.

SUCH parts or passages of the scriptures as inculcate morality, have a tendency to subserve mankind, the same as all other public investigations or teachings of it, may be supposed to have; but are neither better or worse for having a place in the volumn of those writings denominated canonical; for morality does not derive its nature from books, but from the fitness of things; and though it may be more or less, interspersed through the pages of the Alkoran, its purity and rectitude would remain the same; for that it is founded in eternal right; and whatever writings, books or oral speculations, best illustrate or teach this moral science, should have the preference. The knowledge of this as well as all other sciences, is acquired from reason and experience, and (as it is progressively obtained) may with propriety be called, the revelation of God, which he has revealed to us in the constitution of our rational natures; and as it is congenial with reason and truth cannot

not (like other revelations) partake of imposture. This is natural religion, and could be derived from none other but God. I have endeavoured, in this treatise, to prune this religion from those excrescences, with which Craft on the one hand, and Ignorance on the other, have loaded it; and to hold it up to view in its native simplicity, free from alloy; and have throughout the contents of the volume, addressed the reason of mankind, and not their passions, traditions or prejudices; for which cause, it is no wise probable that it will meet with any considerable approbation.

Most of the human race, by one means or other are prepossessed with principles opposed to the religion of reason. In these parts of America, they are most generally taught, that they are born into the world in a state of enmity to God and moral good, and are under his wrath and curse, that the way to Heaven and future blessedness is out of their power to pursue, and that it is incumbred with mysteries which none but the Priests can unfold, that we must "*be born again*" have a special kind of faith, and be regenerated; or in fine, that human nature, which they call "the old man," must be destroyed, perverted, or changed by them, and by them new modeled, before it can be admitted into the Heavenly kingdom.

Such

Such a plan of superstition, as far as it obtains credit in the world, subjects mankind to sacerdotal empire; which is erected on the imbecility of human nature. Such of mankind, as break the fetters of their education, remove such other obstacles as are in their way, and have the confidence publicly to talk rational, exalt reason to its just supremacy, and vindicate truth and the ways of God's providence to men; are sure to be stamped with the epithet of irreligious, infidel, prophane, and the like. But it is often observed of such a man, that *he is morally honest*, and as often replied, *what of that? Morality will carry no man to heaven.* So that all the satisfaction the honest man can have while the superstitious are squibbing hell fire at him, is to retort back upon them that they are priest ridden.

Most people place religion in arbitrary ceremonies, or mere positive institutions, abstractly considered from the moral rectitude of things, and in which religion does not and cannot consist, and thus delude themselves with an empty notion of religion, which, in reality is made up of tradition and superstition, and in which moral obligation is not concerned; not considering that a conformity to moral rectitude, which is morality in the abstract, is the sum of all religion, that ever was or can be in the universe; as there can be no religion in that in which there is no moral obligation; except we make religion to be void of reason, and if so, all argument about it is at an end.

The manner of the existence, and intercourse of human souls, after the dissolution of their bodies by death, being inconceiveable to us in this life, and all manner of intelligence between us and departed souls impracticable, the priests have it in their power to amuse us, with a great variety of visionary apprehensions of things in the world to come, which, while in this life, we cannot contradict from experience, the test of great part of our certainty (especially to those of ordinary understandings) and having introduced mysteries into their religion, make it as incomprehensible to us, (in this natural state) as the manner of our future existence; and from scripture authority, having invalidated reason as being carnal and depraved, they proceed further to teach us from the same authority, that " *the natural man knoweth not the things of the spirit, for they are foolishness unto him, neither can he know them for they are spiritually discerned.*" A spiritualizing teacher is nearly as well acquainted with the kingdom of Heaven, as a man can be with his home lot. He knows the road to heaven and eternal blessedness, to which happy regions, with the greatest assurance, he presumes to pilot his dear disciples, and unfold to them the

mysteries

mifteries of the canonical writings, and of the world to come; they catch the enthufiafm and fee with the fame fort of fpiritual eyes, with which they can pierce religion through and through, and underftand the fpiritual meaning of the fcriptures, which before had been "a dead letter" to them, particularly the revelations of St. John the Divine, and the allufion of the horns therein mentioned. The moft obfcure and unintelligible paffages of the Bible, come within the compafs of their fpiritual difcerning, as apparently as figures do to a mathematician: Then they can fing fongs out of the Canticles, faying, "I am my beloved's and my beloved is mine;" and being at a loofe from the government of reafon, pleafe themfelves with any fanaticifms they like beft, as that of their being *"fnatched as brands out of the burning, to enjoy the fpecial and eternal favour of God, not from any worthinefs or merit in them, but merely from the fovereign will and pleafure of God, while millions of millions, as good by nature and practice as they, were left to welter eternally, under the fcalding drops of divine vengeance;"* not confidering, that if it was confiftent with the peefections of God to fave them, his falvation could not fail to have been uniformly extended to all others, whofe circumftances may be fuppofed to be fimilar to, or more deferving than theirs, for equal juftice cannot fail to apply in all cafes in which equal juftice demands it. But thefe

deluded

deluded people resolve the divine government altogether into sovereignty; "*even so Father, for so it seemed good in thy sight.*" And as they exclude reason and justice from their imaginary notions of religion, they also exclude it from the providence or moral government of God. Nothing is more common, in the part of the country where I was educated, than to hear those infatuated people, in their public and private addresses, acknowledge to their creator, from the desk and elsewhere, "*hadst thou, O Lord, laid judgment to the line and righteousness to the plummet, we had been in the grave with the dead and in hell with the damned, long before this time.*" Such expressions from the creature to the creator are prophane, and utterly incompatible with the divine character. Undoubtedly, (all things complexly considered) the providence of God to man is just, inasmuch as it has the divine approbation.

The superstitious thus set up a spiritual discerning, independent of, and in opposition to reason, and their mere imaginations pass with each other, and with themselves, for infallible truths. Hence it is, that they despise the progressive and wearisome reasonings of philosophers (which must be admitted to be a painful method of arriving at truth) but as it is the only way in which we can acquire it, I have pursued the old natural road of

ratiocination

raciocination, concluding, that as this spiritual discerning is altogether inadequate to the management of any of the concerns of life, or of contributing any assistance or knowledge towards the perfecting of the arts and sciences, it is equally unintelligible and insignificant in matters of religion: and therefore conclude, that if the human race in general, could be prevailed upon to exercise common sense in religious concerns, those spiritual fictions would cease, and be succeeded by reason and truth.

SECTION III.

Of the Importance of the Exercise of Reason, and Practice of Morality, in order to the Happiness of Mankind.

THE period of life is very uncertain, and at the longest is but short: a few years bring us from infancy to manhood, a few more to a dissolution; pain, sickness and death are the necessary consequences of animal life. Through life we struggle with physical evils, which eventually are certain to destroy our earthly composition; and well would it be for us did evils end here; but alas! moral evil has been more or less predominant in our agency, and though natural evil is unavoidable, yet moral evil may be prevented or remedied by

the

the exercife of virtue. Morality is therefore of more importance to us than any or all other attainments; as it is a habit of mind, which, from a retrofpective conlcioufnefs of our agency in this life, we fhould carry with us into our fucceeding ftate of exiftence, as an acquired appendage of our rational nature, and as the neceffary means of our mental happinefs. Virtue and vice are the only things in this world, which, with our fouls, are capable of furviving death; the former is the rational and only procuring caufe of all intellectual happinefs, and the latter of conlcious guilt and milery; and therefore, our indifpenfible duty and ultimate intereft is, to love, cultivate and improve the one, as the means of our greateft good, and to hate and abftain from the other, as productve of our greateft evil. And in order thereto, we fhould fo far diveft ourfelves of the incumbrances of this world, (which are too apt to engrofs our attention) as to enquire a confiftent fyftem of the knowledge of religious duty, and make it our conftant endeavour in life to act conformably to it. The knowledge of the being, perfections, creation and providence of GOD, and of the immortality of our fouls, is the foundation of religion; which has been particularly illuftrated in the four firft chapters of this difcourfe. And as the Pagan, Jewifh, Chriftian and Mahometan countries of the world have been overwhelmed with a multiplicity of revelations diverse from each other, and which, by their respective promulgators, are said to have been immediately inspired into their souls, by the spirit of God, or immediately communicated to them by the intervening agency of angels (as in the instance of the invisible Gabriel to Mahomet) and as those revelations have been received and credited, by far the greater part of the inhabitants of the several countries of the world (on whom they have been obtruded) as supernaturally revealed by God or Angels, and which, in doctrine and discipline, are in most respects repugnant to each other, it fully evinces their imposture, and authorizes us, without a lengthy course of arguing, to determine with certainty, that not more than one if any one of them, had their original from God; as they clash with each other; which is ground of high probability against the authenticity of each of them.

A REVELATION, that may be supposed to be really of the institution of God, must also be supposed to be perfectly consistent or uniform, and to be able to stand the test of truth; therefore such pretended revelations, as are tendered to us as the contrivance of heaven, which do not bear that test, we may be morally certain, was either originally a deception, or has since, by adulteration become spurious.

spurious. Furthermore, should we admit, that among the numerous revelations on which the respective priests have given the stamp of divinity, some one of them was in reality of divine authority, yet we could no otherwise, as rational beings, distinguish it from others, but by reason.

REASON therefore must be the standard, by which we determine the respective claims of revelation; for otherwise we may as well subscribe to the divinity of the one as of the other, or to the whole of them, or to none at all. So likewise on this thesis, if reason rejects the whole of those revelations, we ought to return to the religion of nature and reason.

UNDOUBTEDLY it is our duty, and for our best good, that we occupy and improve the faculties, with which our Creator has endowed us, but so far as prejudice, or prepossession of opinion prevails over our minds, in the same proportion, reason is excluded from our theory or practice. Therefore if we would acquire useful knowledge, we must first divest ourselves of those impediments; and sincerely endeavour to search out the truth; and draw our conclusions from reason and just argument, which will never conform to our inclination, interest or fancy; but we must conform to that if

we

would judge rightly. As certain as we determine contrary to reason, we make a wrong conclusion; therefore, our wisdom is, to conform to the nature and reason of things, as well in religious matters, as in other sciences. Preposterously absurd would it be, to negative the exercise of reason in religious concerns, and yet, be actuated by it in all other and less occurrences of life. All our knowledge of things is derived from God, in and by the order of nature, out of which we cannot perceive, reflect or understand any thing whatsoever; our external senses are natural and so are our souls; by the instrumentality of the former we perceive the objects of sense, and with the latter we reflect on them. And those objects are also natural; so that ourselves, and all things about us, and our knowledge collected therefrom, is natural, and not supernatural; as argued in the 6th chapter.

We may and often do, connect or arrange our ideas together, in a wrong or improper manner, for the want of skill or judgment, or through mistake or the want of application, or through the influence of prejudice; but in all such cases, the error does not originate from the ideas themselves, but from the composer; for a system, or an arrangement of ideas justly composed; always contain the truth; but an unjust composition never fails

fails to contain error and falshood. Therefore an unjust connection of ideas is not derived from nature, but from the imperfect composition of man. Misconnection of ideas is the same as misjudging, and has no positive existence, being merely a creature of the imagination; but nature and truth are real and uniform; and the rational mind by reasoning, discerns the uniformity, and is thereby enabled to make a just composition of ideas, which will stand the test of truth. But the fantastical illuminations of the credulous and superstitious part of mankind, proceed from weakness, and as far as they take place in the world, subvert the religion of REASON and TRUTH.

FINIS.

LaVergne, TN USA
30 November 2009

165581LV00001B/17/A